de Gruyter Studies in Organization 73

Business Networks

de Gruyter Studies in Organization

Organizational Theory and Research

This de Gruyter Series aims at publishing theoretical and methodological studies of organizations as well as research findings, which yield insight in and knowledge about organizations. The whole spectrum of perspectives will be considered: organizational analyses rooted in the sociological as well as the economic tradition, from a socio-psychological or a political science angle, mainstream as well as critical or ethnomethodological contributions. Equally, all kinds of organizations will be considered: firms, public agencies, non-profit institutions, voluntary associations, inter-organizational networks, supra-national organizations etc.

Emphasis is on publication of *new* contributions, or significant revisions of existing approaches. However, summaries or critical reflections on current thinking and research will also be considered.

This series represents an effort to advance the social scientific study of organizations across national boundaries and academic disciplines. An Advisory Board consisting of representatives of a variety of perspectives and from different cultural areas is responsible for achieving this task.

This series addresses organization researchers within and outside universities, but also practitioners who have an interest in grounding their work on recent social scientific knowledge and insights.

Business Networks

Prospects for Regional Development

Edited by
Udo H. Staber
Norbert V. Schaefer
Basu Sharma

Walter de Gruyter · Berlin · New York 1996

Editors

Udo H. Staber, Professor, Faculty of Administration,
University of New Brunswick, Fredericton, Canada

Norbert V. Schaefer, Professor, Faculty of Administration,
University of New Brunswick, Fredericton, Canada

Basu Sharma, Professor, Faculty of Administration,
University of New Brunswick, Fredericton, Canada

⊗ Printed on acid-free paper which falls within the guidelines
of the ANSI to ensure permanence and durability.

Library of Congress Cataloging-in-Publication Data

Business networks ; prospects for regional development /
editors, Udo H. Staber, Norbert V. Schaefer, Basu Sharma.
(De Gruyter studies in organization ; 73)
Papers originally presented at a conference held at the University of New Brunswick 1993.
Includes bibliographical references and index.
ISBN 3-11-015107-3 (cloth)
1. Business networks – Congresses. 2. Strategic alliances (Business) – Congresses. I. Staber, Udo H. II. Schaefer, Norbert V. III. Sharma, Basu. IV. Series.
HD69.S8B87 1996
338.8–dc20 96-11129
CIP

Die Deutsche Bibliothek – Cataloging-in-Publication Data

Business networks : prospects for regional development / ed. by
Udo H. Staber. – Berlin ; New York : de Gruyter, 1996
(De Gruyter studies in organization ; 73 : Organizational theory and research)
ISBN 3-11-015107-3
NE: Staber, Udo H. [Hrsg.]; GT

Typesetting: Converted by Knipp Medien und Kommunikation oHG, Dortmund. –
Printing: Gerike GmbH, Berlin. – Binding: Mikolai GmbH, Berlin. –
Cover Design: Johannes Rother, Berlin. – Printed in Germany.

Preface

Most of the contributions in this volume arise from a conference held at the University of New Brunswick in November 1993. The objective of this conference was to bring together academic researchers, business managers, and government officials to consider the potential of business networking for regional economic development.

Business networks, as a subject of inquiry and practice, have become increasingly prominent in recent years. Many theorists and practitioners believe that businesses are operating in more complex and volatile environments than ever before. One may consider, for example, the growing environmental constraints and market opportunities confronting both private and public sector organizations; the globalization of mass markets and reconfiguration of national and regional economies; the increasing sophistication of available technologies affecting workflow interdependencies both within and across organizational boundaries; and the many articulate stakeholder groups involved in the strategic issues that confront large-scale organizations. These conditions call for business strategies that facilitate continuous learning and innovation, and for public policies that provide the necessary institutional infrastructures.

Networking has been offered as a possible blueprint for economic success, although the universality of its applicability has been the subject of some debate. To some observers, networking is a term that merely glorifies what businesses have long practiced, in such forms as joint ventures, bidding consortia, and cartels. To others, networking is particularly well suited to the intensely competitive and volatile business environments of today, because it facilitates rapid learning and flexible deployment of resources. According to many scholars, business networking also holds promise for economic development if it is embedded in a wider socio-political institutional context that balances interfirm cooperation and competition. The challenge for theorists and practitioners alike is to identify the conditions under which business networks are likely to deliver on their strategic promises.

The aim of this volume is to invite attention to the problematique of institutional interventions designed to foster business networks as a tool for regional development. Networking offers clear advantages, but there are also significant limitations which are often overlooked in the current euphoria for this organizational strategy. The contributors to this volume explore these limitations in various ways and from various theoretical perspectives. Some authors report their findings from case studies of network formation; others formulate policy prescriptions from a conceptual analysis of facilitating and constraining conditions; and still others develop an agenda for further research, based on their review of the empirical literature. An effort was made to move the discussion of business networks and regional development beyond the literature on Italian small firm districts, which are often considered a model for replication. Contributors were invited to report their findings of business networks and policy approaches at varying levels and in varying regions. Their collective contribution is intended to educate the reader about a complex organizational form and development strategy whose implementation is usually problematic and deserves careful scrutiny.

Most of the academic papers presented at the conference are included in this volume. Following the conference, the contributing authors revised their papers based on suggestions provided by the editors and based on their assessment of the debates that took place during the conference. Two chapters were written originally for this volume. In addition, the leading editor prepared an introductory chapter, in an attempt to identify key issues and to synthesize the state of knowledge on networks as a strategy for business and economic development. The authors of Chapters 2 through 7 review the experiences and problems encountered in specific cases of networking, in different regions, and at different levels of analysis. The contributors in Chapters 8 through 10 summarize what they see as the critical variables and conditions affecting the success of networking. In doing so, they also identify an agenda for further research.

We would like to thank all those who participated in the conference, the contributors to this volume, and Margaret Wicken for editorial assistance in preparing the bibliography. We also appreciate the financial support of the Social Sciences and Humanities Research Council of Canada (grant # 804-93-0033), Industry Canada, and the Atlantic Canada Opportunities Agency, which made the conference and, ultimately, this book possible.

Udo Staber
Norbert V. Schaefer
Basu Sharma

Table of Contents

List of Tables

List of Figures

1. Networks and Regional Development: Perspectives and Unresolved Issues

Udo Staber

1.1 Introduction

Network and networking have become popular concepts in business, government, and academia. For example, researchers working in the area of small business entrepreneurship propose networking as a necessary strategy for obtaining critical resources and for connecting to sources of information. Large multinational companies are collaborating with numerous organizations in ways that bind them together in formal networks that can span the globe. Old-style conglomerates are fragmenting into easier-to-manage units and are coordinating them along the line of flexible networks. Many new products and technologies are being developed and diffused through networks. Some researchers focus on the spatial aspects of networking to describe the social organization of production and exchange in regional economies. In general, networking is viewed by many as an organizational survival strategy in today's intensely competitive business environment. Some go as far as to suggest that business networks are part of a new industrial order, one in which production depends on continuous collaboration with external sources of knowledge and expertise (Best, 1990). The "learning organization" (Stata, 1989; Nonara, 1991) of the future, so the argument, depends upon external networking, to ensure that customers, suppliers, and alliance partners can be tapped continuously for new ideas and insights. Some students of organizational change see networking as a defining characteristic of "post-modern organizations" (Reed, 1992).

Despite the current flurry of interest, the idea of networking is not new. Businesses have always practiced some form of networking, as in bidding consortia and buying clubs. They have done so to collect information, obtain material resources, diffuse new ideas, or exercise political influence. The concept of networking is also not new to academic researchers who have studied the subject from various theoretical perspectives which cross-cut the social sciences. Neoclassical economists, from Marshall (1890) to Weber (1929) to Schumpeter (1934), have noted the competitive advantages of interfirm linkages for firms and for the regional economies in which they are embedded. They argued that networks of interdependent and specialized firms can lead to significant external economies of scale and scope (often in form of agglomeration economies), thus compensating for the limitations of small production units. Economists view interfirm linkages also as a mechanism through which innovations are created and diffused. Regional scientists, arguing in the tradition of agglomeration economics, view networks as a set of purchase and sales relationships to be explored through input-output analysis (e.g., Isard, 1956). Some organizational and management theorists, following a strategic perspective, look at networking as a means of managing firms' resource interdependencies and uncertainties in their environments (e.g., Pfeffer and Salancik, 1978; Astley and Fombrun, 1983). Others, working in the organizational ecology tradition, focus more on the competitive forces that constrain firms' ability to cooperate formally and to take collective action on common problems (e.g., Aldrich, 1979; Staber and Aldrich, 1983). Neo-institutional economists, particularly those working within the transaction cost framework (Williamson, 1985), think of interfirm networks as a governance alternative to both open markets and internal organizational hierarchies. They view networks as an efficient mechanism for coordinating strategic action across firms, without sacrificing organizational autonomy, either legally or functionally.

These theoretical perspectives have proven useful for explaining various facets of interfirm networking, but only in a limited way. The richness of networks, combined with their distinctive duality of flexibility and control, makes them difficult to analyze. A network is simultaneously an organizational form in its own right and a product of sovereign organizations, with consequences for its governability (Powell, 1990). Network participants are more loosely coupled than in organizational hierarchies, but they are also more tightly integrated than in open markets. Their autonomy is structured but not tightly controlled. While there is no general theory of interfirm networks (Salancik, 1995), there are various theoretical perspectives on specific issues related to networks and networking. I shall highlight some of the more prominent issues below.

The applied literature on business networking shows the unevenness with which many practitioners attempt to implement theoretical concepts and models. Scholarly research has not been of much help. Researchers are grappling with difficult conceptual and operational issues, and no general theory is in place that would address the multiplicity and complexity of issues raised and integrate previous research into a theoretical whole. There is also no clear consensus on the basic concepts involved. The term network has been used variably and has often been loosely associated with other terms, such as "intelligent enterprise" and "virtual corporation." Some people think of network processes, such as network formation, trust building, conflict resolution, and partnering, when they discuss network arrangements, but they ignore the constraining aspects of network structures. Others are interested mostly in network structures, such as density, composition, and range, and neglect the processual and dynamic aspects. The term network has also been used to account for various developments, from "flexible specialization" in business strategy to the "renaissance" of regional economies. It is the relationship between business networks and regional economic development that this volume addresses.

The aim of the present collection of essays is to invite attention to the problematique of institutional interventions designed to foster business networks as tools of regional development. Of course, questions of institutional regulation are not new. They have been raised and empirically addressed in various volumes on industrial districts and business networks (e.g., Hirst and Zeitlin, 1989; Pyke and Sengenberger, 1992; Ernste and Meier, 1992; Grabher, 1993a). But there remains significant room for developing further insights into the range of possible institutional regimes and problems associated with their implementation. The contributors to this volume come from academic disciplines in which business networks have figured prominently in recent discourse: economic geography, development economics, management theory, and industrial relations. Each author has considered issues related to the institutional environment of business networking. The collective purpose of their contributions is the advancement of theory and practice for public policy and network management.

1.2 The Promises of Networking for Regional Development

While businesses have always practiced some form of networking, and researchers have long been interested in the structures and processes of formal networks and other forms of interorganizational relations, it is only recently that public policy makers have begun to consider more systematically and positively the potentials of interfirm networking for regional economic development. The prevailing attitude toward interfirm collaboration used to be rather negative, more so in the United States than most other industrialized countries. The main concern was with negative externalities (market power, slow innovation, etc.), while efficiency potentials were overlooked or downplayed. Some organization theorists argued that cooperative strategies by firms are often not intended to maximize efficiency but to "obtain market control and oligopolistic advantages" (Perrow, 1981: 377). Similarly, some political economists saw in business networks new accumulations of power, enabling business elites to control the distribution of resources and the terms on which they are available in society and economy (Benson, 1975). Some economists objected to the preoccupation of policy makers with the anticompetitive outcomes of some forms of interfirm cooperation, "when instead the principal objects of the practices is transactional efficiency" (Williamson, 1975: 253).

What went largely unnoticed in these debates was the fact that in some regions the construction of institutional arrangements to support business networks and foster interfirm cooperation was well underway and that at least in some cases public intervention seemed to have enhanced, rather than stifled, regional economic competitiveness. The argument in some policy circles was that, under certain conditions, open markets keep firms from performing at socially optimal levels. Firms are often not able to produce all necessary services in-house, and where these services involve transactional ambiguities (as in technology research or labor training) and asset specificity (as in acquiring and using dedicated equipment) some form of public intervention may lead to more efficient solutions for firms. In the language of industrial economists, networks of independent firms may be superior to an integrated enterprise if they generate economies of scale and scope (Eccles, 1981). If, in addition, these networks are embedded in supportive institutional infrastructures that regulate cooperation they may also be a basis for sustained regional competitiveness and endogenous development (Best, 1990).

The implications of locally embedded business networks for regional development have only recently attracted more systematic attention. During much of the post World War II era governments and policy making bodies tended to look at investment from the outside as an effective way of stimulating regional or local economic development. This approach has recently given way to a greater emphasis on mobilizing and developing the resources that are already available in a given area. Economic development has increasingly become a localized phenomenon, despite the internationalization of the production process in many industries.[1] Localized and bottom-up development strategies include efforts to encourage cooperation among the various actors in the chain of production, from basic research to marketing, within an institutional framework that meets regional needs. The central idea, or hope, is that cooperative networking can unlock important synergies, encourage innovativeness, raise efficiency, and thus strengthen the competitive advantages of the regional economy in which business networks are embedded (Sengenberger, 1993). As a by-product, local network building may also enhance political competencies and social commitments which, some would argue, are necessary for a region's survival in an increasingly global environment.

Examples of institutional possibilities and development options can be gleaned from the accumulating literature on the spatial clustering of networked businesses and public-sector organizations. Piore and Sabel's (1984) work on economic restructuring brought the successes of business networks and their contribution to regional economic development in central and north-eastern Italy (the "Third Italy") to the attention of English-speaking audiences. Since then spatially-clustered and cooperatively linked firms – often referred to as "industrial districts" – have become the object of public policy deliberation in many parts of the world. Also Porter's (1990) work on industry clusters, from a business strategy perspective, has been highly influential in public policy circles. In Québec (Canada), for example, efforts are made to directly apply Porter's (1990) model

1 In some cases, the international investment strategies of companies may have the effect of *localizing* the production process by creating forward and backward linkages in local markets (Fujita and Hill, 1995).

of industry clusters in an attempt to enhance regional competitiveness (Ferland et al., in this volume).

The network approach to regional economic development is now being tried in many parts of the world (Schaefer and Roy, 1993). Some countries, such as Denmark and Britain, have national programs for initiating business networks. In other countries, such as the United States and Canada, business networks are often more local and sector-specific, and governments use a variety of methods to encourage networking (Sabel, 1992). Network initiatives may also span across national borders, as in the case of "growth triangles" in Southeast Asia (Sharma et al., in this volume) and the Cascadia linkages connecting parts of British Columbia in Canada and Washington State in the United States. Regional development is no longer, and everywhere, a purely national matter.

Not all of the network building efforts are successful, for various reasons. In some cases, competitive business instincts tend to override government incentives for joint action, as in the machine-tool industry in Baden-Württemberg, Germany (Cooke et al., 1993). In other cases, interfirm cooperation emerges even without government assistance, as in some manufacturing networks in New Hampshire, United States (Gittell et al. in this volume). Also, not all cooperation is strategically planned and executed, but may "just happen" in the course of normal transactions between firms (Schmitz, 1992: 98). Development initiatives come in many forms, but the conditions under which some are effective and others fail are not always clear. The evaluation literature on local development strategies is disappointingly thin. Thus, there continues to be a need for systematic research on the promises of networking for regional development.

1.3 Business Networks in the New Economic Environment

The last two decades have been a time of major upheavals in the international economic environment, with far-reaching implications for business and macroeconomic competitiveness. Intensified international competition, fragmentation of demand in some markets and saturation in others, rapid debt buildup and relative decline in savings, discontinuities in technological change, and volatile currency exchange rates and raw material prices have raised substantially the level of uncertainty for economic decision-making. The advanced industrialized countries are facing economic difficulties which are not solely the result of prolonged recessions and limited recoveries but reflect fundamental structural changes in the "new global economy."

Until not too long ago, the preferred public policy approach to managing economic uncertainties would have been to focus attention on macroeconomic measures, opting either for traditional Keynesian strategies of aggregate demand stimulation or hands-off strategies limited to broad fiscal and monetary interventions by central governments. An alternative approach might have been for governments to direct, in a corporatist-like fashion, private and public investment towards selected sectors, industries, or firms, usually those which are assumed to have growth potential. The effectiveness of these strategies has been questioned by those who believe that macro-level policies (whether regulatory, fiscal/monetary, or corporatist) need to be complemented by policies conceived and implemented at the local or regional level (Zeitlin, 1992; Sengenberger, 1993).

Two arguments have generally been put forth. First, with respect to national interventionist policies aimed at *specific* sectors or industries, the argument is that central state officials usually lack the local knowledge needed to evaluate investment requirements. Thus, a host of local factors, often intangible and hard to measure, are overlooked, such as community commitment, risk-taking attitudes, managerial capacity, and quality of labor-management relations (Doeringer and Terkla, in this volume). Instead, attention is focused on the available policy options to reduce or stabilize traditional cost variables, such as energy, wages, transportation, taxes, and communication. Centrally planned and coordinated industrial policy initiatives, so the critique, ignore the variability of development options in specific regions and sectors. The problematique of this policy approach is nowhere clearer than in the Southern Italian Mezzogiorno region where plenty of government transfer payments since the 1950s have failed to help the region's economy to catch up with the industrialized and more prosperous North (Faini et al., 1993). Second, with respect to *general* macroeconomic framework policies, intended to influence the aggregate level of prices and employment, the argument is that market failures, where they occur, have differential effects at the local level, and thus aggregate policies do not adequately reflect the particular needs of product, capital, and labor markets in different regions. National policy, so the argument, cannot do justice to local developmental conditions which are heavily infused with historical and socio-political idiosyncracies.

It is not that macro-level policies do not matter or never have intended effects. Their importance lies in determining the broad conditions and time horizons in which firms make investment decisions (Christopherson and Redfield, 1993). National framework policies define the parameters for developmental opportunities at the local level (Ettlinger, 1994). By providing public goods, such as social security, health care, and vocational education, national institutional regimes enhance the efficiency of labor markets. Through tax policy and ownership regulation national policies affect business investment decisions. National policy measures also intend to equalize opportunities for economic development across regions with different natural endowments, to prevent disadvantaged regions from becoming locked into dependence and marginality. However, national policies, to the extent that they focus on macroeconomic aggregates, are not *tailored* to local needs which may vary considerably from place to place and which may have their own developmental logic. This may not be a problem, as long as the general economic environment is relatively predictable and offers reasonable growth opportunities. But economic conditions since the 1970s have become increasingly constraining and volatile, with differential effects at the regional level. These new conditions call for novel approaches to business governance and public policy.

Responding to the growing turbulence and uncertainty in product, labor, and financial markets, firms have experimented with non-bureaucratic and decentralized forms of production and exchange, involving more flexible work practices and dynamic relations with competitors, suppliers, buyers, and service providers, including network arrangements. Collective bargaining structures have come under increasing strain, especially in those countries where bargaining normally takes place at the industry or sector level. Many governments have reacted to economic strain through deregulation and privatization, with the effect of further intensifying market competition and destabilizing firms and industries. But heightened competition also opened up new opportunities for firms and public sector organizations alike, transforming the shape and composition of many business populations and regional economies. These developments have changed the context in which regional economies compete. Because national regimes differ in terms of labor relations, financial systems, degree of government involvement in private business, and so forth, national variations have consequences for economic adjustments at lower levels as well. As a result, more attention has been paid in recent years to the effectiveness of policy interventions at the local and regional level.

While not too long ago national macroeconomic and regulatory policy was considered the *sine qua non* of development strategies, as suggested above, today the pendulum appears to have swung to the opposite extreme, at least in some policy circles. The position pursued with increasing vigor is that *national* policy counts for little in the "new global economy" and that *local* policy initiatives need to be taken more seriously (Stohr, 1990). In Western Europe, some observers have noted a "strong EU-wide trend towards regionalization in policies dealing with craft enterprises and SMEs" (European Network for SME Research, 1994: 26). Consistent with this position is the idea of a "renaissance of regional economies," as well as the argument that increased regionalism presents firms and governments with significant choices about economic development (Sabel, 1989). According to one school of thought (Piore and Sabel, 1984), successful regional economies are populated by firms which are able to adjust quickly to changing economic conditions, not because they use particular technologies, produce particular goods, or are of a particular size, but because they can draw on a "thick" *institutional* and *qualitative* framework which stimulates and supports continuous innovation and learning. The crucial ingredient of successful networking is that the actors involved are embedded in supportive social structures which provide the meaning and motivation for cooperation and innovation.

This position differs from standard agglomeration theory (Weber, 1929; Chinitz, 1961) which focuses on the external *quantitative* economies associated with the co-location of producers. The argument from the standard agglomeration perspective is that specialized firms can obtain the economies of scale and scope (agglomeration economies) that are normally reserved to large and vertically integrated corporations, if they cluster in space and share access to local pools of resources such as labor, capital, energy, and business services. Agglomerated firms can benefit from the concentration of skilled labor, by riding out employment fluctuations or by sharing in training programs. Quantitative agglomeration economies also derive from the ability to share specialized machinery or distribution centers. Spatial proximity may not be equally important for all functional business areas; accounting and financial relations, for example, can be managed quite well over long distances. But some business activities can benefit from spatial closeness, especially if they require frequent face-to-face interaction among organizational "boundary spanners." The advantage of co-location, from the agglomeration perspective, is that it facilitates speedy and accurate exchange of information and other resources (Chinitz, 1961), and that it minimizes transaction costs (Williamson, 1985). Firms in the same industry may be able to imitate one another more readily, and thus also innovate more quickly, if they are located together. Still, the classical agglomeration argument remains largely economistic in the treatment of firms as atomistic and rational (in a narrow calculative sense) profit maximizers.

Piore and Sabel's (1984) analysis of territorially bounded networking goes beyond standard agglomeration and transaction cost reasoning by emphasizing the *qualitative* social and institutional factors which facilitate quantitative external economies of co-location. Quantitative and qualitative economies are intertwined, and they are both embedded within specific contexts of space and time. Piore and Sabel (1984) discuss a number of regions as examples where locally embedded business networking seems to have played a significant role in economic development. Their argument is that geographic proximity generates developmental synergies and stimulates innovation in regions and industrial communities that have a tradition of cooperation as well as a territorial identity. Institutional structures for cooperation are most effective when producers are physically close. Although it is possible that new communication and information technologies make geographic co-location less important in the future, opportunities for social interaction will probably continue to be important in many industries [see, for example, the financial network in the City of London (Amin and Thrift, 1992), and the high-tech clusters in Silicon Valley (Saxenian, 1990) and Cambridge, England (Garnsey and Cannon-Brookes, 1993)]. What may matter most is not proximity per se but whether or not social relations are such that they lead to trust, loyalty, and tacit understandings, and whether these outcomes enhance firms' willingness to make risky deals and to share their resources.[2]

In contrast to the discrete transactions in open markets, network relations are seen as being motivated by norms of reciprocity (Powell, 1990). Reciprocity expectations define the normative logic of economic exchange and impose structure on available choices. Reciprocity is also a reflection of the trust that holds network members together. Sabel (1992) argues that there has to be sufficient trust if firms – or rather, their "boundary spanners" – are to engage in long term relations, exchange expensive and specialized machinery, share innovations, remain committed to continued exchange during temporary downturns, hire partner firms' redundant employees in times of stress, and so on. The question is whether trust emerges "naturally" in the course of continued interaction or whether it can be "engineered" through strategic intervention from the outside (Staber, in this volume). For example, Gittell et al. (in this volume) argue that the Governor of New Hampshire was instrumental in promoting information sharing among firms in this state. But this does not mean that the local political and social culture which may have enabled the Governor's role in *this* instance is readily transferable to other places. Social relations can differ significantly across communities, setting the context for diverse developmental trajectories and strategies for change.

Porter (1990) argues, from a business strategy perspective, that the geographic concentration of firms and industries creates competitive advantages for national economies. Successful firms, according to this analysis, are linked horizontally and vertically with firms in related and supporting industries. Demand conditions in supplier industries create pressures for continuous innovation, and open entry in related industries contributes to rivalry and competitive pressures. Geographic proximity ensures that new innovations are diffused quickly and that firms invest in skill building. However, the ability to innovate depends on firms' willingness to cooperate. Mechanisms that facilitate cooperative exchange include trade associations, personal relationships, community ties, and interlocking directorates (Porter, 1990: 153). But Porter is careful to argue that competitive advantages can be developed only as long as cooperation enhances rivalry. Porter's analysis thus addresses conditions both for competition and cooperation. Factor conditions lead to domestic rivalry and thus create *incentives* for firms to participate in networks, while networking enhances firms' *ability* to engage in continuous innovation (Lazonick, 1993). However, Porter is somewhat vague about the level of aggregation at which rivalry and cooperation create competitive advantages. While he thinks of geographic clustering as facilitating rapid exchange, he refers to the national environment as the context in which factor conditions exert their force. But there

2 Many contributors to this literature discuss proximity independently from industrial organization variables, such as market structure, information flows, and research intensity (see Enright, in this volume, for a discussion of these variables).

is no reason to assume that local linkages have competitive consequences only at higher levels (Enright, in this volume). The point of economic development policy, in its regional version, is to identify the complex of regional forward and backward linkages among firms that can be used to build up strong regional economies.

The common thread in recent writing on business networks, as it relates to regional economic development, is the concern for institutional infrastructures that facilitate information exchange and limit opportunistic behavior. The fate of a regional economy involves more than a localized set of functionally interdependent, but economically atomistic, firms. Business networks involve a set of institutions, not only at the regional level, which define the terms on which cooperation and competition takes place. Regional development is thus also about a "politics of place" (Scott and Storper, 1992: 19), which creates and legitimizes institutional-regulatory structures for balancing interfirm cooperation and competition. Because business networking occurs not among organizations but ("boundary-spanning") individuals who link organizations, it is important to attend to the microlevel social and political aspects of networks. The key units in analyzing economic exchange are sociopolitical relations rather than isolated transactions.

Discussions of interventionist possibilities have considered the role of service providers in both the public and private arena, such as interest associations, economic development agencies, consulting firms, and research institutes. But there is no systematic comparative research to study the conditions under which these organizations are more or less effective in fostering the right balance of cooperation and competition which, according to Piore and Sabel's (1984) model, leads to continuous innovation. Research is needed to explore the conditions under which networking and particular network structures lead to mutually adaptive learning processes, with consequences for innovation. Theoretical debates in this area are heavily infused with arguments from neo-institutional models in economic sociology and organizational theory (Granovetter, 1985; Powell and DiMaggio, 1991), which criticize strictly economic interpretations of business networking for being unrealistic because they are undersocialized (Harrison, 1992). It is also not clear under what conditions industrial restructuring leads to "post-Fordist" arrangements à la Piore and Sabel (1984) or some other outcome (Sternberg, 1991). But comparative empirical analysis has been sparse and unable to sort out the explanatory power of various theoretical perspectives. Thus, it has been difficult to assess how conclusively the available evidence supports a particular theoretical approach, let alone choose between competing explanations.

1.4 The Institutional Framework of Business Networks

Business networks and institutional structures come in many shapes and forms. Their formation and design may be strategically planned, but outcomes are conditioned by many factors, such as resource availability, pressures from competing networks, historical legacies, and pure chance. Network structures may develop in unexpected directions; some core regions become peripheral over time, while others manage to recover from an extended period of decline. Business networks involve important aspects of interorganizational control and spatial aggregation, as shown in Figure 1.1.[3] Distinguishing between these dimensions helps to identify salient issues with respect to institutional governance and regional development. The contrasting properties of interorganizational control and spatial dimensions, as suggested in Figure 1.1, are not necessarily assumed to be empirically correct, but are of interest because they suggest that the institutional frames can vary significantly.

Aggregation	Interorganizational Control	
	centralized	decentralized
local	science park	small firm industrial district
global	Asian growth triangle	international business network

Figure 1.1 Typologizing business networks

The spatial dimension of networks suggests that interfirm linkages may span various levels of aggregation. Firms may be linked only locally, as in the case of the financial sector in the City of London (Amin and Thrift, 1992) or the clothing district in Modena, Italy (Solinas, 1982; Lazerson, 1995). Sometimes, local networks are linked interregionally by firms having subcontracting relations with firms in other regions (Ferland et al., in this volume) or by national employers' associations imposing national standards on member firms. Local networks may lack identity and coherence if they are embedded in national or global networks, as in industries that are dominated by a small number of global players whose investment decisions are indifferent to regional needs. In such cases, capital hypermobility tends to destabilize local identity, in effect colonizing relations at the local level. Local and regional networks may also be embedded in a wider area by administrative fiat, as in the case of government promoted Southeast Asian "growth triangles" (Sharma et al., in this volume).

Differences in the level of aggregation at which businesses are linked have implications for the level at which institutional governance structures are most ap-

3 Network types can be distinguished along a number of dimensions, depending on the research question of interest. The primary dimensions in typologies include content (e.g., information, resources), formality of relations, structural aspects (e.g., connectivity, centrality), and nature of actors (e.g., their demographics, interests).

propriate. The institutional environment of businesses in industrial districts, for example, is determined by the way the region is constituted as a political system. In contrast to nation states, regions are politically not sovereign and their sanctioning capacity is highly constrained. Thus, they can neither legislate the inflow of labor nor prevent the outflow of capital. In such open systems the involvement of interest associations and other political players in regional networks is largely voluntary and interorganizational relations tend to be informal (Streeck, 1992).

Because of the voluntary nature of relations in most business networks and industrial districts, and because of the importance of local norms and traditions, one would expect significant variations in interorganizational structures of power and control. Control structures may be centralized, as in the case of networks that are dominated by "flagship" firms (D'Cruz and Rugman, 1992; Jarillo, 1988). Such networks tend to have a strategic function from the perspective of the firms dominating them (Sydow, in this volume). Examples of such networks include Japanese keiretsu (independent industrial and financial groups) and Western franchise networks. Other networks are more decentralized and power is more evenly spread, as in the case of New Hampshire's leading manufacturing industries (Gittell et al., in this volume). Decentralized control structures prevail in networks with relatively large numbers of equal-sized, specialized, but functionally interdependent actors. The control structures of networks have institutional implications for resource mobilization, agenda setting, and conflict resolution (Gertler and Rutherford, in this volume).

The evolutionary path of a particular network, and its influence on regional development, is affected by the interplay of these two forces: spatial relations and interorganizational control structures. Figure 1.1 indicates that these two forces are orthogonal to each other, permitting us to cross-classify ideal-typical business networks. Science parks which are centrally administered and driven by core firms illustrate a centralized and localized network. Asian "growth triangles" are examples of more globalized and centralized networks. The small firm industrial districts in the "Third Italy" indicate decentralized and local networks. Some international business networks are global and decentralized, such as the strategic alliances network in the semi-conductor industry.

While the spatial and control dimensions are analytically distinct, they tend to be related empirically. Some firms in local networks may, over time, outperform others, acquire power, and integrate local linkages into geographically broader networks, so that initially cohesive networks develop into fragmented and diffuse networks. Or, central firms in local networks may, through mergers or outsourcing, become integrated into supra-regional networks, thus losing their identity as local players (Cooke et al., 1993). The structuring of business networks is subject to competing pressures which determine how uncertainties, risks, costs, and benefits are shared across network actors. How these pressures are resolved in particular networks and regions, given their unique histories, resource endowments, and political cultures, is difficult to predict. It is, however, possible, within the framework of spatial and control dimensions, to identify several key issues, in order to contemplate institutional possibilities and limitations of networks and regional development. Researchers have grappled with four important questions: (1) determining network boundaries, (2) balancing autonomy and dependence, (3) managing the public-private interface, and (4) evaluating network performance. The contributors to this volume address various facets of these questions, as discussed below.

1.4.1 Network Boundaries

Organizing and governing business networks raises some difficult boundary issues. Looking inward, it is not always clear where the networked organization ends and the network begins. Looking outward, the boundary between network and its surrounding environment tends to be fuzzy as well. Demarcating and maintaining network boundaries can pose serious challenges because of the collective nature of organizational action. For example, practical decisions must be made about how much of each firm's resources can be legitimately claimed by the network and to what degree each firm should have control over the network. In networks without well-specified and agreed-upon boundaries, there are likely to be disagreements over the allocation of network assets, with destabilizing consequences. Unlike firm start-ups, networks have an immediate presence in that partner firms have already developed assets and made commitments to a variety of constituencies. But several questions arise: Are these assets and commitments brought into the network? If they are carried into the network, are they adjusted and further developed to suit a collective purpose? How do they affect the performance of the network? Extant theory only partly addresses these questions. Transaction cost theory, for example, would predict that organizational commitments are determined by the relative costs of managing transactions among firms and between the network and its environment. Institutional theory would place more emphasis on the legitimacy and power aspects of these transactions and propose, for example, that the culture in a particular region will define the nature and extent of barriers in the exchange of resources. Ecological analysis focuses on the competitive dynamics of networks and downplays norms of cooperation. Different perspectives provide different explanations for the nature and evolution of network boundaries.

Some networks are consciously constituted by the individuals participating in them, others are largely researcher-derived constructs with no identity of their own. Networks are not purposeful entities in their own right and have no identifiable intentions, unless the formulation of goals *for* networks is an explicit element of business strategy or public policy. Defining a purpose for networks is problematic in most cases, especially when network members lack a common history and come from different domains. Even when firms operate in the same industry and are located in the same region, there may be significant differences in cost functions, organizational maturity, business strategy, and so forth which make it difficult to achieve a common understanding of network goals. Thus, networks have a special need for leadership, especially during the formation stage. Sydow's (in this volume) study of an insurance broker network shows that, while trust and personal friendships can facilitate network building, personal relations need to be continuously nurtured to sustain cooperation. Network building is largely a matter of deciding on the right partners and the appropriate types and strength of relationships. Personal ties are important in defining "who's in and who's out," but they need not necessarily be strong and immediate to have desirable consequences (Granovetter, 1982).[4]

Compared to inter*personal* networks occurring within identifiable boundaries of an organization, investigating inter*firm* relations faces more serious problems of boundary definition. The boundaries of interfirm networks can be very imprecise. If entry and exit are uncontrolled, boundaries are fluid and impossible to maintain. If relations are multiplex (firms being connected in more than one way), boundaries may shift variably and at different rates. Researchers often use rather arbitrary criteria for demarcating network boundaries, making choices on the basis of data availability or using common sense definitions of organizational communities based on product type, business function, or geographic location. Given the fascination of many network researchers with formal analytical techniques, this strategy is understandable. It may also be appropriate, as long as the network data are complete with respect to a clear set of criteria. Substantively, a network must be represented accurately, if the intent is to study the relative importance of relations, the quality of connections, and the degree of actor commitment to relations (Marsden, 1990). For most business managers it is usually sufficient to know at least the immediate ties between organizations, and how well connected they are. They find it less important to have a complete image of all connections, although they may miss potentially valuable information about opportunities at the fringes of their network by ignoring relations among their distant alters. Practitioners are more interested in the *process* of networking and in the subleties and nuances of relations with select organizations than in the analytical *structure* and form of complete networks (Kanter and Eccles, 1992).

For policy purposes, however, it is important that network boundaries are clearly understood and properly delimited. In practice, policy makers tend to identify networks in ad hoc ways, defining network boundaries as being congruent with those of industries or sectors. In doing so they ignore vertical relationships which are an important aspect of corporate "flexible specialization" strategies. Enright

4 Granovetter's (1982) argument, extrapolated to business networks, is that *weak* ties to *distant* others imply competitive advantages, because such connections raise the probability of obtaining information about new opportunities.

(in this volume) argues that the performance of an industry depends significantly on the relations that industry members have with organizations in other industries. The task is therefore to determine the flows of inputs, knowledge, and information that contribute to an industry's performance, and to recognize the possibility that these flows encompass large geographical areas and a wide range of related industries. Competitive advantages may need to be widely (sectorally and territorially) defined. Ad hoc approaches to determining network boundaries are questionable if the aim of policy is to create synergies with the resources that are available in a given region and that are to be married to new resources (Doeringer and Terkla, in this volume). To be sure, identifying all interrelated firms and organizations, as well as all types of linkages and resources that are being exchanged is not an easy task, but is necessary if all possible synergies are to be exploited (Ferland et al., and Scott and Bergman, in this volume).

Questions of network boundary also have implications for institutional governance. Networks with fluid boundaries, such as those in New Hampshire (Gittell et al., in this volume), are more difficult to manage than networks with stable boundaries. Vague and dynamic boundaries may indicate the emergence of new policy domains, with participation in the domain being determined by yet ill-defined preferences, capacity to mobilize important resources, and centrality of organizations in the network (Laumann and Knoke, 1987). Fluid boundaries may limit the coherence and rationality of policy making and implementation, but they may also make it easier for outsiders to "buy into" an existing network and to contribute to its development (Enright, in this volume). One would expect relatively open networks to be less centralized and less localized than closed ones, and to provide multiple opportunities for actors to influence their development.

The boundary issue should be of concern to whose who wonder about the level of aggregation at which industries can gain competitive advantages. The geographic scope of competitive advantages may be very narrow, as in the case of some Italian industrial districts (Enright, in this volume) or industry agglomerations in urban areas (e.g., fur centers, garment districts). Or, there may be significant overlaps in regional networks, linked by firms and institutional organizations operating in several locales, as in Asian "growth triangles" (Sharma et al., in this volume). Doeringer and Terkla (in this volume) argue that policy makers should identify unique regional strengths, instead of applying universal location criteria, when devising policies for nurturing business networks. However, a high degree of localization of the production system does not necessarily mean that government policies and institutional infrastructures must be equally localized or that competitive advantages of regions can be achieved independently of national framework policies (Saxenian, 1989). There is a need for coordinating policies at various levels of government, to avoid unnecessary duplication and self-defeating competition (Scott and Bergman, in this volume). Scott and Bergman fear that government efforts to create an advanced ground transportation industry in Southern California may encounter resistance from other regions in the state which would like to share in the benefits. Institutional coordination needs to be statewide and, if competencies can be found outside the state, may need to go far beyond state boundaries.

1.4.2 Power, Autonomy, and Dependence

There is some debate on the question of whether business networks are an intermediate organizational form between open markets and organizational hierarchies (Thorelli, 1986: 37) or whether they are a distinct organizational form with its own logic, normative basis, and incentive structure (Powell, 1990). The implication of the former perspective is that networks are constantly at risk of dissolving either into markets (as members insist on their independence) or into hierarchies (as members give up their autonomy). From the latter perspective, networks evolve naturally over time and may eventually become an organizational actor with a distinct identity. The dominant perspective seems to be that flexible and efficient networks call for a balance of market and hierarchy.

Networks derive their flexibility and efficiency, and thus their competitive advantage, from the fact that they contain elements of both markets and hierarchies. The ideal-typical network is more reliable (the hierarchical element) than markets and less coercive (the market element) than hierarchies. Market-like flexibility is obtained through loose coupling of network members and through network boundaries that are relatively open. Loose coupling, evident in the absence of formal long-term obligations, prevents firms from getting locked into specific relationships. The open-endedness of networks facilitates interactive learning and innovation to an extent not possible in rigid hierarchies. If there is slack in the system, loose coupling ensures that redundant resources are pooled and redistributed throughout the network (Grabher, 1993b), assuming that actors are willing to share resources. But networks also have certain characteristics of organizational hierarchies which provide structure, loyalty, and stability. Structure reduces uncertainty and facilitates the exchange of tacit knowledge where open markets would fail. Mutual orientation and awareness of shared fates among network members serve as a functional equivalent of tight hierarchical controls by limiting opportunistic behavior, but without administrative fiat.

Networked firms lose some of their autonomy when they specialize in core competencies and share resources with other firms. With the loss of autonomy comes an increase in dependence, but within a network dependencies are experienced as interdependencies. Interdependence of some kind is an inevitable part of cooperation. Without some degree of interdependence with respect to information, location, resource acquisition, and the like, there would be no incentive to assume risks or to explore possibilities for cooperation. If managed effectively, interdependencies can have positive outcomes for firms and the network as a whole. Specialized and networked firms have access to resources when they need them, without having to develop them in-house. At the collective level, firms may *gain* autonomy. Examples are cooperative buying clubs in the textile-apparel sector which enhance members' bargaining power vis-à-vis large producers (Popovic, 1994) and insurance brokers who develop, through networking, expertise vis-à-vis financial institutions (Sydow, in this volume).

Interdependence may or may not lead to mutual orientation and consensus within the group, but it always implies power. What is true for power relations within organizations is also true for power being exercised in and through interorganizational networks (Pfeffer and Salancik, 1978). The structure of resource dependencies affects the distribution of opportunities for influence and power. From a strategic firm-focused perspective, networks are tools for achieving certain ends, but their effectiveness depends on the firm's location in the structure of relations. A firm's position in the network can be an important source of power. But position can also be a constraint, depending on the degree to which the other actors in the focal firm's network are connected among themselves (Burt, 1992). For example, an oligopolist's profit opportunities are limited when transacting with a well-organized group of suppliers.

Notwithstanding the rhetoric in the recent literature on interfirm *cooperation*, power is rarely symmetrically distributed. Some organizations exist on the edge of a network, able to reach others only through dependence on intermediate organizations. Others are connected directly, but they may use relations only for routine or symbolic purposes. Some centrally positioned organizations may appear powerful only because they serve as links for certain other organizations but otherwise may be quite dependent. Position is important, but it rarely tells the whole story. Controls may be unobtrusive and outcomes may result more from premise setting than direct action (Perrow, 1986).

Because a chief aim of policy efforts is to instrumentalize business networks as tools for economic development, to stimulate employment creation and maintenance, it is important to consider the role of labor in network and institution building. Horizontally and vertically fragmented production systems (such as industrial districts) require flexible and cooperative management-labor relations, as well as labor market structures that support flexibility and innovation. Gertler and Rutherford (in this volume) explain why the formation of flexible and innovative business networks calls for full labor participation. They argue that mutual adjustment in such networks depends on the ability and willingness of partner firms to deliver goods and resources on time and to agreed-upon quality standards. To the extent that external relations of trust depend on relations of trust within the workplace a case can be made for union involvement. But there are doubts that labor has in the past been given sufficient opportunity to participate formally in the shaping of business networks. Networks and industrial districts are rarely as "worker-friendly" as is often claimed by those working in the tradition of Piore and Sabel (1984) (Staber and Sharma, 1994). In those few instances where labor groups are explicitly involved in the creation and formation of networks, it seems that policy initiatives are more inclusive of a wide variety of local institutions, but that labor is not given privileged status. Gertler and Rutherford (in this volume) find in their study of network-based regional development efforts in Northern Ontario, Canada, that the climate between labor and management has been highly adversarial and that labor has not been an equal partner with business. This may not come as a surprise, given the voluntary character of network membership and the inability of local or regional governments to impose rules. The limited sovereignty of local political systems forces institutional actors to conform to market pressures, with the consequence that private business interests are usually favored over others. Labor representatives are invited only if needed and only if they "cooperate" (Streeck, 1992).

But this does not mean that business interests with respect to involvement in networks are homogeneous or can easily be reconciled if they differ. Depending on the size, range, and multiplexity of networks, authority structures are more or less complicated, as the actors are accountable to a variety of constituencies. For example, CEOs of individual firms may be held accountable to both local boards and supra-regional institutions, whose interests may diverge significantly. Saxenian (1989) argues that the political environment is an important causal factor in network development (not the other way around). Complex hierarchical network structures have conflict potential, leading to coalition building and agenda setting. The pattern of regional politics is shaped by the participation or exclusion of actors with an interest in regional development, but some of the actors may have extra-regional orientations. Even if supra-regional actors (such as national interest associations, funding agencies, and multinational corporations headquartered elsewhere) are not strongly connected to any particular regional network, they can exercise significant influence in regional matters. The power of such organizations is based on their ability to withdraw resources from the region, given their connections and facilities elsewhere. Gertler and Rutherford (in this volume) find, for example, that labor unions become active only when business has fled the region, or threatens to flee. While power is an inherent feature of networks, it is not always exercised. Power becomes evident when existing networks are reorganized, when actors align with new partners, or when outsiders seek access.

1.4.3 Managing the Public-Private Interface

Networks emerge when the expected payoffs from joint action exceed the benefits of individual action. But the payoffs may be remote and they are not always easy to evaluate. Knowledge of production processes, appropriate labor skills, and innovations at various stages in the value-added chain is often qualitative and difficult to acquire, unless the firm produces everything in-house or is embedded in a dense network of interdependent producers with guaranteed access to the knowledge held by others. One would expect highly specialized firms in networks to have a keen interest in institutional arrangements that help to evaluate and realize the expected payoffs from networking: structures that facilitate mutual assistance, knowledge sharing, and risk pooling (as in New Hampshire business networks, see Gittell et al., in this volume). Using the example of recent efforts in Southern California to promote an advanced ground transportation equipment manufacturing complex, Scott and Bergman (in this volume) outline some key areas of institution building: raising high-risk capital investment funds, promoting technology research, creating a skill base, and building collaborative industry consortia.

How these areas and the institutions that cover them should be related is a matter that has not seen much research. The dominant perspective seems to call for institutional infrastructures that are resource efficient. Understandably, in times of resource scarcity public sector organizations are subject to increased pressures for accountability. The most sensible approach to regional economic policy may therefore be to rationalize network relations and to minimize redundancies. Paradoxically, the outcome of streamlining networks may be a reduction in their learning capacity and adaptability (Grabher, 1993b). Successful industrial districts, for example, are often described as being embedded in "thick" institutional infrastructures, where redundancy is seen as a source of adaptability. Redundant network structures, so the argument, constitute a repository of solutions to the problem of adjusting to unpredictable conditions and thus make the system "error friendly." Hence, a sensible policy approach would be to promote redundancy rather than pursue narrow efficiency objectives. The objective would be not to create a limited number of agencies and to charge them with narrow mandates, but instead to build infrastructures within which a variety of actors can thrive and develop alternative solutions. While this approach is well anchored in systems theory, it is clearly antithetical to conventional thinking in public policy. But whether redundant infrastructures are (over the long term) superior to efficient structures is not known, given the available empirical evidence.

A key question with respect to institutional governance is whether the organizations responsible for governance are best located in the private (e.g., chambers of commerce, trade associations, labor unions) or public domain (e.g., ministries, export promotion agencies, universities). In the United States, the governance capacity of collective bodies in the private sector, such as trade and employers' associations (Staber, 1987), is highly limited. Similarly, R&D consortia are likely to be created at private-sector initiative, their managements rely heavily on member dues (with no or few government subsidies), and technology transfer is hampered by high member drop-out rates (Aldrich and Sasaki, 1995a,b). Many private-sector collective bodies are internally divided and lack the self-discipline necessary for the kind of cooperation that policy makers wish to encourage. This picture of fragmentation in the United States is consistent with the country's general libertarian ideology, buttressed by a national regulatory regime that encourages short-term orientations (Christopherson and Redfield, 1993). Gittell et al. (in this volume) wonder about the appropriate governance system if businesses cannot be brought together in the first place, in the absence of cultural norms of cooperation. They explain the difficulties of creating institutional structures for interfirm networking in the libertarian context of the state of New Hampshire, where many businesses are not accustomed to cooperation.

Whether institutional structures of coordination and collaboration are best privately or publicly controlled is probably a function of the political culture in a particular region. In states with a liberal tradition, such as the United States, Canada, and Britain, public institutions for interfirm cooperation tend to be relatively weak, and private institutions are weaker still. Gertler and Rutherford (in this volume) argue that the regulatory framework in Ontario provides no incentives for employers to invest in worker training and to collaborate in the development of high-skill production sytems. Consultation and bargaining among major private interests, within a larger institutional framework of broad consensus and long term orientation, is more likely in corporatist regimes, such as Austria and Sweden (Katzenstein, 1985). National regimes of institutional regulation set the broad parameters for interfirm collaboration, but there may be significant variations in local social structures and traditions which mediate the overall effect of national policies (Ettlinger, 1994). Thus, there is also the question of the level at which collaboration is best formulated and enforced (Grote, 1995). Should regulatory powers be given to intermediary organizations which are embedded locally or nationally? The answer may vary from country to country, depending upon political culture and economic circumstances. In Italy, for example, regional differences in political structures and resource endowments have had differential effects on the evolutionary pattern of populations of rural cooperative banks (Lomi, 1995). Accordingly, one would expect the networks in which these banks are embedded to be location-dependent as well. Public intervention strategies need to be sensitive to local needs and circumstances.

1.4.4 Performance Evaluation

Several decades of research on organizational performance have not yet led to a consensus on what performance means and what its determinants are. Earlier models of performance, which viewed organizations as essentially rational entities, emphasized structural-functional aspects and degrees of goal accomplishment. Recent models are concerned more with the non-rational, non-linear, and contradictory aspects of organizations. In this imagery, performance is driven not only by the interests of network planners but also by stakeholder preferences, which can be highly variable and unstable.

What is true for organizations with relatively fixed and identifiable boundaries is even more true for interorganizational networks with more elusive and transient boundaries. Much change in networks is largely uncontrolled, and thus the consequences of planned changes are difficult to anticipate. Network outcomes are often decoupled from individual intentions, and short-run consequences may differ greatly from long-run consequences. Therefore, it is not enough to ask whether individual organizations can learn and plan for an uncertain future. One must also ask whether networks of organizations as collective actors display the same capacities.

Assessing the performance of business networks and the districts in which they are embedded is problematic, but the policy-oriented literature has generally only paid lip-service to problems of performance measurement. The tendency has been to borrow from the experience of networks elsewhere which are assumed to be successful, without exploring the particular circumstances that may have led to these experiences (Staber, 1996). There has also been a tendency to make ad hoc judgments about network or regional performance based on a very limited range of measures, typically focusing on economic growth (Doeringer and Terkla, in this volume). In cases where networks are unstable, overlapping, and permeable, conventional performance measures – such as unemployment and economic growth rates – do not capture the independent effects of network characteristics on performance outcomes, relative to other factors that might explain the success of networks and regions. Economic growth and employment levels are a function of many variables, and it is difficult to isolate the net contribution of network arrangements and institutional structures.

Economic growth is also only one of several indicators of success. From a sociological-institutional perspective, the performance of a business network and its individual members is only indirectly linked to economic efficiency. More immediate performance indicators include "soft" variables such as conformity, trust, flexibility, reciprocity, and cooperation. It is not clear, however, whether these variables should be treated as measures of network performance or as independent variables explaining the effectiveness of networks. Cultural factors have figured prominently particularly in discussions of the evolution of industrial districts, with reference being made to things like entrepreneurial spirit, industriousness, and religious beliefs (Staber, in this volume). But such variables are difficult to measure and, even if they could be measured, knowing that values and traditions can make a difference for network performance is of limited use, from a policy perspective, unless the variables can be influenced by government programs. Innovation processes in networks can be very complex and chaotic, so that different criteria need to be applied when measuring behaviors and outcomes. Even if "soft" variables are difficult to measure, it is important to be aware of their influence, for they define the *processes* of building and maintaining network relations (Staber, in this volume). Regardless of whether one takes an interpretive (Kreiner and Schultz, 1993) or structuration approach (Sydow, in this volume), network structures cannot be divorced from their processual aspects. Dynamic processes shape the reality of networks over time. Processes should be of particular interest to practitioners, for they need to know the competencies necessary for motivating network members, negotiating and enforcing contracts, buffering the network from external demands, and so on.

But while human agency may open up possibilities for effective design, these possibilities are circumscribed by contextual constraints. Most organization researchers agree that performance outcomes are not independent of the contexts in which organizations operate. This is especially true for business networks whose participants may have multiple goals and constituencies with conflicting demands. These external constituencies may prevent firms from constructing a network as they see fit. The implication for government agencies, or anyone else interested in fostering cooperation, is that their network building efforts are constrained by the linkages that firms have with constituency organizations. In effect, these constituency organizations also become part of the network, and their preferences will influence the network's performance.

Ambiguities in measuring the performance of networks and the effectiveness of government programs for network building are compounded by opportunities for private actors to capture public programs. Under conditions of market failure, there may also be incentives for public agencies to oversupply services for networks (Gittell et al., in this volume). Interdependencies with other actors in the network determine how firms respond to and make use of public initiatives (Hall and Quinn, 1983). Information asymmetries, for example, may lead to lower quality service providers driving higher quality service providers out of the market (Gittell et al., in this volume).

Performance assessment is difficult not only because of the existence of multiple network constituencies who may bring divergent preferences and performance expectations to the exchange. Network performance is difficult to evaluate also because of changes in network memberships and affiliations over time. By definition, the competitive advantage of networks lies in their capacity to adapt quickly to changing circumstances. Not only do network members reconfigure themselves by changing their particular contributions to network exchanges (for example, by investing in new activities or by re-assigning personnel), but network membership itself may be highly fluid, as actors come and go, change their affiliations, and discover new preferences. Networks shape and transform the interests of actors, thus leading to their own transformation. Such changes contribute to dynamic network structures, with no apparent equilibria and with indeterminate outcomes. The result is that performance indicators need to be flexible themselves, informed by changes in constituencies and changes in contexts both within and outside of the network.

1.5 Conclusion

It has been suggested that networks are particularly well suited for rapid learning, mutual adjustment, and flexible deployment of resources. If supported by local governments and interest associations they may also make a positive contribution to endogenous regional development. Obviously, there is much we still do not understand about the institutional infrastructures in which business networks are embedded. At this stage in theory development, there are no clear and coherent models from which testable hypotheses can be derived. So far there has been no systematic and comparative research on the conditions under which particular institutional arrangements make identifiable differences (Staber, 1996). Much of the evidence has been descriptive, anecdotal, and case oriented. Research is usually conducted on units selected from samples of convenience or opportunity, often the most visible networks and districts. Theory building on the contribution of business networks to regional economic development has also been constrained by cross-sectional methodologies and additive and linear thinking. The tendency has been to generate simple check-lists of "things to do" and "things to keep in mind."

Policy makers have been tempted to assume that successful institutional arrangements can be transferred from regions that are thought to have model character, without first exploring the particular circumstances that have shaped the evolution of network structures in specific places. Local social structures and traditions ensure that agglomerations of firms and institutional organizations have an evolutionary logic of their own. But agglomerations are never completely self-contained. In the age of global hierarchies local economic prospects are shaped by global economic and organizational forces (Amin and Thrift, 1992). These larger forces place serious limits on policy intervention, and to ignore them is to risk that business networks, intended as an instrument of economic development, become another fad in the tool kit of governments concerned with job creation and social welfare.

In the absence of a strong theory, the trial-and-error approaches of policy makers and business practitioners are understandable. Researchers have only begun to piece together the puzzles of a complex set of antecedent and consequent conditions. They are still grappling with important specification problems in modelling network relations in a dynamic and multivariate context. There continues to be an unfortunate lack of dialogue among network analysts (particularly those with a strong mathematical-technical bend), business strategists, policy makers, and social theorists. There is also a need to make the findings of network research, as it applies to regional development, more accessible to practitioners, while improving upon the theoretical and methodological sophistication of that research. This volume is intended to be a modest step in that direction.

2. Flexible Specialization in Regional Networks

Jörg Sydow

2.1 Flexible Specialization, Regional Networks, and Strategic Networks

Much of the popularity and understanding of flexible specialization is owed to the oeuvre of Piore and Sabel (1984). Since then a lively debate has developed not only in Northern America but also in Europe, and attention has been paid to this debate by practitioners in firms, governments and government agencies.[1] *Flexible specialization*, according to Piore and Sabel (1984), is an adequate organizational response to ongoing product market differentiation and technological development. This organizational form, in their eyes, seems very suitable for small and medium-sized firms operating in niche rather than mass markets, although big mass-producing corporations have also adopted some kind of flexible specialization. Most importantly, the organizational form of flexible specialization implies an extensive horizontal and vertical division of work among technologically dynamic and organizationally flexible firms, which tend to concentrate on their core-competencies (Prahalad and Hamel, 1990). The nature and extent of this inter-firm division of work is often coordinated among the firms with the help of trade associations or other collective institutions. It is of equal importance that this organizational form emphazises the development and maintenance of co-operative rather than competitive relationships among firms embedded within a particular region or industrial district. A *regional network*, then, is an organizational arrangement among distinct but related small and medium-sized for-profit organizations. This organizational arrangement, above all, is characterized by complex reciprocal, co-operative rather than competitive, and relatively stable relations between legally independent though economically interdependent firms which co-operate in spa-

1 For the U.S e.g., Scott (1988a), Sabel (1989), Sabel et al. (1989), Storper and Scott (1989, 1992), Saxenian (1990), Storper and Harrison (1991), Nohria (1992), Perrow (1992), Alter and Hage (1993) or Harrison (1994), for Europe e.g., Aydalot and Keeble (1988), Goodman et al. (1989), Hirst and Zeitlin (1989), Sayer (1989), Amin and Robins (1990), Best (1990), Pyke et al. (1990), Bergman et al. (1991), Ernste and Meier (1992), Illeris (1992), Pyke and Sengenberger (1992), Grabher (1993a). In additon, see the contributions within this volume.

tial proximity (Sydow, 1992a).[2] And it is these kinds of relations which allow small firms to act like larger ones. Financial, educational and research institutions are usually as closely tied into these networks as are government agencies, trade associations, chambers of commerce and trade unions (e.g., Sabel et al., 1989).

As to whether a regional network is a hybrid organizational form between markets and hierarchies (e.g., Thorelli, 1986) or neither a market nor a hierarchy, i.e., an organizational form on its own (e.g., Powell, 1990), is still debated. Compared to markets, a network has more structure, produces more interaction among the network organizations, provides "thicker" information channels, demands more loyalty, exhibits more trust, prefers voice to exit, and puts less emphasis on prices. Compared to hierarchies, a network is somewhat "underorganized" (Brown, 1983), due to the loose coupling of the network organizations and due to the open boundaries of the network. Moreover, it calls for negotiation rather than for command, puts more emphasis on boundary spanning roles and is more open towards the entry and exit of members. The market test is still applicable and thus, "networking introduces a cost discipline that may be absent in an integrated firm" (Jarillo, 1988, p. 35). Confronted with increasingly differentiated product markets, this (inter-)organizational arrangement, it is assumed, allows firms in the network to gain or sustain a competitive advantage vis-à-vis their competitors outside the network. The prototype of this kind of network may be found in the Emilia Romagna of the Third Italy (e.g., Brusco, 1982; Goodman et al., 1989; Best, 1990; Inzerelli, 1990; Pyke et al., 1990; Harrison, 1994).

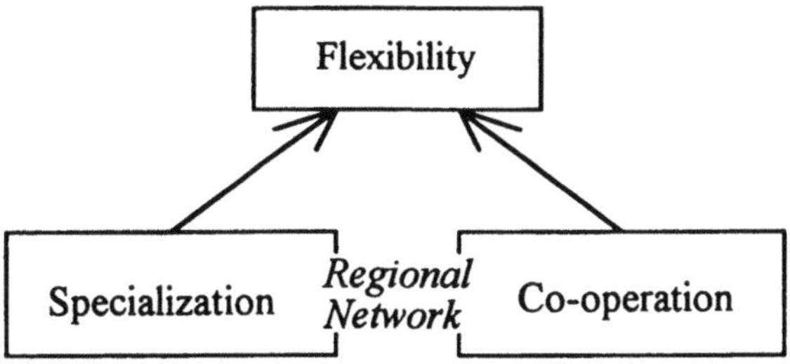

Figure 2.1 Flexibility through specialization and co-operation

Both characteristics, specialization and co-operation within a network, are mainly responsible for the high level of numerical and, above all, functional flexibility of this organizational form (see Fig. 2.1). However, a regional network is

2 The notion of regional networks emphazises the interorganizational relationships between the network firms rather than the regional milieux or any other spatial conditions which are usually associated with the notion of regional economies, industrial districts or decentralized industrial order.

just one of at least two types of interorganizational networks.[3] A *strategic network*, the second type of network, exhibits similar characteristics to the regional network, though this type of interorganizational network is neither situated in a particular region or industrial district nor does it comprise only small and medium-sized firms but all types of firms. The most important difference, however, is that this type of network is strategically led by a focal or hub firm (see Table 2.1 for a summary).

Table 2.1 Regional and strategic networks

	regional network	*strategic network*
strategic leadership	none, perhaps collective leadership	focal or hub firm
size of network firms	small and medium-sized firms only	large, medium-sized, (small)
organization	self-organization, culture	formalized interorganizational structure
network boundries	relatively closed	relatively open
prototypical examples	Emilia Romagna	Japanese Keiretsu, franchising networks

A strategic network is, on the one hand, an outcome of the present "co-operating rather than merging"-philosphy. On the other hand, it is an outcome of the current downsizing, demassing, demerging and restructuring wave sweeping over Germany as well as other highly industrialized countries. More precisely, strategic and regional networks are an outcome not only of quasi-internalization but also of quasi-externalization of economic activities (Sydow, 1992b). Probably the networks led by Japanese car manufacturers come closest to the organizational form of strategic networks but they can also be found in other industries. Prominent examples are IBM (especially in Japan), Bosch, Ikea, Benetton and Marks & Spencer. Multinational companies are sometimes organized in a form which comes close to that of a strategic network. This is particularly true for "transnational corporations" (Bartlett and Ghoshal, 1989) which, similar to some regional networks, may be conceived as embedded in *international* networks.

Strategic networks and regional networks may well be *interrelated*. Strategic networks grow from industrial districts, and firms embedded in regional networks may quasi-integrate into strategic networks. Even spatially distant networks may be interlinked to networks of small and medium-sized firms within a particular

3 A somewhat more differentiated typology may be found in Storper and Harrison (1991).

region through a strategic network, as the case of Benetton and the regional networks of small textile producers in Northern Italy clearly demonstrates. The question of whether the organizational form of small and medium-sized firms linked up in a regional network converges, as Sabel (1989) suggests, with that of big firms quasi-externalizing business functions, still remains an open question which will not be answered here. Instead, assuming there is a difference between these two organizational forms (Amin and Robins, 1990), this chapter addresses mainly regional networks.

A necessary precondition not only for effective network management but also for successful public policy aiming at regional economic competitiveness and development is understanding the processes of network building, of the inter-firm division of work, of the balancing of the autonomy and dependence within the network and of the measures taken to create and sustain trusting relationships. The analysis of a particular case of regional networking which we came across in an empirical study on interorganizational relationships in the German financial service industry may deepen this understanding. This analysis takes a management and organizational perspective highlighting the processes of network building on the firm and inter-firm level, but without ignoring regional, sectoral and public policy aspects. A short overview of the experiences with flexible specialization in Germany, especially in Baden-Württemberg, will precede this analysis.

2.2 German Experiences: Baden-Württemberg and Beyond

The German region where flexible specialization is considered most common is the south-western state of Baden-Württemberg. This region with its rather large number of small and medium-sized firms, often closely tied together in regional networks, has been analyzed not only by German researchers (e.g., Maier, 1987; Schmitz, 1992; Semlinger, 1993, 1994) but also by Sabel and his colleagues (e.g., Piore and Sabel, 1984; Sabel et al., 1989; Herrigel, 1993) who compare it with presumedly similar regions in the United States.

The research of the latter scholars identifies central elements of flexible specialization and regional networks especially within the machine-tool, special machine and auto supplier industry of Baden-Württemberg, obviously rather traditional industries, at least if compared with the prospering high-tech and financial services industry of Massachusetts. Baden-Württemberg firms have resisted attempts to diversify into new product areas. Instead, they have specialized in the manufacturing of highly sophisticated products and continously improved and customized existing product lines, in particular by adopting and integrating technological innovations from computer and software businesses. Since specialized firms are systematically more dependent on the success of complementary products and services, their economic success depends significantly not only upon the existence of private firms and public institutions which supply these products and services but on their own *relational capabilities to co-operate* with these firms and institutions in a regional network.

Baden-Württemberg firms, as Sabel et al. (1989) demonstrate in the case of the textile-machinery industry, have pursued the strategy of flexible specialization up to the present. This strategy has recently been complemented by extensive sub-contracting practices and, since then, has increased even more the numerical and functional flexibility of the firms co-operating. Sub-contracting is not entirely new to Baden-Württemberg firms, but the nature of the sub-contracting practices has changed. Firms do not only externalize simple manufacturing tasks to sub-contractors but delegate to them complex manufacturing and even design tasks, including the responsibilities for developing new components and processes. Sabel (1989, pp. 30-31) himself rightly points to the learning advantages of this organizational form. Since many firms now pursue this strategy of flexible specialization, much of Baden-Württemberg's textile-machinery industry has developed in what may be called regional clusters or "small-firm networks" (Perrow, 1992). Large firms in the Stuttgart region such as Daimler-Benz, Alcatel-SEL, IBM and especially Bosch have contributed to the spread of this organizational form because they have also started to concentrate on core-competencies, to farm out the manufacturing of components and the provision of producer services, and to coordinate their production in networks.

The state, the regional government of Baden-Württemberg in particular, has facilitated the development and spread of flexible specialization in regional networks via the provision of technical and vocational training, of technical and commercial consultancy and of a variety of other services. Apart from the state, local banks, venture capitalists, but also non-financial intermediaries such as sectoral associations (VDMA and ZVEI, in particular) and chambers of commerce provided the appropriate milieux for the spread of this organizational form (Sabel et al., 1989; Herrigel, 1993; Semlinger, 1993).

While clusters of technologically dynamic and organizationally flexible firms co-operating in regional networks are not only to be found in the textile-machinery industry of Baden-Württemberg but also in other machine-tool, special machine industries and the auto supplier industry of this area, this picture tells only half the story of Baden-Württemberg (Schmitz, 1992). What is true for the textile-machinery industry in particular and for the machine-tool and special machine industry in general, does not necessarily apply to the electronics and auto supplier industries which are also of particular importance to the Baden-Württemberg economy. Networks of firms in these industries are dominated by large hub firms and, hence, should be considered as being members of strategic rather than regional networks. Schmitz (1992) -in contrast to Sabel et al. – thus concludes that "Baden-Württemberg cannot be characterized as a small firm economy. On the contrary, the main industrial agglomeration of the Stuttgart region is dominated by large firms. It is true that there are some small industrial centres outside the Stuttgart region which bear a closer resemblance, in size and structure, to the industrial district model. One of the most interesting examples is Tuttlingen, a world leader in the production of surgical instruments (Maier, 1987). However, such small firm industrial districts have relatively little weight in the Baden-Württemberg economy – particularly if compared with the "Third Italy" (Schmitz, 1992: 95).

The type of network-character of the Baden-Württemberg economy is still disputed. On the one hand, Semlinger (1993) reports some successful cases of the more complicated and fragile type of horizontal networking in different Baden-Württemberg industries. On the other hand, Staber (1996) reports empirical evidence suggesting that firms in Baden-Württemberg do not co-operate extensively, and, if they do co-operate with other firms (apart from financial institutions), they rarely do so within their immediate region.

The fact that the region has been hit by the recession in the early 1990s as much as the entire German economy has not only taken some glamour away from the region but has also given rise to *doubts on the flexibility of flexible specialization*. The recent recession has not bypassed the Baden-Württemberg economy for at least four reasons. Firstly, firms in this region, more than in other parts of Germany, manufacture industrial goods affected most by this recession. Secondly, firms co-operating in regional networks are often tied to strategic networks led by large firms, and these large firms are of course affected by the recession. Thirdly, as pointed out above, small and medium-sized firms co-operating in flexible networks may have little weight in the Baden-Württemberg economy. Fourthly, organizational flexibility hardly protects firms from general economic downturns. As opposed to the first reason given, these last three reasons are closely related to the organizational form of flexible specialization in regional networks. Nevertheless, the regional government, now a grand coalition of Christian and Social Democrats, the latter even providing the Secretary of Economic Affairs, has continued its interventionist industrial policy which aims at small and medium-sized firms in particular. This policy is now labeled "dialogue-oriented economic policy," and the unions in the meantime have joined this dialogue. The government continues to stimulate not only direct co-operation of small and medium-sized firms but also the provision of marketing services, the exchange of technical and professional specialists, the provision of organizational and technical consultancy and the coordination of research efforts in the fields of biotechnology, information technology, new materials, recycling and soft energy (Behrens and Böhmer, 1993).

Although the model of flexible specialization may be found not only in Baden-Württemberg but also in other regions of Germany as well as in other industries, evidence on this is rather limited. Two recent studies of the Institut für Arbeit und Technik show that firms are much less interlinked in other regions of Germany. Kilper and Rehfeld's (1991) analysis of four urban agglomerations (Munich, Frankfurt, Hannover and Hamburg) adds further evidence that there is hardly any "pure" Emilian-like industrial district characterized by a high degree of flexible specialization and regional networking, while elements of this organizational form may be found in almost all industries and regions of Germany. Rehfeld (1994) argues that even in the car industry, which has been thoroughly investigated in terms of network relationships, regional networks are hardly to be found outside the Stuttgart region and nowadays outside the area of Regensburg, Bavaria, and of Eisenach, Saxony, – both more recent locations of flexible specialization. However, present public policy interventions (by the regional government of North Rhine-Westphalia, for instance) could increase the networking activities of firms on a regional basis, although a recent survey of 719 manufacturing firms in North Rhine-Westphalia shows that especially small firms are little inclined to co-operate (Belzer, 1993). Hence, general doubts exist as to whether the German economy is correctly labelled an example of "cooperative managerial capitalism" (Chandler, 1990). Nevertheless, more research using a network perspective is likely to discover more strategic and more regional networks in the German economy.

2.3 InBroNet: A Regional Network in the Financial Service Industry

The international debate on flexible specialization in regional networks up to now has focussed on the nature and spread of this organizational form in manufacturing industries. The provision of services by private firms or public institutions has been considered a condition which stimulates or facilitates co-operation on a regional basis (e.g., Maillat and Vasserot, 1988; Brusco, 1992b; de Jong et al., 1992; Semlinger, 1993). However, only few studies have investigated *regional networks of service firms* in their own right (e.g., Traxler et al., 1991; Bryson et al., 1993). Flexible specialization in regional networks may be an effective organizational form for this kind of industry too, for these firms face a differentiation of demand and a respective individualization and customization of services as much as the manufacturers of consumer and industrial goods.

2.3.1 Insurance Brokers and their Role within Financial Services Networks

Differentiation of demand, and individualization and customization of services, also affect firms in the financial service industry which up to now have hardly been analyzed from a network perspective (for exceptions, see Fombrun and Astley, 1983; Eccles and Crane, 1987; Buono and Hachey, 1993). Since insurance intermediaries, especially insurance brokers, more than others are likely to organize financial services networks, they were the focus of an empirical study of network relationships we conducted within the German financial service industry (Sydow et al., 1995).[4] *Insurance brokers* are considered independent intermediaries who buy coverage from insurers on behalf of their private or commercial clients. Typically, an insurance broker analyzes the client's risks, advises on risk aversion and management, and, of course, searches for an insurer who underwrites this risk at a minimum premium and yet offers good service. If necessary, the broker him- or herself designs the coverage in co-operation with insurers and reinsurers. In the case of damage, he or she manages the claims and advises the client on how to minimize the financial consequences. The service of the broker is usually remunerated by a commission which the broker may deduct from the premium he or she collects from the client and transfers to the insurer.

Although depending upon the specific kind of coverage, this business involves a vast expertise which, in the case of commercial lines at least, can only be provided by brokers beyond a minimum size (or who have access to the necessary expertise via network relationships, for example). For insurance brokers in the commercial lines may closely resemble what Starbuck (1992) calls "knowledge-intensive firms," as distinct from "information-intensive firms"; the latter may become computerized much more easily.

The role of insurance brokers in financial services networks cannot be understood properly without acknowledging the existence of *alternative distribution channels*. These are provided on the one hand by agents[5] tied to one insurance company only and by direct insurers on the other. While the insurance markets of countries such as the United Kingdom, the Netherlands and the United States are largely "broker-controlled markets," insurance brokers in most other countries, including Germany, constitute a distribution channel of only minor importance if one looks at the industry as a whole. However, in the commercial lines, brokers have a significant stake even in these countries.

If one looks at the insurance broker being tied into a bundle of network-like relationships to insurance companies (as well as to clients) many insurance brokers

4 Funds for this study which were provided by the ISDN-Forschungskommission des Landes Nordrhein-Westfalens are gratefully acknowledged. This study follows -in terms of theory – a structurationist perspective developed by Anthony Giddens (1984) and outlined and applied to the analysis of inter-firm networks by Sydow and Windeler (1996). In terms of methodology, a qualitative network analysis has been applied to discover the number and nature of network relationships that insurance brokers maintain with clients, insurers, and among themselves. I thank André Kretschmann and especially Arnold Windeler for collecting valuable information on the particular case presented in this paper.

5 These may be self-employed or employed by an insurer. They also include banks, building societies and retail chains used as distribution outlets for insurance.

in these "broker-controlled markets" occupy a role which comes close to that of a hub firm in a strategic network. In these markets brokers rather than insurers develop new products, design new coverages and build up interorganizational information systems. However, in insurance markets of countries which are dominated by tied agents, and that means more precisely by insurers, even large industrial brokers are somewhat remote from taking on this role of a strategic leader of the network.[6]

In our empirical study of network relationships within the German insurance industry focussing upon the role of insurance brokers and other independent intermediaries, we discovered not only *vertical* network relationships between insurers, intermediaries and clients but also *horizontal* forms of co-operation (cf. Sydow et al., 1995, pp. 316-429). Some of the latter are rather conventional: they simply aim at the pooling of premium income in order to increase their commissions or, which is much more demanding, at the joint development and use of inter-organizational information systems. Furthermore, commercial insurance brokers increasingly tend to operate on a global basis and therefore co-operate in international networks of corresponding brokers, although they are not very likely to become "neo-Marshallian nodes in global networks" (Amin and Thrift, 1992). Some other co-operative arrangements we discovered among insurance brokers are less conventional: while some brokers are developing franchise-like arrangements, others employ the concept of flexible specialization in regional networks.[7] One of these regional networks, labelled "InBroNet" as a pseudonym for "Industrial Broker Network," will be described and analyzed in the remainder of this chapter.

2.3.2 InBroNet: Insurance Brokers on their Way to Flexible Specialization

InBroNet, situated in an industrial region in northern Germany, has been formed by seven medium-sized insurance brokers who do much of their business in commercial lines, although some of them are considering more involvement in the pri-

6 Although this may well change due to the creation of the Single European Market in the financial service industry in 1994, the German insurance market at least seems very unlikely to turn into a "broker-controlled market" (see Sydow et al., 1995).

7 Moreover, as Gentle (1993) reports from Britain, big insurance brokers, "mega-brokers" in particular, have adopted more decentralized, specialized and, hence, market-driven organizational forms. Some of these, lean holding structures in particular, closely resemble (strategic) networks. This example, by the way, demonstrates that network-like forms of organization may well go hand in hand with the creation of financial conglomerates.

vate lines business. Many of the network relationships among the InBroNet brokers have been developed in regular meetings which for some time constituted the main forum of interorganizational interaction (see Figure 2.2).

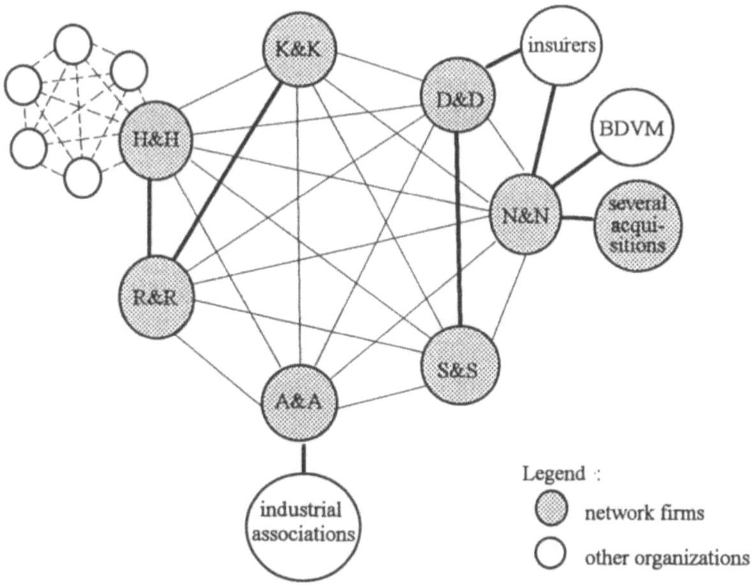

Dimension	K&K, H&H, R&R *	D&D, N&N, S&S *
Size	smaller	larger
Business	commercial, but significant private included	commercial, private insignificant
Age	newcomer	established
Products	innovative	conservative
Attitude towards flexible specialization	promotors	some of them waverer

* A&A which is somewhat isolated, takes a medium position in every respect.

Figure 2.2 InBroNet – attributes of the network firms

All seven network firms conceive themselves as "real" insurance brokers, i.e., as the client's rather than the insurer's agent. One of the brokers (H&H) is not only a member of InBroNet but also tied to a very loose network of brokers and agents operating in the private lines business. The size of the brokers varies between four and over 30 employees, including several self-employed salespersons, so that some of these brokers are (strategic) networks themselves.

2.3.2.1 Setting up the Network

InBroNet as a regional network of independent insurance brokers evolved as a response to an insurer's initiative to set up a strategic network. This network was planned to be based upon modern interorganizational information systems and to comprise not only "real" insurance brokers but also semi-professional alleged brokers. Both network features did not meet the needs of independent insurance brokers who do much of their business in commercial lines so that they started to form their own network which suits their interests.

Despite significant differences in detail, the seven broker firms shared a similar size-related position before starting to network:

(1) The increaing complexity and volatility of the insurance business does not allow small and medium-sized brokers to serve all the needs of their commercial clients.[8]

(2) In view of the increasing business complexity and volatitily, the broker's independence, which is of overwhelming strategic importance, can only be sustained if brokers succeed in extending their expert knowledge. This knowledge is a significant resource in the managing of interorganizational relationships with clients and insurers.

(3) The ongoing efforts of insurers to rationalize their relationships with agents tied within their traditional distribution channels put brokers under pressure to rationalize their organizational and interorganizational operations. Improved accounting practices, optimum utilization of experts, coordinated use of information systems and joint cashing in of insurance premiums could be suitable measures to reduce production and transaction costs.

(4) Faced with a saturation of demand on the part of big industrial clients, the "mighty players" among the insurance brokers penetrate into the market of small and medium-sized customers which were traditionally supplied by intermediaries of the size of the InBroNet bokers; partly they even do so by acquiring brokers of this kind.

In the case of the seven industrial insurance brokers, specialization and cooperation (including mutual allocation of business) seems a more adequate response to any of these four challenges than internal growth. External growth, quite popular among large insurance brokers (Gentle, 1993; Sydow et al, 1995 pp. 300-316), was out of question for them due to the lack of capital. However, the mastering of the expertise issue for insurance brokers, as much as for any other knowledge-intensive firm, is the basis for gaining or at least sustaining compet-

8 The increased complexity stems from the demand side as well as from the supply side. For instance, risks are becoming more complex and interdependent, insurance products are connected to other financial services, customers increasingly go international, and the supply of coverage by brokers in a Single European Market is less surveyable.

itive advantage in the distribution channel. As one of the seven brokers stated, "For insurance brokers like us it is too expensive to keep available the knowledge necessary to serve commercial clients in a reasonable way."

Co-operation in a regional network not only enables insurance brokers to specialize on their core-competence but also enhances the possibilities for interorganizational learning via "knowledge-links" (Badaracco, 1991). Furthermore, it may enable them to diversify their services without broadening their own expertise and strengthen their network position in relation to insurers and other providers of financial services.

2.3.2.2 The Influence of Personal Relationships

More than a similar starting position, trust and at least some shared understandings were a necessary condition for setting up InBroNet. Trust and mutual understanding, although far from being perfect, did indeed facilitate the evolution of InBroNet. Both stem from long lasting personal ties between the members of two subgroups (D&D, S&S and N&N on the one hand, H&H, K&K and R&R on the other), some of them could even be considered friendship ties (see thick lines in figure 3). Moreover, apart from one firm (N&N), all are members of the same German association of insurance brokers (BDVM). One of the brokers even holds an influential position in this association. The spatial proximity contributes further to the "social embeddedness" (Granovetter, 1985) of economic transactions within this network which, as any network, has evolved through several phases.

Trustee relationships and shared understandings, despite significant differences in opinion about the prospects, form and intensity of networking,[9] were able to compensate for a lack of organizing capabilities which are necessary even in the very early phases of network development. All seven firms were neither familiar with the concept of flexible specialization nor did they have much knowledge about how to set up a (regional) network. This became particularly clear when we were called upon to consult on the visions of regional networking and on the process of organizing networks several months after we had finished the network analysis of InBroNet.

2.3.2.3 Phases of Network Formation

The idea of setting up a regional network of independent insurance brokers was first discussed in a regional group of the BDVM. Although almost 30 insurance brokers participated in this *first* phase, only seven of them agreed on more intensive networking and started to develop an organizational form which now, more

9 Some of the InBroNet brokers wished to exchange kowledge via regular meetings only, while others – at least implicitly – pursued the strategy of flexible specialization, others still could hardly be prevented from setting up a referent organization providing services to all network firms.

than two years later, closely resembles the model of flexible specialization in a regional network.

The phase of discussing the idea was followed by a *second* phase in which the remaining seven brokers tried to gain a shared understanding about the goals of the effort and the scope of choices concerning the external division of work and the form of network relationships. In this phase an outside consultant significantly facilitated this learning process, even if it became clear soon that he did not have enough capabilities to moderate the process of network building.

Formalizing the network was the main issue in the *third* phase. Among other things, the network partners reached agreement on some professional norms and decision rules, set up some kind of strategic plan, founded a formal association (Verein), elected a chairman and – finally – started operation. At this stage InBroNet had reached a level of network density and interconnectedness which bears all the *potentials* of successful flexible specialization in a regional network but certainly does not guarantee long-term stability.

2.3.3 Managing the Formation of InBroNet: Tensions and Contradictions

We investigated in some depth the *processes of network building*, focussing in particular on the inter-firm division of work, the balancing of the autonomy and dependence as well as of competition and co-operation within the network and on the measures taken to create and sustain trusting relationships despite necessary controls. From a structurationist perspective, which guided our qualitative network analysis, these tensions are as much an outcome as a medium of managing inter-firm networks (see Sydow and Windeler 1996, for details on this perspective.

2.3.3.1 Flexible Specialization and Inter-firm Division of Work

All InBroNet-brokers have been concentrating on their core-competences. They all renounced the employment or acquisition of risk consultants, engineers, risk experts, tax consultants, lawyers and certified accountants. Instead, the seven brokers co-operate closely with independent firms which provide these professional services via *vertical* network-relationships. Currently they are negotiating with their main coverage providers about rearranging the division of work between brokers and insurers. Moreover, the seven brokers have started to co-operate in the area of information management, advertising, and personnel development. In addition, the InBroNet brokers have set up small task forces of experts who try to design new coverages, a task which corresponds to developing new products in other industries (see Sydow et al., 1995, pp. 364-378, for details).

In terms of *horizontal* relationships, the seven insurance brokers have stopped diversifying any further the financial services provided by each network firm. Instead, they want to mutually allocate their business to each other. In the distant future, an interorganizational information system may assist this allocation process. However, the still somewhat contradictory interests and visions of the seven brokers on the prospects and forms of networking may delay more intensive flexbile specialization and co-operation within the network.

2.3.3.2 Flexible Specialization, Autonomy and Dependence

Flexible specialization is a two-edged sword with regard to autonomy and dependence. This also proves to be true in the case of InBroNet. On a *horizontal* level every network firm loses some of its autonomy when it specializes and quasi-externalizes some functions to either one of the other firms of the network or to some referent organization.

With regard to *vertical* relationships, specialization usually increases dependence too. Flexible specialization in a regional network, however, increases the autonomy of the entire network and thus of every single organization with respect to providers and customers of financial services. This is the case when the network firms, as in the case of InBroNet, pool their premium (and thereby increase their bargaining power), develop their expertise, or set up their own interorganizational information system. However, the insurers with whom InBroNet do most of their business found it difficult to accept the network as a unified agent. The struggle about the recognition of the network by the insurers still continues.

2.3.3.3 Flexible Specialization, Competition, and Co-operation

As argued in the literature on inter-firm networking (e.g., Semlinger, 1993) and in this chapter, a clear distinction should be made between vertical and horizontal relations. This is particularly relevant with repect to the issue of competition and co-operation. For *horizontal* relations, which are essential for regional networks, imply a higher level of competition. They are, therefore, more likely to break up than *vertical* relations. On the other hand, many gains of networking depend significantly upon successful horizontal co-operation.

Due to the prospect of better products and services, some economies of scale, and increased commissions, the brokers of InBroNet had strong incentives to co-operate horizontally. Moreover, measures have been taken to avoid competition as much as possible. For instance, it was necessary for the InBroNet-brokers, who all operate within a specific region of northern Germany, to pay attention to the regional distribution of their clients. For insurance brokers, in the commercial lines at least, provide services to clients not only in their immediate localities but also to firms from a wider area. Although the seven brokers, by and large, managed to avoid competiton within the network, this issue is on the agenda of regular network meetings from time to time.

However, there is another kind of competition which interpenetrates co-operative relationships among the network members: a more subtle kind of competition about who has the best expertise in the network, who is most influential in the relations with insurers and who performs best at the network meetings. This kind of "personal" competition is also a two-edged sword. On the one hand, it is a driving force of network development, on the other it is an additional cause of conflict and disruption. After initial competition of this kind within InBroNet, the different personalities and roles played in the network have been largely accepted by the network members.

2.3.3.4 Flexible Specialization, Trust, and Control

Trust seems to be a necessary condition for specialization and co-operation in a network (e.g., Jarillo, 1988; Lorenz, 1989; Ring and Van de Ven, 1994). One reason for this is the loss of independence among the network firms, another concerns the open exchange of knowledge whose abuse may undermine the competitive position of the network partners. While pre-existing personal ties, shared understandings and spatial proximity provide the basis for trust within InBroNet, concrete action taken by the network firms – and not least concrete success – strengthened the trust base. The early disclosure of the respective rate of commission and of the cost structure of the individual network firms has been particulary important in this respect. In the case of InBroNet, person-based and experience-based trust are likely to develop into institutional trust in the near future (Zucker, 1986). However, control systems (e.g., control for an appropriate allocation of business and for a fair payment system of services provided by any of the other brokers or a referent organization) still have to be developed and may once more put pressure upon the trustee relationships of the seven insurance brokers. In order to avoid this pressure, such control systems should be of a kind that does not lose sight of reciprocity expectations.

2.3.3.5 Flexible Specialization and Economic Performance

The costs and benefits of InBroNet have not yet been evaluated by the network partners because it is much too early for such an evaluation. Although each of the network firms has profited from the co-operative venture, the network is not yet likely to have a big economic impact upon its members. This is because, among other things, the most immediate and substantial benefit which was expected from the pooling of the premium and the bargaining with insurers over higher commissions, has not yet been realized. All insurers resisted this request, arguing that they will not place their tied agents at a disadvantage. However, it seems likely that the size argument will pay off: the network firms can remain small and yet profit from economies of scale and scope similar to larger organizations. Nevertheless, it will remain an open question whether co-operation in the case of InBroNet – as in many other instances – is only a temporary phenomenon which will be turned into a pure hierarchical organizational form by means of mergers and acquisition. One of the network organizations may grow faster than others and take over one of the other network firms. Or, as reported from other regional networks (cf. Harrison, 1994), InBroNet may become a target for acquisition by large firms, either by an insurer or by one of the "mighty players" among the German insurance brokers. While this would not necessarily imply the end of flexible specialization in regional networks, InBroNet could become just one node in a larger *strategic* network.

Although flexible specialization in regional networks may still be quite uncommon in the German financial service industry, economically it does seem to be a viable organizational form, at least for small and medium-sized insurance brokers. For this particular form provides an effective way to overcome the structural contradiction between diversification (in order to follow market differentiation) and specialization (in the face of the constantly increasing complexity of business in the commercial lines). This insight may well be extended to include financial services other than insurance, which is important, since financial services in general increasingly occupy an autonomous role in the restructuring of regional economies and affect the economic development of a region as a whole (Gentle, 1993).

2.4 Organizing Regional Networks: Some Conclusions for Business and Public Policy

In conclusion, flexible specialization in regional networks may not be the dominant form of organizing production, neither of goods nor of services, neither in Germany in general nor in Baden-Württemberg in particular. However, the spread of this organizational form is neither restricted to this region nor to the manufacturing industry. At least some cases of flexible specialization may be found, as shown in this chapter, in the financial service industry. Although this organizational form is not immune to economic recession and management failures, by emphasing co-operation it may provide a viable alternative to concentration.

The formation of a regional network depends, as argued in the case of InBroNet, not only on shared goals and a common understanding of the inter-firm division of work, but also on the mastering of structural contradictions between autonomy and dependence (including in strategic networks), co-operation and competition, and trust and control.

As much of the literature on industrial districts and regional economies demonstrates, public policy can facilitate this complicated process of network formation in many ways (e.g., Bianchi and Bellini, 1991; Pyke and Sengenberger, 1992; Semlinger, 1993). For instance, the state government, government agencies or professional associations may help to make network structures explicit by encouraging single firms to consider themselves part of an inter-firm network, provide information about who is considering network building of one kind or another, give advice on the interorganizational division of work and pooling of resources via subsidized expert opinion or consultancy, initiate and organize inter-firm cooperation by means of funds or services, or support institutions who are able to do so. Although the case of InBroNet illustrates that networking is possible *without* external support, government agencies and other institutions should in fact stimulate the organizing of mostly underorganized networks by means of "transorganizational development" (Cummings, 1984). Transorganizational development or TD, which, however, has up to now and to our knowledge only been applied in settings with non-profit organizations, uses many of the techniques of organizational development (OD), but takes the special structural properties of inter-firm networks[10] into account (cf. Gray, 1990; Sink, 1991). TD may be used in a design-oriented approach to inter-firm networking as well as in a more evolutionary developmental approach, as the one choosen by InBroNet.

And although some scepticism towards the effectiveness of purposive external intervention in network formation is certainly in order (Staber, 1996), such intervention may well improve the organization of the co-operative relationships within networks. In the case of network building among firms which have not yet developed relational capabilities to co-operate such interventions may even be a necessary but insufficient condition of networking.

But any business and public policy approach to networking presumes a deep understanding of the problems, tensions and contradictions involved in setting up and managing a regional network. To the extent that regional networks will increasingly be tied into strategic networks, so that the region may lose importance in view of the increasing globalization of economies, it is also important for managers and public policy makers to develop a better understanding of strategic networks.

10 E.g., the autonomy of the network firms, the mostly long-term character of network development, and the different political character of networks.

3. Regional-Industrial Networks and the Role of Labour

Meric S. Gertler and Tod D. Rutherford

3.1 Introduction

There is now a growing consensus that the face of manufacturing is changing in response to a set of shifts in the dominant terms of competition in capitalist societies. Where previously most producers competed largely on the basis of the cost of production, and sought to lower this by achieving economies of scale within their plants, now quality, responsiveness to customers' particular and increasingly differentiated needs, and time-to-market with new products have joined cost as the principal arbiters of competitive success. Producers are developing and adopting new production processes, built around new, versatile machinery, new ways of organising work and operations within the firm, and – perhaps most fundamentally – a growing awareness on the part of management of the need to encourage the full participation and empowerment of their workers.

However, not all of the changes in manufacturing are confined to internal structure, strategy and operations. In some of the world's most dynamic industrial regions, an equally significant set of changes seems to be taking shape in the interfirm organisational structure of industries as well. Furthermore, there appear to be important links between the changes observed *within single plants* and the transformation of *interfirm relations*. What is now emerging has been described by some as a new regime of interfirm cooperation, in which private manufacturers in the same industries – or those related by buyer-supplier linkages – forge new relations based on collaboration, information-sharing, and mutual trust.

This new organisational form represents a *social model of production*, which seems capable of providing participating firms with several distinct advantages. For small and medium-sized enterprise (SMEs), such collaborative production *networks* allow them to cooperate with other firms that have complementary strengths, permitting greater specialisation and rationalisation by each member firm. SMEs can retain their well-recognised agility in designing new products and responding quickly to changing market demands, while also exploiting the efficiencies arising from their participation in an extended production system based on linkages outside the firm. In essence, instead of achieving competitive success through increasing *internal* production scale, these firms can instead exploit *external* economies of scale. There is further evidence to suggest that these benefits will be especially strong when the members of such production networks are clustered within the same or nearby regions.

However, production networks are not the exclusive domain of SMEs. Recent work has brought attention to the benefits that these organisational forms can bring to large firms as well. Large firms are increasingly engaging in collaborative agreements with one another, such as strategic alliances, to exploit the same possibilities for specialisation that arise from cooperation. But they are also forging new links with smaller firms in network relations that provide benefits for both parties.

Not surprisingly, much attention has been directed recently to the idea of stimulating the development of industrial networks in disadvantaged regions, to emulate the successes of regions in Germany, Italy, Denmark, and elsewhere. This interest has been further fuelled by the work of scholars such as Piore and Sabel (1984), Scott (1988b), and more recently, Porter (1990, 1991), who have underscored the territorial foundations of competitively successful economic activity. However, this growing international literature has had surprisingly little to say about a subject of considerable importance -namely, what role has labour played in contributing to the shape and success of these various industrial agglomerations?

This is an important question for at least one compelling reason. There appears to be a growing realization that if the economies of the industrialised countries are to retain or enhance their competitive position, they can only do so by fostering high-value production built on the foundation of truly participatory employment relations in the workplace.[1] And yet the overwhelming majority of those writing on business networks seem not to acknowledge this insight. Instead, the literature is awash with descriptions of emerging buyer-supplier relationships and forms of interfirm cooperation, but little time is given to the significant role played (or the share of benefits received) by other equally important stakeholders in the production process. As we argue below, the characteristics of individual network-based industrial districts vary substantially from one case to another, and a good deal of this variation can be attributed to the nature and extent of labour's contribution to institution-building and competitive strategy in each regional setting. Hence, as local, regional, and national policymakers begin to deal with the question of how network principles might be adapted and employed so as to stimulate regional economic development, it is important to be aware of the interaction between how such networks are constructed – in particular, the nature and extent of labour's involvement – and the kind of benefits arising from their creation.

1 Witness the mantra-like frequency with which the term "empowerment" has come to be used within the lexicon of government of the Province of Ontario (Province of Ontario, 1990), labour (United Steelworkers of America, 1992), and business (D'Cruz and Rugman, 1992b).

This chapter considers the following set of questions. First, what role has organised labour played in contributing to the formation and maintenance of network-based regional-industrial systems in Europe and North America? Second, what kinds of outcomes have been produced for the workers involved in such networks, and how are these outcomes linked to the role that labour plays within each regional economy? What benefits accrue to major stakeholders when labour unions play an active role in network creation and maintenance, and what might a "worker-friendly" industrial network look like? Third, how feasible are such networks within the Canadian context, and what are the major obstacles to their implementation? In providing some answers to these questions, this paper draws from the findings of a year-long study sponsored by the United Steelworkers of America (Toronto), and the governments of Canada and Ontario to examine the prospects for employing a network approach to stimulate regional development in Northern Ontario.[2] Prior to considering these questions, the following section offers a brief examination of the network concept, and the broader notion of "network paradigm" which is central to the later arguments of this paper.

3.2 Regional-Industrial Networks and the "Network Paradigm"

Interfirm networks represent a form of industrial organization in which private firms (including actual or potential competitors) cooperate with one another to perform a set of tasks from which each will gain some benefit not available through private action alone. Although these are based on interaction between firms, these exchanges of goods and services are not limited to simple market transactions. Instead, they are characterised by the sharing of large amounts of information (including proprietary knowledge) based on *relations of trust* built up over time. In this sense, they exhibit some of the characteristics of relations within single, large organisations (hierarchies), though they are built on external transactions. Furthermore, it has been suggested that the geographical concentration of firms bound by network relations offers at least two distinct advantages. First, given the transaction-intensive nature of these production systems, spatial clustering is said to facilitate the more frequent, often unplanned nature of exchanges of goods and information between network members (Scott, 1988b). Second, spatial concentration also fosters the sense of trust between firms on which network relations are built by providing the opportunity for repeated, face-to-face interaction (both formal and informal) over time (Harrison, 1992).

2 The steelworkers' interest stems from their involvement in the recent employee buyout of a 60 per cent ownership stake in one of the region's major employers, Algoma Steel Corporation.

DeBresson and Amesse (1991) note the increasing use of network forms of organization in the "pre-competitive" innovation process. This has become increasingly common in industries such as pharmaceuticals, telecommunications, aerospace, computing, and microelectronics, where the combined effect of very high product development costs and increasing pressure to bring new products to market quickly has made non-cooperative research an increasingly expensive, risky, and insufficiently timely option. Firms participating in such innovation networks may agree on technological trajectories for the industry as a whole and reduce duplicative research projects being carried out by individual firms, without reducing competition for alternative designs. As a result, all members of the network stand to benefit from participating.

Network organisations have arisen not only around research/development and production relations (inside and outside individual firms), but have also been used to provide cooperative market research, product distribution and marketing, labour training, and pooled procurement of goods and services for their member firms. Further, networks may develop around some kind of "hub" entity, such as a dominant large (buyer) firm that orchestrates the distribution of functions across (or cooperation with and between) supplier firms in a particular industry and region. Alternatively, networks may be relatively "headless," consisting instead of looser associations of SMEs that cooperate with one another for the purposes enumerated above (see Smith et al., 1991; Fournier et al., 1992; and Sydow, 1992b for alternative ways of classifying networks). The international literature on interfirm networks has suggested that the typical network organisational structure may include the following four elements:

Private Firms – These are usually drawn from a single industry, or a group of industries related to one another through buyer-supplier linkages.

Non-Governmental Institutions – These institutions correspond to the industries mentioned above, and their organisational scope may be national or regional. Most important here are producer associations, labour unions, local chambers of commerce, research centres, and educational institutions.

Government Development Agencies – These are typically agencies with a mandate for regional development, technology upgrading, training and industrial (especially SME) assistance.

Network "Hubs" – These are either large, dominant companies ("hub firms") or "hub organisations" set up through the cooperation of the entities described above. They provide a focal point for the network's organization and governance. In addition, hub organisations typically offer an array of common services available to network members.

Where a network is structured around one or a few large firms, the hub role will normally be played by these private companies. Such firms may orchestrate collective action within their sector to stimulate the provision of industry-specific services, or may simply occupy a central role themselves within the industry's input-output system in the region. In either case, the hub firm would exert influence on regional firms in the same or related sectors to increase the general level of technological sophistication within the local industry.[3] In other cases, where there is no large, leading firm able or willing to perform such a role, one or more hub organisations may be created to serve the collective needs of, or to stimulate collective behaviour amongst, numerous SMEs in a region.

While many forms of networking behaviour have been around for a long time, there is a strong sense in the social science literature that its importance has grown in response to recent changes in the nature of capitalist societies and the terms of competition (for example, see Boyer, 1989; Sydow, 1992a). Networking is seen as part of a broader set of changes in the way that manufacturing firms approach product development, design, production, and marketing. Elaborating the more general concept of the "*network paradigm*," Cooke and Morgan (1993) argue that network forms of organization have developed not only between, but also *within*, firms, and that these two sets of changes are strongly interrelated. Indeed, Cooke and Morgan see the successful achievement of external network relations as depending upon the successful implementation of network principles inside participating firms. Further, they argue that network organization is becoming evident not only amongst SMEs but also in the interfirm dealings and intrafirm organization of large, multinational enterprises, as such firms recognize the need to respond more effectively to these new realities.

Cooke and Morgan outline a set of changes which they understand as forms of network relations being established *within* the firm. First, as reduced time-to-market for new or modified, increasingly customised products becomes a more important determinant of competitive success, the integration of research and development with marketing and production on the shopfloor to speed up and improve the product development process has become ever more important. Second, firms are seeking to decentralise production decisions as far as possible within smaller and less hierarchical (often self-directed) units to enhance productivity, quality, and product-process improvements. Finally, in emulation of Japanese competitive strategies, firms both large and small are aiming to achieve high quality at reasonable cost, by pursuing the "zero defect" objective at each stage of the production process. Within a competitive setting in which production occurs increasingly on a just-in-time basis (with assemblers keeping much smaller parts

3 The case of Baden-Württemberg in Germany demonstrates the central role that large firms can play in the organization and governance of network relations involving large numbers of medium-sized and small firms in a region (Cooke and Morgan, 1993). The Japanese structure of interfirm organization, particularly in industries such as consumer electronics and automobiles, illustrates many of the same structural characteristics (Florida and Kenney, 1990a). For a more general discussion of the role of large firms in network formation and maintenance (what the authors refer to as "flagship firms"), see D'Cruz and Rugman (1992).

inventories), it becomes all the more crucial for firms to be able to provide a consistently high quality and low defect rate for supplied parts. In order to achieve this, firms are finding it necessary to impose more stringent controls on the quality of their production by adopting new, advanced manufacturing technologies and monitoring systems. These manufacturing technologies also offer the benefit of versatility and relatively quick changeover to accommodate new product specifications.

Such buyer-supplier relations entail close cooperation and the liberal exchange of information between transacting firms over long periods of time. It appears to be increasingly common for buyers to forge close, long-lasting partnerships with their key suppliers in order to ensure that suppliers are able successfully to upgrade their product and process technologies (thereby ensuring consistently high quality and low defect rates). At the same time, buyers seek to benefit by developing easier access to their supplier's innovative ideas and, in industries such as automotive, are increasingly requiring suppliers to perform their own R&D to develop products that match assemblers' performance specifications. The ability to achieve such an enriched relationship appears to hinge on the success with which a strong degree of trust can be built up between buyer and supplier. The most common route to achieving this is through the signing of longer-term contracts, in which the supplier is insulated from the annual, cost-based, competitive supplier bidding process.

However, it is crucially important to point out that the successful achievement of collaborative network relations with buyer or supplier firms *also requires a whole new set of relations between management and workers within individual firms*. As I shall argue in the following section, the improvement of quality, the reduction in defect rates, the enhanced ability to customize products to smaller segments of the market, and the technological upgrading of production processes necessary to achieve these objectives are simply impossible to achieve without an accompanying reorganisation of the workplace in order to *promote the empowerment of workers*. Furthermore, if just-in-time supply links are to be maintained, then supplier firms must ensure that they remain on good terms with their workers, so that the possibility of disruptions to supply are minimised. As I argue below, the success of either of these strategies will, contrary to the popular wisdom, be enhanced by the presence of unions in the workplace.

3.3 Unions and the Network Paradigm

There is a large body of evidence to suggest that the successful implementation of both flexible *interfirm* relations based on collaboration, networks and just-in-time exchange, as well as flexible process technologies and new forms of work organization *within individual plants* can best be achieved in unionised workplaces. Since this argument suggests that there is a strong and compelling logic for inviting full union participation as one seeks to rework industrial production systems through the fostering of network relations, it deserves closer scrutiny.

First, the firm's ability to respond flexibly and quickly to its customers' needs, to provide a high-quality product, will depend on its success in harnessing the full productive powers of its technology. This can only be achieved by marshalling the full creative powers and effort of its workforce.[4] Second, mounting evidence argues persuasively that fundamental and lasting change to work organization, including successful implementation of new process technologies, is far more likely to be achieved when organised labour plays a central role as an equal partner with management.[5] The basic argument here is that workers will more readily accept the changes in workrules and job descriptions that accompany the adoption of flexible production systems when they have played a meaningful and significant part in contributing to adoption decisions in the first place, and are assured of reaping their fair share of the benefits. Furthermore, their willingness to cooperate actively in the implementation of these new systems will be greater when they have received some reliable offsetting guarantee of job security. Both of these circumstances are far more likely to apply when workers are formally represented by a union. As Marshall (1992: 76) notes upon engaging in an exhaustive review of the relevant literature:

"... high performance work organisations are likely to be most effective where workers have an independent source of power to protect themselves and ensure an equitable sharing of the benefits and costs of change. ... worker participation systems are most effective

4 The growing literature on the *effective* implementation of advanced manufacturing technologies is highly consistent in supporting this assertion. For a review, see Gertler (forthcoming).

5 For recent comprehensive surveys of this evidence, see especially Marshall (1992) and Bluestone and Bluestone (1992). For earlier evidence on the positive influence of unionization on workplace productivity, see Freeman and Medoff (1984). Even D'Cruz and Rugman (1992a), despite representing a distinctly pro-business perspective, acknowledge that successful network relations can only be developed when each participating firm actively promotes worker empowerment within its own organization. Though they profess to "show that the current attitudes and policies of organized labour have become a major impediment to... the development of networks" (p. 39), they concede that recently some Canadian unions (especially the United Steelworkers) have changed their attitude. In place of their traditional exclusive concern for "protection of the wages and rights of workers" (p. 41), these unions have subscribed to the goal of successful competition in the global marketplace, achieved through changing product mix, skills upgrading, and work reorganization. Furthermore, they even go so far as to acknowledge that, for this kind of attitude shift to occur, senior and middle management must also change their mindset and seek to establish an environment of support, collaboration, and trust in the workplace. For other Canadian evidence on workers' attitudes towards new technology and work reorganization, see Meurer et al. (1987).

where workers are unionised. The general conclusions are: (i) that genuine worker participation improves economic performance, but that superficial processes do not; and (ii) labour organisations help improve productivity where unions are accepted as true partners in production processes. The crucial factor appears to be the nature of labour management relations. Relationships characterised by conflict, a lack of trust, and a refusal to acknowledge each party's legitimacy are unlikely to have high economic performance."[6]

The German and Scandinavian experiences suggest that high wages, the tight control of layoffs, and the relative absence of labour market dualism serves as an incentive for managers to innovate in higher-value added, higher-skilled production (Streeck, 1986, 1990). This is part of a virtuous circle driving firms to upgrade their products and processes, instead of competing on the basis of cheap labour. Hence, unionisation compels firms to invest in advanced manufacturing technologies, and to make a considerably greater commitment to the establishment of *meaningful* participatory employment relations in the workplace. Furthermore, the success of implementing workplace reorganisation, including new and enlarged roles for workers, depends heavily on the training effort engaged in by firms. Here too, there is compelling evidence to suggest that firms' training efforts will be greater when the institutional structure of their employment relations fosters stability of tenure and a long-term association between the employee and the firm (Sorge and Streeck, 1988; Christopherson, 1993). These conditions are most likely to be met in a union, rather than a nonunion, workplace.

In Germany, IG Metall (the national metalworkers union) has played an active role not only in training and skill acquisition, but also in product development (Muster, 1992). It has in recent years begun to press management to develop more durable and ecologically friendly automobiles. It has also been instrumental in helping defence-based German firms move successfully into civilian product markets. Hence, a proactive stance by unions can push firms to introduce many progressive changes to products, processes, work organization, and even basic corporate strategy.

Third, recognising that interfirm networks seek to change production practices in a fundamental way, and that much of this change hinges on the development of trust between partners, it is only logical to conclude that union involvement (as a prerequisite for building trust between workers and managers) will also contribute to this process of trust formation between firms, and its attendant benefits. If a firm's ability to trust its suppliers depends on the supplier's ability to provide the requisite goods on time, to agreed-upon quality standards, and if (as indicated above) the supplier's ability to do so depends on its success in achieving a trust-based, participatory relationship with its workers, then it is clear that external relations of trust depend heavily on relations of trust within the workplace.

6 For an empirical study of the US metalworking industry that reaches similar conclusions, see Kelley and Harrison (1991).

3.4 The Difference that Labour Relations Make

3.4.1 European Cases

The literature on "successful" regionally based industrial networks in Europe is now well-established and voluminous. The tales from the Emilian landscape, the Tuscan hills, the cities and town of southwestern Germany, and other regions are by now well-rehearsed and need no retelling here.[7] Generally, their success has been explained by the role of network relations between local firms (many of them small), supported by a rich matrix of educational and other social institutions in the region.

Yet, despite some apparent resemblance between regions like the Third Italy and Baden-Württemberg, it is clear that they each provide starkly different work experiences for the employees of networked firms. As I shall argue below, these differences in outcome reflect the very different roles that individual workers and unions have been able to play, as determined by rather divergent industrial relations systems and regulatory regimes.

The "realities" of Third Italy employment practices have been most thoroughly explored by Murray (1987), Amin (1989), and Amin and Robins (1990). All take issue with some of the rosier portrayals of the Third Italy offered by the likes of Piore, Sabel, and others. Murray is critical of Sabel's claim that many small firms are unionised, instead pointing to a study of the metalworking industries in Bologna which found that unionisation was "scarce" amongst that proportion of the workforce (constituting roughly one-third of all workers) who were employed in the small-firm sector (firms with fewer than 16 employees). In fact, this study found that total unionisation in Emilian manufacturing was probably under 50 per cent and in some areas as low as 6 per cent (Murray, 1987, p. 89). Furthermore, there was a marked gender division of labour in the metalworking industry, with 96 per cent of women workers occupying the three lowest skill grades. In fact, due to competition from lower-paying firms, it would appear that unions in Emilia-Romagna have been undermined and forced into a reactive position.

Meanwhile, the situation in southwestern Germany is very different. While unions in Baden-Württemberg have been innovative and provided leadership to other German regions, they have benefitted from an industrial relations system which is fundamentally *national* in scope. In particular, two key post-war pieces of legislation – The Work Constitution Act (1952, amended in 1972) and the Co-Determination Act (1976) – have played an important role in the formation of this system. The Works Constitution Act made Works Councils the only legal representative of the shopfloor (although only unions could actually call a strike). These Works Councils were given one-third representation on the supervisory boards of

7 For the now mainstream view, see Piore and Sabel (1984) and Sabel (1989).

companies. The 1972 revision gave the Works Councils the legal means to resist mass layoffs (Mahon, 1987, p. 41). Under this system, layoffs are strictly controlled since management must gain consent from the Works Councils and individual workers (Windolf, 1985, p. 462).

Co-determination applies at two levels: at the shopfloor level in firms which employ more than five workers and at the supervisory board level in (publicly quoted) firms employing more than 2,000 employees (Cooke and Morgan, 1991, p. 28). Workers have the right to influence the introduction of new technology and any subsequent redistribution of skills and jobs. These restraints have led employers to depend heavily on the internal labour market, which managers have an incentive to use as a reservoir of skills, given the generally high level of technical skills produced by the German training system (Streeck, 1986, p. 24). However, there is considerable variation at the regional or plant level in the success of works councils in offsetting deskilling or skill polarisation (Windolf, 1985).

German workers in the metal industries have also benefitted from the representation of IG Metall. With over 2.5 million workers (in West Germany), it represents all workers in the metals sector regardless of skill, and has been effective in ensuring that wage gains keep up with productivity increases, as well as fighting for a shorter work week. Furthermore, IG Metall also benefits from German industrial legislation which makes settlements won by unions applicable to non-union members (Mahon, 1987, p. 39). This has significantly reduced the segmentation of the domestic workforce, preventing the kind of situation that is prevalent in Italy and North America. The high labour costs and shorter hours are offset by the very high levels of productivity and quality enjoyed in Baden-Württemberg's plants, which in large part is derived from the highly skilled character of the regional workforce.

It is clear then that there are important differences between employment practices between the Third Italy and Baden-Württemberg. Outcomes in the latter case are, despite some shortcomings, considerably more attractive to workers, as they have been more successful in securing their share of the benefits of quality-based production. Finally, while the networking model offers some important advantages to workers, its emphasis on firm- and local-level solutions to problems neglects the continued relevance of *national* policies that foster very different roles for labour in the two systems.

3.4.2 The North American Experience

Since the late 1980s, growing awareness of the apparent success of European regional industrial networks has triggered a new interest in exploiting network concepts as a basis for improving industrial competitiveness or for fostering regional economic development. In the United States, the absence of a Federal government presence in economic development policy during the Reagan/Bush years created something of a vacuum that came to be filled by public policy initiatives at the state and local level.[8] Many of these initiatives have sought to exploit the idea of regionally based networking and cooperation as a way to turn around the fortunes of ailing regional economies. In Canada, similar initiatives have been getting underway two to three years later.

As these initiatives have most commonly proceeded in regions possessing few natural advantages, where such developments had not previously occurred on a spontaneous basis, they are normally founded on attempts to foster collaborative behaviour between individual (often small and medium-sized) firms, through the creation of some form of hub organization. The collaborative behaviour supported by these hub organisations may range from research and product development, to the actual production process, to the ultimate marketing of the good. In their more passive incarnation, hub organisations serve as a common source for pooled business services (accounting, business planning, market analysis). They may also orchestrate joint marketing initiatives, facilitate access to finance, coordinate joint procurement of inputs, assist in the diffusion and implementation of new technology, and provide industry-specific worker and manager training, quality monitoring, testing, and advising. They may also offer assistance in helping firms introduce new "softer" technologies (reorganising work flow, job descriptions, reporting relationships, and worker-management relations). Further, they may provide a location for specialised (often pre-competitive) research and development on industry-specific products and processes, or may serve as a conduit to other research institutions performing work with direct applications in the sector of interest. Finally, they provide a forum in which members of the industry interact with one another on a frequent basis. This last function may vary from a relatively passive process, based on chance encounters and meetings, to an active one in which a "*brokering*" process seeks to bring together firms with complementary interests to engage in true collaborative production.[9]

As part of our broad review of the networking approach on behalf of the United Steelworkers, the Government of Canada, and the Province of Ontario, we were asked to appraise some of the more notable US case studies (particularly those of some relevance to the Northern Ontario economy – i.e., focussing on metalworking, resource industries, or rural areas). Our purpose, beyond documenting the approach pursued by each case, was to determine the role played by workers and

8 Evidence of this trend, and descriptions of recent initiatives, are provided by Goldstein (1987), Shapira (1990), and Wolfe (1993).

9 Useful and highly influential reviews of networking activity in the US and abroad can be found in two special issues of *The Entrepreneurial Economy* devoted to FMNs. See volume 6, no. 1 (July/August 1987) and volume 9, no. 3 (Spring 1991). This journal is published quarterly by the Corporation for Enterprise Development in Washington, DC. See also Rosenfeld *et al.* (1992).

unions (if any) in the formation or operation of networks, and to see what kinds of implications this might hold for the structure, strategy, and objectives chosen by each case. As most of these projects were no more than a few years old, it was considered too early to engage in a comprehensive evaluation of each network's achievements. Nevertheless, even the limited assessment of goals, participants, organisational structure, strategy, and activities was able to yield a number of useful insights.[10]

Although all the US networking projects studied paid lip service to the role of networks as a vehicle for regional development, the actual level of commitment to bringing it about varied significantly from case to case. Furthermore, the precise nature of the hub organization created varied substantially from case to case. Some have been set up in a manner that resembles the cooperative, multifunctional, multistakeholder models of Baden-Württemberg (MAP, ACEnet), while others define their role more narrowly as one of simply brokering cooperation between individual firms with complementary assets or objectives (WoodNet, EMN). Still others have set themselves up as private (even for-profit) firms offering specialised services to *individual* local firms through standard, one-on-one market transactions (TSMA). In such cases, the objectives and range of activities are extremely limited.

Our review determined that those network organisations whose goals remained confined to improving the competitiveness of individual firms will generally limit themselves to providing services emphasising technology transfer and marketing. On the other hand, networks which view themselves as a means to achieving regional development are attempting to engage in a broader range of activities designed to encourage collaboration among firms, various regional institutions, and other stakeholders (such as workers). Thus, although it is clearly too early to make any definitive judgements, it appears that the success of a flexible manufacturing network *as a tool for regional development* will depend largely on the strength of its explicit commitment to that cause, as well as on how comprehensive its activities are.

At the same time, there is also evidence that many of these networks began as relatively modest entities, and hope to take on broader roles with the passage of time and the gaining of experience. It is still too early to discern any concrete ev-

10 Our review included case studies of nine regionally based manufacturing networks: the Appalachian Center for Economic Networks, Inc. (ACEnet), and the Heat Treating Network (HTN) (both in Ohio); the Export Manufacturing Project (EMN) in Illinois; the Machine Action Project (MAP) in Massachusetts; the Metalworking Connection, Inc. (TMS) in Arkansas; the Mon Valley Initiative (MVI) in Pennsylvania; the Textile and Apparel Labor-Management Innovation Network (AIN) in Pennsylvania; the Tri-State Manufacturer's Association (TSMA) in Minnesota and the Dakotas; and WoodNet in Washington.

idence of meaningful interfirm cooperation and the breaking down of the traditional individualist business ethic. However, it is already clear that a number of these networks have chosen to define a distinctly American form, one that tends more often than not to *exclude organised labour* from its formation and operation. When they choose to do so, our review indicates that the mandate of the network initiative will generally be quite limited, and less oriented to a *regional* approach to development than to one that is based on individual private *firms*. Consequently, it seems that when labour groups are explicitly involved in the formation and operation of network organisations, the goals and mandate of such initiatives are considerably more comprehensive and inclusive of a wider variety of local institutions and stakeholders. If the arguments advanced in the earlier part of this chapter are correct, then one would also expect such worker-based initiatives ultimately to be more successful and have a longer-lasting impact.

The first systematic review of networking behaviour in Canada has recently been completed by researchers at Wilfrid Laurier University, on behalf of ISTC (Fournier et al., 1992). This study's findings indicate that the functions performed by what are largely only recently established networks *seem to be confined largely to activities either preceding or following the actual production of commodities.* The two most commonly reported activities are cooperative R&D (primarily between potential competitive rivals) and joint marketing alliances (especially export promotion). There is little of what one might regard as truly collaborative manufacturing (only about 20 per cent of projects even mention this as an objective), and surprisingly little attention is given to stimulating the development of specialised suppliers, technology transfer, industry-specific training, or quality improvement. Only in one or two instances does one see a truly comprehensive approach to network development. Furthermore, in the overwhelming majority of cases, the target constituency for the network activity is the private firm itself. Given the dominance of R&D activities, it should come as no surprise that the most commonly reported partners, apart form government development agencies, are universities and research centres. Only in one network (based on the furniture industry in Ontario) are unions singled out as an explicitly identified participant in the collaborative activities.

This review of the early Canadian experience indicates at least two interesting points. First, as in several of the US cases, many founders of Canadian networks have explicitly adopted a developmental approach to network formation. Consequently, they have pursued relatively modest and limited initial goals, with the hope that some early successes from relatively short-term, superficial activities (for example, in leveraging government funds for network members) will build up private firms' commitment to cooperation. Related to this is the observation that many networks begin with activities around which interfirm cooperation is relatively easy to induce. A common example is to adopt an international focus to joint marketing initiatives, so that firms which normally compete with one another in the Canadian market can more easily cooperate and build trust on market terrain that is, for them, currently uncontested. The unfortunate side effect of this strategy is that labour is not actively courted as a partner at the time that such networks are established.

Second, in those few networks with a strong production (versus research or marketing) orientation, spatial clustering of members appears to be especially important – particularly when member firms are relatively small in size. This proximity between network members seems to facilitate the sharing of commonly purchased production equipment, the diffusion of know-how concerning process and product technologies, and the development of a trained regional labour force possessing skills needed by the industry in question. Furthermore, collaborative production depends upon the establishment of strong mutual trust between partners, and this seems to be built up best by the kind of frequent face-to-face interaction which spatial proximity enables.

Hence, it would seem that the "Canadian model" of networking, at least as it has developed thus far, is rather similar to the American one, given the emphasis on SMEs, the apparent lack of involvement of organised labour, and the focus on non-production activities. These latter two features should come as no surprise, given the general similarity of individualist business cultures on both sides of the border. Furthermore, so long as network organisations continue to focus on pre- and post-production activities, it is unlikely that union participation in these ventures will grow. Nevertheless, it is both significant and revealing that, even in those networks where production-related activities *are* within their area of interest, those involved in network formation have apparently not (for the most apart) thought it important or necessary to invite the meaningful participation of workers.

The recent American and Canadian literature on network formation reviewed above emphasises that networking efforts often embrace the twin objectives of industrial "modernisation" (upgrading of technologies, improving quality, and adopting new forms of work organization) *and* interfirm cooperation. The message running throughout this literature is that cooperation can be an important means by which individual firms (especially SMEs) can receive assistance in their efforts to modernise – i.e., "*cooperate to modernise*".[11] However, this same literature appears to be largely oblivious to the arguments reviewed earlier in this paper suggesting that the reverse is also true – that "modernising" (including not only use of new processes but also the new relations within the workplace which ensure effective and lasting implementation) provides many of the requisite changes within individual firms that ultimately enable more fruitful and productive inter-firm cooperation to develop. In other words, it is also necessary to "*modernise to cooperate*". To the extent that successful modernisation will depend on the full involvement of labour, then, it seems clear that worker participation is likely to be a vital determinant of the degree of success of attempts to build production-

11 See, for example, Shapira (1990).

oriented networks. The apparent lack of interest in soliciting the cooperation of labour unions does not augur well for the future achievements of network experiments in North America in general. However, one would expect the prospects for those few exceptions that do have union participation to be markedly more positive.

3.5 Obstacles to Industrial Network Formation in Canada's Regions

As the above review indicates, efforts to establish industrial networks in those North American regions not already blessed with spontaneous network activity are comparatively recent. Despite this fact, there is a growing awareness among those involved that the task is more difficult than it first seemed. There seem to be at lease three different ways of conceiving of the problems at hand. A first set of concerns centres around the issue of how to get private firms to cooperate when the Anglo-American business ethic of rugged, competitive individualism is so strongly engrained in the mindsets of managers. A second set of concerns relates to institution-building – that is, how to "fill in the gaps" in the regional institutional matrix in order to provide the requisite ambient level of SME support and inducement to cooperations in the region. A third set of concerns speaks to the issue of the particular deficiencies or disadvantages of "peripheral," non-metropolitan and rural areas as sites for network-building.

Recent work in some of Europe's less obviously successful regions suggests that the task of instituting network relations in already mature industrial areas in Canada or the United States will not be easy. Cooke and Morgan (1993), in contrasting the experiences of Emilia-Romagna and Baden-Württemberg with those of older "reconversion" regions such as South Wales and Spain's Basque Country, note that the problems may indeed be considerable. The rapid decline of established industries, the lack of integration between existing and new sectors and the lack of any real tradition of networking, constitute major obstacles to policy-makers. This is particularly true of South Wales, where the absence of regionally-based private-sector initiatives and dependence on foreign multinationals make the creation of a thriving network of indigenous firms and institutions difficult. There is clearly an awareness of similar challenges on this side of the Atlantic, where issues such as the difficulty of inducing firms to cooperate, and the general shortage of entrepreneurship are well-recognised. There has also been considerable attention devoted to the special problems of small town and rural settings. Rosenfeld (1991: 28) argues that many rural areas of the US can build on important advantages stemming from their agricultural heritage, particularly participation in cooperative movements and organisations:

"Many rural residents have at some time been exposed to cooperative efforts in agriculture and remember when farmers learned from each other, shared mechanised equipment, and helped their neighbours in times of need. Nearly 5,000 rural marketing, supply, and related service cooperatives with more than four million members were operating in 1988. Cooperative extension agents reoriented to economic development have links to universities and may be able to locate resources and information for rural firms. And areas with a strong tradition of agricultural education are likely to have local leaders who are willing to tackle new problems. In fact, the strongest proponents of networking in rural areas often are firm owners who were raised on farms and are accustomed to cooperation."

Nevertheless, despite this possible advantage, rural and small town settings suffer from a number of weaknesses or deficiencies: a shortage of labour skills (and difficulty in retaining skilled labour in the region); strongly engrained competitive instincts (fostered by the small size of local markets); absence of regionally based producer associations and other cooperation-fostering institutions; long distances between potential network participants (which make planned and unplanned personal interaction – and hence, trust-building – difficult); remoteness from major markets and customers (making market intelligence more difficult to gather – a major problem for the would-be flexible firm); an underdeveloped local supply base of specialised services, information, assistance and capital (also a serious problem for firms looking to compete on the basis of innovation, quality, and responsiveness) (Rosenfeld, 1991; Rosenfeld *et al.*, 1992).

These problems are especially germane to the case of Northern Ontario, whose economy has been dominated for many years by natural resource extraction - especially in forestry and mining – and, to some extent, by the limited processing of natural resource products (pulp and paper, sawmilling, ore smelting). Secondary manufacturing in other sectors is limited, the two most prominent examples being Algoma Steel in Sault Ste. Marie and Bombardier's CanCar plant (making urban transit and rail vehicles) in Thunder Bay. Service activities have also made an important contribution to the region's economic base – especially port-related material-handling activities in Thunder Bay, and tourism activities related to outdoor recreation and vacation travel throughout the region. Nevertheless, as a comprehensive study of the Northern Ontario economy made clear a few years ago,[12] dependency on natural resource-related activities remains the dominant economic characteristic of the region.

For the purposes of our study, we conducted a survey and review of three major constituencies within the Northern Ontario region: firms (especially manufacturers, mining and forestry companies), key institutions (unions, universities and colleges, chambers of commerce, producer associations and financial institutions),

12 *Final Report and Recommendations of the Advisory Committee on Resource Dependent Communities in Northern Ontario*, May 1986, Province of Ontario (1986).

and government actors (municipal, provincial, and federal).[13] Our objectives in this work were to determine the following:

- What is the state of current practices *within* individual workplaces in the region? What types of competitive strategies are most commonly employed? How much experimentation with new forms of internal work organization (e.g., empowerment, self-directed teams, work cells, etc.) is taking place? What kinds of relationships exist between management and workers?
- What is the state of current practice in terms of relations *between* firms within the region? Is there any existing evidence of cooperative or collaborative interfirm relationships? How reliant are firms on local (versus non-local) suppliers or markets, and what barriers prevent greater reliance?
- How well-developed is the base of *local institutions* to support collaborative, network-based behaviour? How well-suited are those institutions to the task of fostering closer cooperation between firms and unions, and closer collaboration between private firms? What are the major gaps in this base, and how feasible is it that these might be filled?
- What *level of interest* in networking, and in closer cooperation with labour, is evident within the business community? What are the major obstacles to such cooperation? How willing are firms to accept a more active role for labour (especially organised labour) in economic decision making?

The results of the study are of interest, as we found evidence to suggest a relationship between the adoption of progressive *internal* practices by individual firms (recognition of unions, work place committees, shopfloor empowerment, high levels of R&D and training) and progressive *external* practices (such as information sharing between firms in the same sector, and more collaborative customer/supplier relations). Furthermore, these "progressive" cases tended (with a few exceptions) to be the larger and older firms in the region, concentrated in forest products, mining, primary metals, and transportation equipment sectors. There was also some evidence of development of key upstream supplier industries in the region (particularly in the mining machinery/equipment and explosives sectors), some maturation of the region's service sector, and growing use of the region's recently upgraded telecommunications system and services.

13 A postal survey brought responses from sixty firms in the region, representing over one-third of all employment in the primary and manufacturing sectors in Northern Ontario. We also received completed surveys from roughly 100 government and non-governmental institutions. The surveys were followed up with day-long workshops held in two of the larger communities in the region (Sault Ste. Marie and Thunder Bay), to which representatives of all major economic stakeholder groups were invited for a joint consideration of the prospects for (and obstacles to) network formation in the region. These workshops also afforded us the opportunity to visit the plants and conduct interviews with the major employers in each community.

Perhaps most significant was the manifestation of a strong community ethic in several urban centres (such as Sault Ste. Marie, Sudbury, Thunder Bay, and Kapuskasing) that had experienced the threat of major layoffs or shutdowns by their dominant employers. In these cases, collective, broad-based actions (often spearheaded by unions such as the Steelworkers in Sault Ste. Marie) were successful in averting shutdowns, illustrating the presence of innovative leadership, imagination, cooperation, and risk-taking. Such events have left in their wake a growing number of worker-owned enterprises which now offer considerable promise as laboratories for developing network relations inside and outside the firm (Saunders, 1995). The central role played by unions and unionised enterprise in the region stands in stark contrast to the North American experience reviewed earlier. Unionisation levels are higher in Northern Ontario than in many other regions, with unionisation amongst full-time employees approaching 40 per cent. Moreover, in a region characterised by single-industry communities, unions have long played a wider, active social and political role. In a region where distances often isolate communities, unions were one of the few institutions which have developed any intra-regional links across individual workplaces and communities.

Despite these strengths on which to build a new set of economic relations in the north, it was widely agreed that the region faces some serious challenges and liabilities. The most prominent of these are listed below:

(1) *Many leading large firms are currently in difficult financial shape.*

- This is due to recession, low world prices, import penetration, and growing protectionism abroad (e.g., recent steel import rulings in the United States; FTA and NAFTA.
- This means that these firms are less likely to have the resources, time or inclination to devote themselves to playing a lead role in the establishment of regional industrial networks (and this problem is exacerbated by the high degree of non-regional ownership of many large employers).
- In order to perform this role effectively, firms must be technologically sophisticated, sensitive to changing market demands, and willing and able to work with their suppliers to establish long-term, trust-based, mutually beneficial relations. While some progress has been made (see previous section), these qualities are apparently not yet widespread throughout Northern (or Southern) Ontario.

(2) *The base of SMEs in the region is quite small.*

- The large, dominant regional employers remain highly vertically integrated, retaining in-house many manufacturing functions that could easily be spun off to external firms, thereby improving the socially available supply base of inputs in the region.
- Key support sectors such as business services also remain underdeveloped or excessively internalised within large firms in other sectors; hence, the

specialised service base to support producers in the region is still inadequate.
- Few SMEs (or larger firms) in the region are using inputs from the resource-based industries to add further value to these commodities in the region (not enough downstream value-adding) -the region's major exporters are still largely in commodity markets.

(3) *Long distances between centres may frustrate interaction within the region.*

- Subregional specialisation may mitigate this problem somewhat (e.g., mining, primary metal smelting in the Northeast; forest products in the Northwest), but distances between communities are still very large.
- Almost complete absence of *regional* producers associations makes this problem considerably worse (the dominant industry associations are national, with most activity occurring in centres such as Vancouver, Toronto, and Montreal; most collaboration within these institutions revolves around pre-production phases, such as joint R&D, or post-production phases, such as joint international marketing).

(4) *A well-entrenched legacy of employment in large, dominant industries.*

- The traditional "culture of employment" and "culture of management" do not provide the most fertile conditions in which to encourage greater risk-taking and innovativeness.
- There is a well-recognised undersupply of generally diffused business skills.
- The local institutional support base is not yet well enough developed to compensate for these deficiencies.

(5) *Lack of cooperative ethic and collaborative practice.*

- This problem exists at several different levels – within the firm, in interfirm relations, and within the broader community.

Of all these problems, the last one is ultimately the most significant. Within *individual workplaces*, the legacy of adversarialism and the entrenched mindsets of managers and workers was highlighted in both the institutional survey and workshops as an important obstacle to overcome. Generally, the relatively active role played by labour in the region has *not* been as an equal partner with business. Instead, unions like the Steelworkers have been forced into assuming active roles when private industrial capital has fled (or threatened to flee) the region. Hence, despite a promising degree of initiative on the part of the regional labour movement, the extent of labour-management cooperation has, until the recent experiments with worker ownership, been rather limited. Indeed, it is more accurate to say that labour relations in the region's major workplaces have often been highly confrontational, as the lengthy 1990 strike at Algoma suggests. This is absolutely crucial, given the demonstrated link between collaborative relations, based on trust, empowerment and mutual respect, *within* the workplace, and collaborative relations *between* individual firms. Our analysis of the institutional infrastructure of the region indicates that only a few organisations actively promote closer co-operation between workers and managers.

Our industrial survey revealed that, while there is some evidence that *interfirm relations* have begun to take on the characteristics of collaborating firms, it is worth noting that nearly 60 per cent of establishments surveyed indicated that they share absolutely no information with firms in the same or related industries. And those that do are considerably more likely to share information with *nonlocal* than local firms. Furthermore, many of these firms really only share more superficial forms of information. For small firms in particular, buyer-supplier relations remain dominated by arm's length transactions in which price is the key determinant. The cooperative and collaborative relations that have been shown to be the hallmark of the more successful industrial districts of Europe are distinctly scarce in Northern Ontario. As for regional buyer-supplier links involving large firms, these too have hardly been a model of successful networking in action. For example, although there is a significant cluster of metal fabricating firms in the Sault region (many of which had, at one time, purchased locally-made steel), Algoma (prior to the employee buyout) progressively alienated most of these customers by consistently assigning their orders a low delivery priority in favour of serving the needs of larger customers outside the region. One by one, most of Algoma's local customers stopped buying from them, turning instead to steel sources outside the region (the 1990 strike also did little to build strong, collaborative buyer-supplier relations locally).

Northern Ontario firms (like most Southern Ontario firms) clearly lack any experience with a more collaborative mode of organization, as this runs directly counter to a strongly engrained ethic of individualism and competition. For example, our discussions with local stakeholders revealed that poaching of skilled labour between firms in the region is a widespread and well-established practice. This not only suggests an absence of interfirm cooperation within the region, but also serves to discourage private training within the workplace. Even in industries such as steel, where significant initiatives on training have been achieved through interfirm collaboration, the major Canadian steel companies still remain suspicious of (if not openly hostile to) one another. However, it is a form of behaviour which is also reinforced by the regulatory framework for manufacturing in Ontario and Canada. Until firms are supported by a regulatory framework for labour markets that promotes job security and removes wages and work practices from the competitive field, the conditions for supporting closer relations between firms will remain inhospitable. Similarly, the incentives against collective action by firms, through the more aggressive and comprehensive use of producer associations, will remain weak. This too stands in stark contrast to the situation in European regions like Baden-Württemberg, where producers' organisations have played key roles in designing and delivering training programs, and in helping to set industry-wide standards for wages, benefits, and work practices.

Within the broader community, although local economic crises such as the impending closure of Algoma have had a galvanising effect to forge alliances between major economic stakeholder groups within communities like Sault Ste. Marie, our investigation revealed that these coalitions have not withstood the test of time. Once a looming crisis is averted, even if only on the basis of a short-term solution, old animosities and divisions seem to resurface. In the case of the Sault, many local residents still harbour resentment toward the Steelworkers for the bitter strike they conducted – a job action that some feel was instrumental in bringing Algoma to the precipice. Although most industry analysts would dispute this claim, many such feelings linger within the community. Hence, the self-described inhabitants of "an island with warring tribes" argue over whether or not labour should play a prominent role on the board of the local economic development corporation, even though they are already a major force in the local economy by virtue of their equity position in Algoma.

Finally, and here we return to an earlier theme, it must be pointed out that the macro-regulatory environment has not been highly conducive to the development of a high-skill, quality-based production system and the effective implementation of advanced manufacturing technologies. Despite a system of educational and training institutions in most of the major centres across the region, the general training effort in the workplace is very weak by international standards. Lamentable though this situation may be, it is entirely rational and understandable within the context of a broader labour market regime in which there are such strong disincentives to invest in worker training. While the recent attempts by the NDP government of Ontario to install a new training culture in individual workplaces and communities must be recognised, this change has been slow to materialize, and policymakers will have a difficult time overcoming the entrenched attitudes of employers and the existing training and education hierarchy.

3.6 Reflections on the Northern Ontario Case Study: Lessons for Future Action

It is clear that, for firms and regional economies, *the benefits of network relations can be considerable*, including an enhanced ability to respond flexibly and quickly to changing market demand, the ability to serve profitably smaller niches in otherwise stagnant markets, and the opportunity to learn through closer interaction with other firms in the network. To the extent that interfirm networking is supported by network relations within the firm, this gives firms the opportunity to tap more fully the expertise and wisdom of their workers. It is therefore important to stress that, in the leading industrial networks around the world, inter- and intra-firm cooperation are motivated not by altruism or some culturally determined sense of social commitment, but by the *enlightened self-interest of the participants*.

However, those participants are fundamentally economic beings who respond rationally to the system of incentives they face. We have tried to show how firms' responses, as manifested in the kinds of collaborative behaviour they exhibit, flow fairly directly from the nature of the macro-regulatory context within which they are operating. We have also argued that it is the nature of this macro-regulatory framework which also serves to differentiate one industrial network from another. Hence, *there is no single "model" of an industrial network, either in Europe or North America*. Instead, different regions and the economic actors therein have developed individual approaches that build on their own particular institutional legacy and inherited industrial structure. Where workers and unions participate fully (as a result of the "space" created for them by national-level industrial relations legislation), the network approach offers a number of attractive attributes for workers and management alike: in particular, the possibility of well-paid employment in a setting where unionised workers – in both large and small firms in the region – actively contribute to management's drive to engage in innovative, high-quality, collaborative production.

Other regions in North America, including some with industrial structures not unlike Northern Ontario, are currently exploring network approaches. In a few of these cases, the *labour movement* has been integrally involved in their development and operation. When they *have* been involved, they have played a major part in defining the scope, objectives, and nature of the network. In doing so, they have helped to ensure that the resulting organization is not only "worker friendly," but also closely tied to the broader objectives for development of the host region and community. Hence, the labour movement's role in contributing to the potential success of network initiatives is absolutely fundamental. However, this contribution has gone largely unacknowledged in much of the literature on industrial networks and districts. That this remains so is unfortunate, since a considerable body of empirical evidence suggests that: (i) the achievement of progressive practices within the firm (and the productivity and other competitive gains flowing from them) are most positively supported by a union workplace environment, and (ii) only when firms have successfully instituted internal network practices, through the meaningful empowerment of their employees, will they be in the optimal position to participate in (and exploit the benefits of) interfirm network relations.

It is clear that regions such as Northern Ontario are characterised by many disadvantages related to their degree of isolation, low density of settlement, industrial structure and history. However, without wishing to make light of these very real obstacles, the above arguments suggest that the really fundamental difficulties encountered in the pursuit of more cooperative relations in the region stem from the broader macro-regulatory framework established through provincial and federal labour market, training, and industrial relations legislation.[14] Such arguments also cast doubt upon alternative diagnoses of the obstacles to networking in North America which seek explanations by reverting to *cultural* arguments (the idea that North American business people are just inherently more competitive and less cooperative than their European counterparts). There is both good and bad news in this realization. On the positive side, it demystifies the sources of these cross-national differences, and also suggests that the possibilities for altering the behaviour of managers are considerably greater than cultural explanations alone would allow. On the other hand, it suggests that the full potential of the network approach cannot be realised unless policy to support *local and regional networks is approached as one piece of an integrated and more fully articulated industrial strategy*. Just as obstacles to the achievement of network relations do not reside exclusively at the level of individual firms, so too must solutions also be pursued at provincial and national scales of action.

Undoubtedly, achieving such change will not come easily. There is good reason to expect that both business and unions will be sceptical or reluctant to adopt this path. The traditional antipathy between these parties in the North American context is difficult to overcome. Furthermore, it is also important to note that the present decentralised structure of collective bargaining in Canada, in which agreements are struck at the level of individual workplaces, represents a further impediment to the labour movement's willing acceptance of certain aspects of the network approach. In particular, the absence of the kind of sector-wide bargaining that is commonly seen in western European countries raises the unsavoury spectre for the labour movement that outsourcing by hub firms within a network will simply lead to work being lost to low-wage competition, and to a downward pressure on wages. A further obstacle, seen from the perspective of individual bargaining units, is that the transfer of work to an outside firm (even a unionised one) might be viewed as a loss of clout, since the original bargaining unit would be reduced in size. Finally, it should be emphasised that the existence of more 'network-compatible' labour law (based on sectoral bargaining) in countries like Germany and Sweden not only fosters labour-management cooperation within individual workplaces, but also strongly facilitates cooperation *between* individual firms, since interfirm differences in wages, benefits, and work conditions are min-

14 Christopherson and Redfield (1993) make the further point that the regulatory structure of capital markets, as determined by nation-states, also comes into play here. The Anglo-American system of corporate finance, based on publicly traded stocks, exerts pressure on publicly held firms to emphasize short-term returns at the expense of longer-term considerations. This serves to weaken the incentives for firms to enter into long-term agreements with suppliers, or to commit funds to research and development. In contrast, the German and Japanese systems of finance, being more privately based, afford firms the ability to accord long-term competitive considerations their top priority.

imised. Consequently, the present state of Canadian and Ontario labour law represents something of a barrier to the achievement of network relations on "worker-friendly" terms.

Networks can only function properly if the participants are strongly motivated. Both producers and members of the labour movement need to be convinced that their participation in a regional network is a matter of enlightened self-interest, not altruism. Once this realization has been achieved, meaningful participation of these parties will be much easier to secure. Since the establishment of successful interfirm networking seems to depend on the prior existence of network relations within individual workplaces, unions can help establish the right preconditions by engaging management in bargaining that leads to the real empowerment of workers and the building of trust. If the first objective has been achieved, then both parties should be motivated by enlightened self-interest to bargain in good faith towards this end. Unions could also contribute to the establishment of network relations within the region by engaging in political activism at the federal and provincial levels to bring about "network-compatible" legislative change. This recommendation recognises the key role that has been played by sympathetic regulatory environments in countries such as Germany to encourage firms to establish the kinds of long-term relations with workers and other firms that are conducive to network behaviour. In the absence of similar attention to such issues in the Ontario and Canadian context, it will be much more difficult to achieve significant beneficial results solely on the basis of local action.

Of course, there are certain countervailing influences that are already undermining unions' abilities to effect such changes in Canada. We refer here to the Canada-US FTA, and its likely successor NAFTA. To the extent that these agreements exert greater pressure on Canadian legislators to "harmonize" our regulatory regime with the lowest common denominator (the southern US or, ultimately, Mexico) or face the prospect of capital flight, it will become increasingly difficult to achieve the kinds of national and provincial reforms suggested here.

4. Rationalizing State Economic Development

Ross Gittell, Allen Kaufman, and Michael Merenda

4.1 Introduction

Much controversy surrounds state government economic development efforts in the United States: what interests motivate these programs; who benefits and who pays for them; and do these programs provide net social gains? To examine these questions, we use collective action theory to analyze one type of state development activity, industrial extension service. However, whereas most scholars apply collective action theory to admonish state activism, we employ the theory to highlight both the potential benefits and costs associated with these programs. By recognizing the socially beneficial and harmful forces motivating these programs, we offer rational means for maximizing public and private benefits.

4.2 Background

Over the last two decades state economic development programs have proliferated (National Governors' Association, 1992). Prior to the late 1970s, most state economic development policy makers practiced a "traditional" approach. The traditional approach presumes that new investment flows to areas with the lowest costs and that state government priority should be on the maintenance and promotion of "good business climates" with: (1) low factor (e.g., taxes, labor and energy) costs; and (2) receptivity to business interests, with incentive packages and direct subsidies to firms (e.g.,tax abatements and free training programs).

In the late 1970s and early 1980s, many states, particularly in the declining industrial Northeast, reconsidered their approaches under the pressures of economic recession, international competition and cut-backs in federal aid to states. Empirical investigations added to this reevaluation. For example, the empirical evidence suggested that reducing broad-based taxes to affect business location or expansion decisions was often misdirected policy, especially, if lower taxes lead to lower quality public services (e.g., infrastructure and education) that adversely affected the competitiveness of industry and the quality of life (Ferguson and Ladd, 1988). Policy reformers no longer emphasized the supply side of the economic development equation. Rather, they looked to the demand side, attempting to identify, anticipate and even help create markets on which private producers could capitalize. Eisinger labeled the demand side approaches taken by state governments as "entrepreneurial" (Eisinger, 1988).

In formulating state entrepreneurial policies, reformers distinguished between high growth/high technology and mature/"old-line" industries. California's Silicon Valley and Massachusetts' Route 128 became the archetypal examples for the first industry category. States acted on the belief that geographically concentrated activity including the formation of high tech businesses and the provision of "complementary" support services (e.g., research, education and training centers and financial and venture capital) provided the greatest prospect for future economic growth. To encourage these high technology agglomerations, state economy policy makers advocated policies that fostered industry and university partnerships (e.g., Pennsylvania's Ben Franklin Program) and research parks (e.g., North Carolina's Research Triangle).

Policies to revitalize older industries similarly called attention to technology and to the needs of small and medium-size enterprises (SMEs). Only here the new policy advocates emphasized the need to modernize existing enterprises through industrial extension services that would facilitate technology transfer and worker training. Pennsylvania's Industrial Resource Centers (IRCs) perhaps best illustrate this clamor for industrial modernization. As advocates for entrepreneurial state governments honed policies suited for both high growth and mature industries, these policy analysts systematized their shared assumptions, concluding that a region's economic growth depended on home-based firms, usually SMEs, and that competitive advantage could be sustained by upgrading factors of production (Porter, 1990; Best, 1990).

During the 1980s this emphasis on assisting SMEs through an industrial extension service and through programs that linked business to the states' educational/research institutions and venture capital sources found wide acceptance both among the states and the federal government. This consensus emerged among the states cyclically. The first states to adopt these policies were those effected by the 1980-82 recession; the word spread later in the decade to other states, such as New Hampshire and California, with the US military build-down and its accompanying recession. Indeed, by 1987 forty-three states had some type of entrepreneurial policy that linked university and vocational research to industry, including industrial services aimed at diffusing new technologies to SMEs (US General Accounting Office, 1991).

The United States federal government, too, became involved in this movement as it attempted to address America's declining international position. In 1988 Congress passed the Omnibus Trade and Competitiveness Act. As part of this legislation, Congress reorganized the Department of Commerce's National Bureau of Standards, a research agency responsible for national manufacturing standards, into the National Institute for Standards and Technology (NIST). The new agency's mission was to advance manufacturing practices among the nation's SMEs (US Department of Commerce, 1991). To carry out this objective, Congress gave NIST authority to establish manufacturing technology centers and to provide technical and financial assistance for state technology programs under the Manufacturing Extension Partnership (MEP). Subsequently, the Clinton administration worked with Congress to increase NIST's budget from $1.4 million to $384 million in 1993 and proposed that NIST's budget reach $1.4 billion by 1997 and that MEP's budget be increased from $18 million to $91 million.

After the election of November 1994, and the Republican party take-over of the US Congress and Senate, NIST's and MEP's budgets were subjected to increased scrutiny. At the writing of this chapter, it appeared that these programs' budgets would be cut. However, the extent of the cutbacks were not clear as industry groups, including the Coalition for Technology Partnerships and the Aerospace Industries Association of America Inc., lobbied against proposed budget rescissions (Morrison, 1995).

As industrial modernization policies advanced both at the state and federal level, a controversy over their efficacy emerged. While admitting difficulties in measuring success, proponents argued that state assistance to SMEs provided net social benefits. Their claims rested primarily on comparative studies that showed foreign, particularly German and Japanese, SMEs to be more productive than their US counterparts. These two nations had comprehensive industrial services that proponents claimed accounted for much of the differential. To further bolster their case, these advocates cited surveys that demonstrated business' receptivity to existing programs, reported benefits from program administrators and provided anecdotal success stories (Osborne, 1988; Pennsylvania Economy League, Inc., 1993; Kelley and Arora, 1995).

None of these arguments convinced critics. Opponents questioned whether the early successes depended on the program's proficiency or the economy's robustness (Feller, 1992). Since no precise means existed to measure these programs' contributions to a state's economy growth, fiscal conservatives and newly elected governors targeted entrepreneurial initiatives as state economies slowed. Massachusetts followed this pattern. After the state's economy receded in the late 1980s, newly elected Governor William Weld dismantled some of the earlier entrepreneurial efforts (put in place by his predecessor, Michael Dukakis).

While many critics pointed to specific abuses, the arguments drew on established propositions found in collective action and public choice theory. Essentially, these theories contend that special interests, including the interests of private firms, political entrepreneurs and implementing agencies, can easily capture governmental programs (Olson, 1982; Niskanen, 1971). According to these theories, captured programs misspend taxpayers contributions, interfere with market mechanisms, bias investments, and cause sub-optimal economic growth.

In this chapter, we enter the debate over the wisdom of an industrial extension service. However, we join the debate in a nonpartisan manner, with no intention of settling the issue. Indeed, such an effort would require econometric tools that could decompose an industrial extension program's contribution to a state's economic growth. But analysts have as yet not developed such instruments because of the number of explanatory variables to control for. In the absence of such measurements, reconciliation seems unlikely.

Yet, as we have observed, these programs have proliferated. This reality demands that policy makers act prudently, especially given the lack of rigorous performance measures. Here, collective action theory may be of great assistance, if adopted analytically rather than polemically. While collective action theory recognizes that these programs have sufficient political incentives to inspire institutionalization, the same theory also acknowledges benefits that arise if these services efficiently correct market imperfections. We draw on collective action theory in this balanced manner to consider the utility of public policy and alternative types of institutional arrangements in providing industrial extension services.

The chapter divides into three parts. First, we use collective action theory to consider industrial extension services, both as a corrective to market failures and as a means for political entrepreneurship. Then, we make these ideas tangible by examining one state's discussions to create an industrial extension service. New Hampshire provides an excellent case, since the state's conservative biases work against interventionist policies. Furthermore, the New Hampshire case provides the opportunity to consider the utility of public entrepreneurial effort and cross sectorial (i.e., public and private sector) institutional arrangements to foster business networking. In New Hampshire the main instigators for industrial extension services were public agency officials, while the primary institutional vehicle created to foster extension services (through which business networking could be facilitated) was the Governor's Technology Partnership (GTP), a joint effort of the public and private sectors.

The business network in New Hampshire is highly decentralized with significant linkages to global markets (i.e., lower right hand cell in Staber's matrix, Figure 1.1 in this volume). NH's leading manufacturing industries are dominated by small and medium-sized firms which operate as specialized problem-solving component parts suppliers in vertical production chains (Kaufman et. al., 1994). These firms have excelled at forming close ties to original equipment manufacturers (OEMs) who are mostly located outside the state and region.

While NH's leading firms have established close ties to their out-of-state customers, linkages among firms within the state are less well-established. The GTP was intended in part to foster horizontal networking among firms in the state and to promote inter-firm learning and information sharing.

In New Hampshire, as we will see, the political incentives seem to have persuaded public administrators to forge ahead in planning a public industrial network, even though the business community did not seek the service. In explicating these arguments, we raise questions about the real social benefits from a state subsidized industrial extension service and explore the tendency for a "government-led industry initiative" to supply client services without justification and without sufficient understanding of industry needs. By raising these questions, we do not offer condemnations. Instead, we add to a growing understanding about the need to undertake these efforts more prudently: (1) by consulting with private industry and workers; (2) by demanding cost-sharing between the public sector and the intended beneficiaries; (3) by developing credible measures to hold the programs socially accountable; and (4) by adjusting activity appropriately over time.

4.3 Political Entrepreneurship and the Creation of an Industrial Extension Service

This section reviews collective action arguments concerning the formation of an industrial extension service: why the private market tends to under-invest (less than the desired level) in industrial extension services, and why intervention to correct this market failure might result in appropriations not matched to industries' needs and/or exceeding the desired level.[1]

Essentially, we argue that under conditions of market failure (information asymmetry, externalities and free-rider problems) the private sector will not organize a state-wide industrial extension network/service, resulting in an undersupply of this service. However, if private firms do not have good reasons to act collectively to secure an industrial extension network, we also suggest that political entrepreneurs within the economic development community do. The political entrepreneurs' incentives include the opportunity to expand the apparent efficacy of their agencies and to bolster their personal reputations.

4.3.1 Market Failure and Industrial Extension Services

Industrial services are intended to help firms upgrade capabilities to secure or sustain competitive advantages. The main activities of industrial extension service networks are the dissemination of technical and managerial know-how/information and workforce training. Many private consultants and organizations (including public and private educational institutions) provide these services.

In the absence of government intervention, individual firms can estimate the costs and benefits of industrial services and invest in a level of services which maximize their long term profitability. A market failure can arise when there is asymmetry in information between service suppliers and users, and significant uncertainty and variance in the costs and benefits of services exist.[2] Individual firms,

1 Collective action and public intervention does not require a market failure, but a market failure is often used to justify public intervention.

2 When there is asymmetry in information, i.e., when consumers have a difficult time distinguishing the quality of competitive products and providers have superior informa-

especially those that rely on service providers only occasionally (such as SMEs), can have a difficult time evaluating the value of services and assessing the differences among service suppliers; on the other side of the market, service suppliers have better information about the quality of the services they are selling.

In other words, the market for industrial extension services may contain "lemons." Once firms perceive that lemons exist, companies will discount appropriately for these services. Such discounting may result in lower quality service providers driving higher quality service providers out of the market. The net effect would be either for SMEs to underuse the market for industrial services or for the market to collapse altogether. Such circumstances could justify government intervention.

We can further specify this problem if we consider industrial extension services as a public mechanism for facilitating business networking that substitutes for firms' privately sharing technical information. The sharing of information among firms helps them reduce search costs for finding new, complementary technologies and best managerial practices. The sharing of technological information has benefitted from recent developments in electronic networks, which have improved service efficiencies and expanded their potential scope.[3]

In some cases, firms, usually large firms, can convert existing information externalities into privately appropriable goods. Where companies interact in a vertical supplier/buyer chain, some companies have cooperated to rationalize their technical interdependencies, even where direct market relationships do not exist. Rationalization occurs as firms oversee the flow of technical and business information first between the original equipment manufacturer (OEM) and its primary suppliers and then between the primary suppliers and the secondary and tertiary suppliers. Large OEMs in general have led this rationalization process by introducing managerial procedures such as value engineering and supplier associations that allow technical and business information to flow vertically and horizontally throughout the OEM/supplier chain, promoting innovation and shortening adoption time of best known practices. Once managers institute this information network they can better identify savings and negotiate long-term contracts that include target pricing formulae for equitably distributing these savings.

tion, a market for lemons can exist. The "prototype" market for lemons (in the absence of government regulation) is the market for used cars (Hardin, 1982).

3 Economists have long recognized that firms may gain from external economies arising: (1) from unpaid third party arrangements, as in the government's provision of public goods such as education and highways (Marshall, 1920a); (2) from consumer preferences, for example, through product standardization (Katz and Shapiro, 1985); or (3) from the technical interdependence created by intermediary products, for example in innovations that diffuse through an industrial system (Scitovsky, 1954; Rosenberg, 1963).

Among small firms that collaborate in flexible networks to manufacture finished goods or component parts, similar mechanisms have developed to enhance information flows and to privately appropriate the externalities created by these firms' technical interdependence. The Italian ceramics and furniture industries provide the best known examples of these flexible, horizontal networks. Companies engaged in flexible networks benefit from the specialized skills that each company brings to the project and the information flows that transpire among the participants. As in the case of the vertical OEM-supplier chain, firms within these horizontal arrangements devise contractual methods to allocate the information and/or productivity savings that the network facilitates.

Still, not all information/business networks arise spontaneously as part of ongoing production relationships. Many state governments have initiated public information networks as part of their industrial extension programs for SMEs (Clarke and Dobson, 1992). Governmental action seems necessary in forming these networks because they possess qualities similar to public goods that make their private provision unlikely. An effective system requires a large user base and consequently, significant capital investments to interconnect the various service providers. The system can only provide smaller firm's with useful practices when these are "benchmarked" against national or even international standards. Yet, because of the information asymmetries ("market for lemons") SMEs may find it difficult to calculate accurately a private consultant's benefits and so may discount heavily in purchasing services. This would result in private industrial service entrepreneurs having inadequate incentives to make the large investments needed to build an effective network. In this situation the private market will not deliver a good which could bring ample social returns by enhancing SME productivity. Hence, the need for governmental action to establish a "SME information network" for disseminating best known business and manufacturing practices.

While these efforts seem to have potential benefits for the smallest firms, what interests do medium-size manufacturers that employ between 250 and 2,000 workers have in establishing such a public information network? And what difficulties do medium-size firms have in estimating the system's benefits and costs that the system will bring? In general, these firms have the staff and external connections to assess and implement best known practices as well as the resources to hire consultants where internal expertise are lacking. Thus, these companies could view a public information system as a vehicle for nurturing rivals and so resist collective efforts for instituting this policy. However, medium-size firms need not interpret the system in this manner; they could instead view it as a public endeavor to strengthen a region's competitive advantage by upgrading small firms to be sophisticated, suppliers and customers. Indeed, medium-size firms could even go a step further by recognizing that strong local competitors usually force firms to adopt best practices and to remain competitive internationally (Porter, 1990). And communication linkages could offer the medium-sized firms benefits gained from cooperation. Locally, the network could serve both as a facilitator among local firms on issues of common concern, e.g., worker training, supplier certification, precompetitive research and development, etc., and as a broker uncovering and coordinating flexible manufacturing opportunities. Because the system itself could be integrated into a national network, individual firms would have a low cost method for finding solutions to advanced product or process problems beyond their own expertise. These kinds of situations have become more numerous over the last five years as large OEMs have systematically adopted strategic outsourcing policies that demand their suppliers to design, as well as, manufacture component parts. Given these demands, medium-size firms could benefit from an electronic network which could inexpensively access research centers, such as universities, the national laboratories or the National Institute for Standards and Technology's advanced manufacturing centers. Finally, a public information system could provide medium-size firms with a standard to evaluate alternative private consulting firm services.

Whether medium-size firms finally interpret the formation of a public information network as a competitive threat or an advantage depends largely on the organizational process used for establishing a public information network. And, given the complex nature of the alleged benefits, a precise calculation as to how any individual firm might gain from the system remains speculative.

Even if medium-sized firms recognize these potential benefits, they, nonetheless, may not invest in coordinated efforts to secure this public good. These firms may find it rational to free ride, i.e., to wait until others have expended time and money to attain a public industrial extension service. Indeed, as state governments across the nation initiate and expand industrial extension services, individual firms have less of an incentive to invest their own time in the design and provision of industrial services. Instead, proprietors might wait for political entrepreneurs to take the lead in creating programs that subsidize private industry.

Private industry can choose yet another alternative to collective action, in essence "voting with their feet" (Tiebout, 1956). Firms can move to those states that offer the desired industrial services. This alternative becomes credible only when the information costs on industrial services and the costs of relocation are minimal.

4.3.2 The Creation of an Industrial Extension Service

In sum, asymmetric information suggests market failure, while unenlightened and enlightened self-interest poses problems for private sector collective action. If a network of industrial services to SMEs is to be assured, then the public sector must take actions. Usually, public intervention requires a governmental entrepreneur who views the project's success as a positive benefit to her own career or organization (Kingdon, 1984). Given the industrial extension services dual character, that it serves locally-based firms yet its potency depends on its national user base, any entrepreneurial activity would have to include both federal and state players. Only the federal government can assure the network's inclusive structure, both regarding its technical uniformity and its broad user base, and only on the national level can there be accounting for the benefits from broad/national upgrading of SMEs. Nonetheless, federal action does not necessarily precede state action; nor does the federal government function as the principal coordinator. State governments assume this role because only they can coordinate resources for erecting a system dedicated to local needs.

Hence, the collective action problem remains a "local one," where state government entrepreneurs function as the principal coordinators, even when federal grant programs induce state action and the federal government sets national standards to assure the system's uniformity and effectiveness. In constructing an industrial services network for SMEs, the political entrepreneur must offer local SMEs attractive short-term incentives to induce them to join a public SME initiative. For example, a state entrepreneur might promise that participation will give a firm advantages in shaping public policy and gaining access to public officials; that a state-wide industrial extension service will preserve or upgrade the state's competitive advantages (and reduce the need for firms to move their operations elsewhere, thereby avoiding relocation costs, including the switching costs to establish new supplier and governmental links); or the entrepreneur might simply persuade the firm to participate to attain civic status.

This last incentive will have greater import among states that value civic activity and the maintenance of social capital (Putnam, 1993). In states with a tradition of *voluntary* association an extensive civic network linking individuals instills trust that mitigates opportunism and promotes collective action (Casson, 1991). Civic networks with strong cooperative norms educate their members on how voluntary, collective action bestows benefits, if not immediately than sometime in the near future, and if not in one undertaking then in another.

Once enlisted into the process, the political entrepreneur can help instill collective trust in and commitment to the enterprise. This involves educating the private sector participants of the rewards that their collective action might bring, garnering the appropriate public support for the undertaking, and implementing an administrative structure that can both deliver the public services and legitimate itself by designing means to calculate social returns. To assure the program's success first in finding public support and then in its operation, the political entrepreneur must select private members who both represent the appropriate client base and have the reputation needed to assuage other private entities to join the effort.

So far we have considered the entrepreneur's actions only with respect to the private sector; yet, the formation of public sector supported industrial extension service requires the participation of governmental agencies outside the entrepreneur's direct control. Typically, these include the governor's office, vocational institutions, the university system, small business development centers, and regulatory agencies that oversee manufacturing installations. Each of these institutions have specific services to offer and their participation in an industrial service network could enhance its value.

The entrepreneur's task will be made easier should her institution be rich with resources and be a legitimate lead organization. To elicit endorsements, the entrepreneur must enumerate benefits that each public institution will receive. This task will be substantially less complicated should the governor find the project desirable. Although research has indicated that voters do not hold state governors accountable for the economy as they do the President (Peltzman, 1987; Chubb, 1988), state governors still need to deliver beneficial programs, if they are to keep their electoral coalitions solidified. The entrepreneur will gain leverage if she can persuade the governor that a public industrial service network will in fact please the governor's business constituency.

Even without the governor's endorsement, the entrepreneur may be able to win support from other, public institutions, if she elicits private sector support, and if she convinces the various public institutions that each has a interest in the program's success. The entrepreneur can promise her counterparts reduced transaction costs in delivering services to their clients. For example, she can suggest that by participating in the design and administration of a state manufacturing network, vocational schools will gain detailed information to serve their client firms and students. Universities, too, will gain knowledge regarding local industries' advanced skills and research needs. This information will become increasingly important as Department of Defense (DOD) research funds dwindle and universities seek alternate ways to finance faculty research.

In all, our conceptual discussion suggests that firms may tend to undersubscribe to private industrial services, opening the way for government intervention. And because these public benefits are not easily calculable, private firms in all likelihood will not incur the costs and cooperative encumbrances that collective action demands. Nor can public policy makers easily calculate the social benefits needed to meet stringent, Coasian conditions for state intervention (Feller, 1992). Still, public officials have incentives to promote these programs, as testified by the 43 existing programs. Thus, the private market tends to undersupply industrial services, while the public sector has a bias to supply them.

This understanding suggests the need for policy makers to strike some balance between the two extremes. We review New Hampshire's recent efforts at creating an industrial extension service to give our theoretical discussion some perspective and to illuminate policy guidelines.

4.4 The Case of New Hampshire

New Hampshire (NH) affords an excellent case, for few states have such a conservative/libertarian bias. Yet, even here strong support among public administrators for industrial extension services has arisen. However, the political climate has confined these efforts, limiting the dollars to be spent and forcing public officials to elicit private industry support. That support did not come automatically; public administrators induced private industry leaders to volunteer by having the Governor directly ask for their participation. And, once public officials gained industry's assistance, they had to educate these industrialists on the potential benefits from industrial extension services. Even when enlightened, private sector participants agreed with the Governor's directive that no new state funds be spent in creating an Industrial Extension Program (IEP). Thus, NH provides a story consistent with collective action theory, one that includes policies for striking a balance between under-and-oversupplying industrial services.

In every respect, NH's political composition encourages a weak, noninterventionist state. Its bicameral legislature consists of a 24- member state senate and a house of representatives with over 400 members with terms lasting 2 years. Legislators truly volunteer their services, receiving $200 per biennium. The low compensation contributes to a lack of legislative expertise, as typically a third of the legislators are freshmen. And unlike many other states, NH's legislators lack advisory staff to help them assess complex scientific and technological issues (Myers, 1990). The executive branch contains similar institutional constraints. The Governor serves only a two-year term, giving him insufficient time to develop a program independent of his constituency. Furthermore, the Governor is constrained by his dependence on a 5-member Executive Council (elected every two years) which must approve all major executive branch appointments and budget allocations. The Governor has weak control over the executive branch; its commissioners (approved by the Executive Council) serve longer terms than the Governor, making them less dependent on the Governor and more receptive to their client base.

New Hampshire remains (except for Alaska) the only state without both a broad-based personal income tax and a state sales tax. Although the state has other sources of revenue, principally its (highway) toll revenue, profits from the State Liquor Authority and a meals and rooms tax, NH's state and local tax revenues per capita remain well below the US average. Because of its limited revenues, NH's state expenditures fall below both regional and national averages on a per capita basis (KPMG, 1992). These figures capture NH's citizens' reluctance to amplify the state's authority.

4.4.1 New Hampshire's Low Cost Economic Development Strategy

Well into the 1980s, NH politicians claimed that the state's economic successes had occurred because of its libertarian values. While other states were busy subsidizing business to relocate or adopting entrepreneurial policies to spur economic development, NH's Department of Resources and Economic Development (DRED) adhered to the belief that the state's low taxes assured job creation. Over the past two decades, NH's economy grew at a faster rate than the national average. Between 1977 and 1987 NH's service sector employment expanded at an annualized compounded rate of 7.1 per cent as compared to the 5.6 per cent national average; manufacturing employment increased 0.6 per cent between 1967 and 1987, compared to the national average which declined by 0.1 per cent per annum. Even though the service sector led in job creation, manufacturing showed substantial strength: between 1967 and 1987, productivity advanced at an annualized growth rate of 7.3 per cent, output at rate 6 per cent, and wages at 3 per cent. In each of these categories NH outperformed the nation. New Hampshire's growth came largely from (1) Massachusetts' computer companies investing in NH to benefit from cost advantages; and (2) from the state's DOD contracts between 1980 and 1985. However, after this period of impressive growth, manufacturing employment in NH dropped over 21 per cent between 1984 and 1992 and unemployment more than doubled to over 7 per cent (Kaufman et. al., 1994).

4.4.2 New Hampshire Reconsiders its Economic Development Strategy

As public officials understood the severity of NH's recession, they reviewed the state's economic development efforts and moved cautiously toward entrepreneurial economic policies. DRED issued a "Strategic Plan for Economic Development," in March, 1991. This document emphasized that economic development primarily depended on retaining and expanding small businesses that make up the vast majority of the state's economy. The Report called for local public-private partnerships to provide infrastructural, marketing and financial assistance for SMEs. The Report claimed that these efforts would benefit from an understanding of the state's leading and emerging industries.

The NH Post-Secondary Education System (Post-Secondary) likewise reviewed its mission. In New Hampshire post-secondary education's main emphasis is on vocational and technical education. The Post-Secondary education system in the state developed a working relationship with the National Institute of Standards and Technology's (NIST) Northeast Manufacturing Technology Center (NEMTC); and through this contact coveted a NIST grant to plan a Post-Secondary-based IEP. New Hampshire's hard times also forced a rethinking about the University of New Hampshire's (UNH) linkages to the state's economy. Many legislators argued that NH needed a center where private firms could collaborate with UNH researchers on specific product and process problems. In June 1991, the Industrial Research Center (IRC) was created. This legislation pleased UNH's new President, Dale Nitzschke. He had pledged to the Trustees that UNH would contribute to the state's economic development efforts. To keep his word Nitzschke looked to the Whittemore School of Business and Economics (WSBE), where he found a receptive Dean who encouraged the formation of a New Hampshire Industry Group (NHIG) to work with DRED and the IRC. Thus, by 1992 an informal network had formed among these three groups, but it did not include the state agency which would become the most prominent player, Post-Secondary Education.

That changed in the summer of 1992 when NIST requested formal proposals (RFPs) for planning state IEPs. The possibility of federal matching funds became a powerful incentive to coordinate these public groups. Although DRED and NHIG initially attempted to coordinate the state's effort in responding to the NIST RFP, three separate proposals emerged only two weeks before the deadline, one written by NHIG, another by IRC and a third by Post-Secondary. When the bargaining process concluded merging the proposals, Post-Secondary emerged as the lead agency in what was to evolve into a public-private partnership effort. The NHIG still remained an informal body with a limited mission, to provide independent analytic input into the state's economic development efforts. The IRC had an operating budget, but it was only large enough to employ one staff person, its Director. As a new agency, it had no clout with other state offices, nor had it developed an independent client base among NH's SMEs.

The logical leadership choice appeared to be DRED, the state's economic development organization. Yet, DRED's organization and its resource base prevented it from being the Partnership's coordinator. Unlike many state economic development agencies, DRED also has responsibility for the state's tourist and natural resource industries. The Office of Business and Industrial Development (OBID) remains among DRED's smallest units. The Office followed a two-prong approach: (1) it assisted local development through a Business Visitation Program; and (2) it marketed these locales to firms interested in relocating to NH. These activities made the Office a captive of the local development authorities, reproducing NH's decentralization biases (NH Department of Resources and Economic Development, 1991).

Post-Secondary confounded this bias. It consists of seven associate degree granting colleges, coordinated by a central administration. Each college offers training and technological assistance to local businesses. Given these resources, the System's Commissioner, Jeff Rafn, declared that Post-Secondary would be the leader in the state's industrial extension efforts. To implement this vision, Post-Secondary maintained important connections to the federal government, which allowed Rafn to design programs in keeping with national trends such as those promoted by NIST. Among Rafn's initiatives two stand out: (1) the electronic integration of the colleges through Internet, which now serves as the federal communication system for the nation's emerging industrial extension services network; and (2) plans to build Technology Deployment Centers at each college, that provide general and specialized technological and educational services to industry. Through these Centers, Rafn hoped to make Post-Secondary NH's primary SME service provider and communication link to the national industrial network. To implement this strategy, Rafn had ample funds; in 1992, Post-Secondary's central administration had a budget of nearly $3 million. Thus, Rafn was able to assure the program participants that action would occur even without federal funding (NH Post-Secondary Technical Education System, 1992).

4.4.3 Forging a Governor's Technology Partnership

Post-Secondary, DRED, the IRC and NHIG, had initiated the state's effort at building an IEP. But, such a network required private enterprise input. Indeed, NIST made this a condition in its review process. Ironically, then, these public agencies pursued SMEs to join a partnership that – unknown to these firms' managers – would be beneficial to them. The NHIG and IRC led this effort by approaching members of WSBE's advisory board. In each case, the firms agreed to participate in the partnership, primarily because of the civic status associated with membership. With only one exception, no invited member had any knowledge of public industrial extension systems or of NIST. To guarantee these participants' long-term involvement, the public partners devised a process to educate these industrialists and to vest them in this collective undertaking.

When the NIST grant was put together, the New Hampshire Technology Partnership had a planning budget of approximately $150,000 that doubled for the NIST RFP matching funding requirement. The bulk of these funds came from Post-Secondary, with DRED contributing only $3,000 of in-kind services. Not one of its five private partners contributed to the budget. And, control still rested in the public sector. With an operating budget, the Partnership began work even though it lost the NIST grant. However, all work stopped after Senator Warren Rudman announced his retirement, and Governor Judd Gregg declared his candidacy for the vacancy. The Partnership waited for the new Governor, which turned out to be Steve Merrill, a conservative Republican. Both Commissioners Rafn and Rice tried to inform the new Governor of the Partnership's activities. Delays occurred as Merrill dealt with the state budget. Yet, the delays played to the Commissioners' advantage, for during this period NIST announced a New England Conference on Industrial Modernization and the DOD's Advanced Research Projects Agency (ARPA) announced a $471 million grant program. Because of its excellent conference facilities, NIST selected UNH as the host for the regional meeting. This fact plus NIST's letters requesting each Governor to send a delegation to the two-day conference gave Commissioners Rice and Rafn the opening they needed to discuss the Partnership with Governor Merrill. The expected ARPA RFP added credibility to the Commissioners' arguments.

Induced by the federal government, Merrill endorsed the Technology Partnership, renaming it the Governor's Technology Partnership (GTP) and rearranging its membership. The Governor appointed 6 of his Commissioners, while he slightly modified the private sector composition. He named two Co-chairs: Commissioner Rafn (affirming Post-Secondary's lead) and Andy Lietz, the Chief Operating Officer of HADCO, the nation's leading merchant circuit board manufacturer. Later the Governor met with the Partners in his Council Chambers where he asked them to draft an IEP plan, one that relied on existing services and did not require new funds. When the Governor left the meeting, the GTP's Co-chairs had to consolidate the individuals into a working group. With one exception, the private sector Partners had no working contact with the Governor or the Commissioners.

The NIST conference provided an excellent opportunity for getting this process underway. At the conference, the Partners learned about extension services' alleged benefits and about best practices in the US and Europe. The conference, too, helped build solidarity among the members, particularly between the two Co-chairs. At this meeting Jeff Rafn and Andy Lietz built enthusiasm for the project and set the agenda for future Partnership meetings, including a series of industry forums to gather information about "user needs." Over the course of the next four months industry forums were held for firms in the software, transportation, metals manufacturing and computer/electronics industries. The forums were conducted as focus groups and designed to get detailed input from industry members on their needs for industrial services. At the Partnership meetings and at the industrial forums, formal and informal agreements and exchanges occurred both between public officials and participating firms as well as among the firms themselves. On October 29, 1993 the GTP reported to the Governor. Their plan called for an electronically connected delivery service to facilitate information flows, networking and training. Post-Secondary would be the major service provider, while the electronic system would interconnect Post-Secondary and NH to other state and national industrial extension programs. The GTP made specific recommendations about governance and private contributions. First, the GTP would remain as the oversight board. Second, member firms would lend executives for one year to be center directors. Finally, each participating firm would adopt smaller companies to improve their business capabilities.

The Partnership's efforts (including an ARPA proposal and another NIST grant application) continued primarily because of: (1) Rafn's desire to build Post-Secondary into the state's "industrial service provider;" (2) the Governor's desire to remain linked to the state's manufacturing community; and (3) the new commitment and interest of private sector partners on the GTP board. In the fall of 1994, the state was awarded a $250,000 NIST grant to develop a pilot IEP in Nashua, the center of manufacturing activity in the state, just north of the Massachusetts' border and Route 128.

4.4.4 Lessons from New Hampshire

New Hampshire's experience provides evidence that an industrial extension service's intended beneficiaries, SMEs, may have little if anything to do with its initiation. In New Hampshire, leadership came from public agencies that could benefit from a state industrial network. The private sector joined the effort primarily out of perceived civic duty. Yet, voluntary association brought its own benefits as firms gained connections to important public officials and as firms learned from one another. Thus, where the public agencies had incentives to oversupply services, private industry remained skeptical, wanting documentation on industry needs and evidence that existing services were being rationalized to meet these needs. On the other hand, public officials persuaded industry leaders about the program's potential benefits and secured private commitment through in-kind services. In New Hampshire, at least, public and private partners worked together to find the middle course between too much and too little public intervention in the market.

But New Hampshire's balanced initiative would not have occurred without the federal grants. Earlier, vocational education grants cultivated the state's lead industrial extension organization, Post-Secondary, and acted as a carrot to motivate state officials to form a partnership. In a peculiar way, the federal government undermined New Hampshire's libertarian biases by fostering the state's efforts in industrial services. Indeed, the federal government's ability to lure this libertarian state suggests just how powerful federal programs can be in influencing state and local economic development practice.

4.5 Conclusions: The Need to Rationalize State Development Efforts

Collective action theory simultaneously provides arguments that justify public action and warn against its excess. Information asymmetry suggests social benefits from a public industrial extension network; however, difficulties in calculating its benefits and free rider issues inhibit spontaneous private collective action. Yet, public officials have powerful organizational and status incentives to design and implement services independent of private demand. Left solely to private or to public means, one would expect either too little or too much industrial extension services. Hence, the need for a public-private partnership, both to moderate the supply and to assure its relevance.

An effective public-private partnership must begin with cost sharing measures. Both parties must bring something to the table, whether in cash or in-kind contributions. At the same time, procedures must be used to assure the services' pertinence and cost-effectiveness. For example, a state might institute a (public-private) state certification board to certify and monitor private services; this certification process could overcome asymmetric information and would encourage private competition, especially against public service providers. Alternatively, public extension services could charge fees (i.e., cost sharing) which allow for different levels of state subsidy depending on the needs of firms and ability to pay.

The best approach will vary by state. States should select the approach to industrial service provision that takes advantage of and enhances their existing capabilities and reflects industry needs. In larger states with an existing private industrial service infrastructure, e.g., New York, Pennsylvania, Michigan, state certification or "grading" of service providers might be most beneficial. In smaller, less densely populated states, e.g., New Hampshire, state provision of services and the charging of user fees might be beneficial.

Regardless of a state's policy orientation, each state must develop methods to assess businesses' current and future needs and to evaluate industrial service performance. This would allow the public and private sectors to monitor program effectiveness and to adjust programs to correct for deficiencies or changing economic conditions.

The lessons from the states' experience with industrial extension efforts could apply to other state development activities, including financing and export promotion. Here, too, "partnership" activities make sense for rationalizing programs through joint planning, cost sharing and evaluation. Leaving state development activities to either the private sector or the public sector, without some form of partnership can be detrimental – allowing for market failures to go uncorrected or public agencies to go unchecked.

5. Québec's Strategy to Foster Value-Adding Interfirm Cooperation

Marc Ferland, Benoit Montreuil, and Diane Poulin

5.1 Introduction

Interfirm cooperation is increasingly recognized all around the world as a key to business competitiveness, be the firms small or large. However, interfirm cooperation is clearly not a way of life for most industrial enterprises at the current time. Following the example of governments having taken leadership positions in this domain, as in Denmark, Italy, and Japan, several states have engaged in efforts to provide an infrastructure aimed at fostering cooperation between firms. The Province of Québec in Canada is among this group of states.

This chapter reports Québec's initiatives and experiences in catalyzing interfirm cooperation. The government's dual approach integrates the implementation of two complementary strategies: a top-down clustering strategy and a bottom-up networking strategy. In this chapter, we examine these strategies within the perspective of Québec's implementation of its general economic strategy, and we emphasize the network enterprise model as the key to a successful networking program.

5.2 Québec's Economic Strategy

Québec's government has decided to focus its strategic efforts on developing a competitive value-adding economy (Gagné and Lefèvre, 1993). The intervention approach of the government with investors, company heads and their partner centers is based on a broad view of long-term economic development.

Québec's economy has always been very open. In 1992, the province sold nearly 30 per cent ($45 billion) of its output on external markets. In proportion to its gross domestic product ($160 billion), it exports three time as much as the United States and twice as much as Japan. In 1990, finished products accounted for over half of Québec's exports (MICT, 1993a). To obtain the maximum economic spinoff from foreign trade, the Québec government intends to increase this proportion.

The governments's strategy is to bolster the value added of Québec's industrial output, notably by ensuring the secondary processing of the province's natural resources. The main objective is to boost output by relying on operations that add the most value to Québec products in all sectors of the economy. By acting now, with the medium and long terms in mind, Québec aims to create permanent and quality jobs.

The success of this undertaking is believed to depend on the ability of businesses to meet the following challenges: achieve sound capitalization, train competent workers, engage in extensive R&D and innovation, integrate design into the production process, foster a labour climate conducive to the long-term development of businesses, engage in the integral management of quality and the development of export markets, and to do all this without overlooking environmental protection (MICT, 1993b).

Given the globalization of production, the success of an individual company is less and less an isolated phenomenon. The competitiveness of a firm's suppliers and sub-contractors and the quality of the links that it maintains with them, the support of the company's workers and partners, sound emulation within the particular sector of activity, solid worker training, and a well-developed R&D infrastructure are all crucial to success (Topolsky and Bernstein, 1992).

Québec's government is aware of the salutary effect of interaction between businesses and institutions in the same industrial sector, both with respect to trade relations and non-trade operations, and it has decided to make this synergy a driving force in its industrial strategy. In this way, it intends to encourage the pooling of efforts in promising sectors, whose development the government is fostering in order to maximize economic spinoff (Pellerin, 1992).

As shown in Figure 5.1, Québec's government has developed an industrial strategy which is orchestrated around two intricately related facets. The first facet aims to increase the competitiveness of firms through initiatives which have significant impact on the identified key success variables for an enterprise. These variables include the qualification of a firm's human resources; its sound capitalization; its working environment; its dedication to total quality; its engagement in research and development, technology, innovation and design; its orientation toward exportation; and its commitment to environmental protection.

The second facet aims at fostering interfirm cooperation through dynamic synergistic industrial clusters. This facet centres on the notion of *grappe industrielle*, a loose French Québec translation and adaptation of the notion of industrial cluster introduced by Michael Porter (1990). Such a *grappe* (in English, pronounced *grap(s)*) is a group of businesses in the same sector that share common challenges and demands as regards development. The firms within *grappes* are interdependent as a result of sub-contracting, competition, outsourcing of intermediate products, and partnerships. Through complementarity or competition, such firms can strengthen their overall position and spur growth by means of concerted action in the realm of manpower training, subcontracting and outsourcing, strong alliances, and so on.

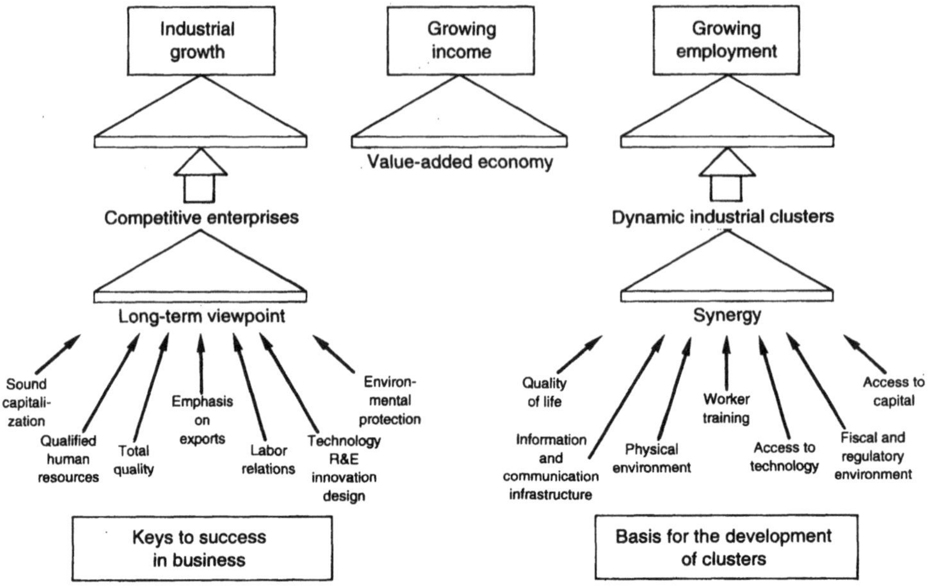

Figure 5.1 Quebec's industrial development

5.3 Strategy Phases

The implementation of the strategy has been planned in two phases. Both of these phases focus on strengthening Québec's industrial fabrics through enhanced levels of competition and cooperation among enterprises. These phases can be loosely called the clustering phase and the networking phase. The clustering phase is based on a macroscopic top-down approach, while the networking phase is built around a microscopic bottom-up approach. The clustering phase was launched in 1993, while the networking phase is being launched at the time of this writing (Gagnon, 1993). Below we discuss some details of both phases, emphasizing the networking phase which is much less well documented than the now highly mediatized clustering phase.

5.3.1 The Clustering Phase

The clustering phase was begun with a rigorous study of the industrial fabrics of Québec's economy. This study led the Ministry of Industry, Commerce and Technology (MICT)[1] strategy planners to identify thirteen *grappes* which are either

1 In 1994, the Department of Science was transferred to the former Ministry of Industry,

perceived as being world-class competitive, or as being strategic due to either their strong potential for reaching world-class competitiveness or their criticality to Québec's industrial fabrics and economy. These are respectively: ground transport equipment, forest products, cultural industries, housing, pharmaceutical products, energy products, information technology products, aerospace, agrifood products, metal and mineral transformation, fashion and textile, petrochemical and plastics, and environment. Each of these *grappes* includes hundreds of enterprises and organizations in Québec.

The *grappes* cannot be analyzed separately, but call for a macroscopic perspective which shows that all of them are closely interdependent in terms of resources, markets, information, communication and legal infrastructures, markets, technology, and so on. They contain a large potential of synergy which the Québec economic strategy seeks to exploit.

For example, the thirteenth *grappe* of information technology has distinct characteristics. It would be a mistake to think that this *grappe* can be isolated and treated separately from the others. Production technology is perceived as being so critical that the MICT has created a bureau especially devoted to it. Biotechnology and materials technology appear in most documents related to industrial strategy due to their huge potential impact on the underlying fabric of Québec's industry.

The MICT planners have then elaborated what is believed to be the foundation for the development of the *grappes*. This is critical since for Québec's government the *grappes* are not to be merely analytic outputs from some theoretical clustering study. They are to be real entities which are to be developed and nurtured to enhance Québec's economic prosperity. *Grappes* are to be dynamic and evolving realities (MICT, 1992). Key foundations for their synergetic development are the availability of capital, training and education of human resources, availability of technology, fiscal environment and legal rules, physical infrastructure, information and communication infrastructure, and quality of life.

In order to better understand the nature of the *grappes*, Figure 5.2 depicts the example of the *grappe* pharmaceutical products. It illustrates the relationships between the various types of actors in the *grappe*. Enterprises include, for example, part suppliers, raw material producers, subcontractors, finished products producers, integrators, consultants, distributors and customers. The *grappe* also includes public sector actors such as research centers, universities and colleges, institutions, government agencies, and so on. The aim is to develop and maintain synergic value-adding relationships between the various types of actors.

Commerce, and Technology, whose name was then changed to Ministry of Industry, Commerce, Science, and Technology (MICST).

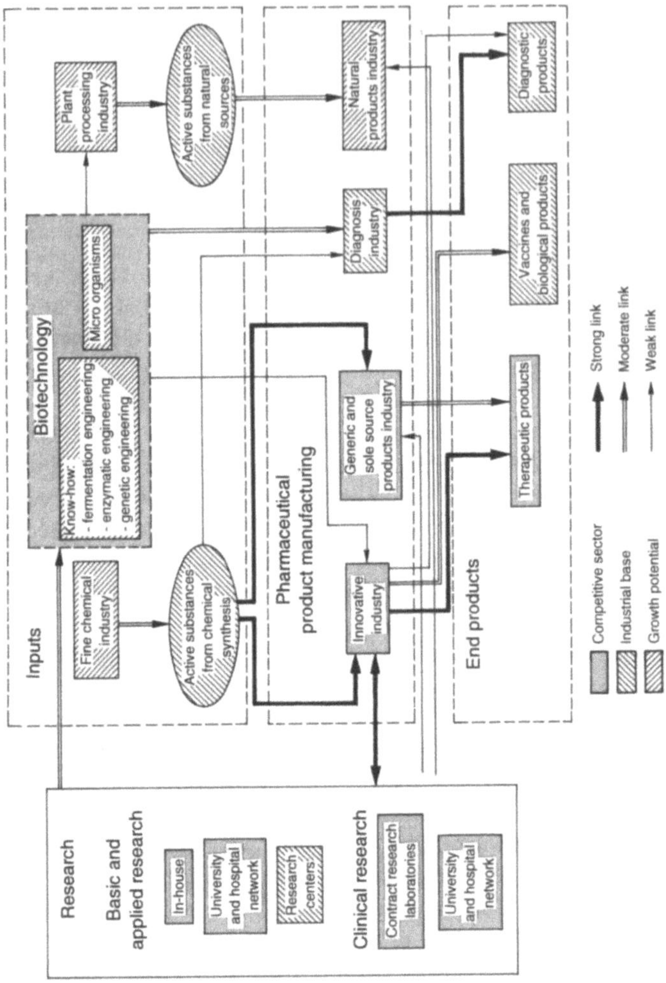

Figure 5.2 Pharmaceutical products

As a first public step, this set of *grappes* has been widely documented and reported in the media, highlighting the fact that the vitality of these thirteen *grappes* is decisive in terms of Québec's industrial and technological development. To enhance this criticality, highly respected leaders from both industry and unions joined government officials to support the initiative.

MICT has then launched a comprehensive concertation oriented program in order to catalyze the synergy building process within each of the thirteen clusters (Côté, Bordeleau, and Pellerin, 1993). The concertation program is structured according to a top-down approach. First, in each cluster, MICT has assembled a main concertation table which groups a selection of industrial leaders within the cluster. The mandate of each table is to identify and discuss what are perceived to be the key issues for the overall cluster, and ultimately to propose initiatives for action. Each table has itself created a number of focused tables aimed at investigating further each key issue. The process has generated a lot of enthusiasm among industrial leaders and has been translated into a number of cluster-wide initiatives. It is also starting to have an impact on the way industrial leaders think about competition and collaboration.

Through this process, the growth potential of each *grappe* has been examined. More precise information has been generated on the niches which should be developed or strengthened, and the networks which should be established or consolidated within the *grappe*. Based on this information, both investors and businesses can adopt a long-term vision of their development and incorporate it into a broader approach aimed at ensuring that their longlasting efforts are profitable.

It is particularly important for investors to have a good understanding of the valuable ways in which they can invest in Québec's industrial clusters. Privileged forms of investment include direct investment leading to the establishment of a R&D center or a manufacturing facility; the expansion or alteration of an existing firm; a partnership with a firm already established in Québec, in order to pool know-how; and the formation of a strategic alliance with an established company, with a view to transferring know-how and production technological systems, and the conclusion of trade agreements.

5.3.2 The Networking Phase

MICT decided in 1993 to engage in a second phase of implementing its industrial strategy, with the aim of better anchoring the relationships between the enterprise-oriented micro facet and the cluster-oriented meso facet of the strategy (Gagnon, 1993). The basic idea was to directly foster networking activities among enterprises, especially small-and-medium-size enterprises (SMEs), and to do so by exploiting MICT's own internal network of over 200 industrial development agents already interacting regularly with SMEs.

One has to realize that 99.4 per cent of Québec's manufacturing firms qualify as SMEs (MICST, 1994). Most of these SMEs have major weaknesses relating to at least one, and often several, of the seven key success variables identified by the MICT (see Figure 5.1). For example, the vast majority of firms have severe handicaps inhibiting their exporting potential and capacity (GREPME, 1994). Yet, through their small size, they have some of the characteristics most saught after by leading-edge firms. For example, many firms are constantly achieving high performances in terms of time and flexibility. States such as Denmark (Hatch, 1991; Kristensen, 1992) and Italy (Trigilia, 1990) have clearly demonstrated that government stimulated interfirm cooperation may help small firms to achieve economies of scale and/or economies of complexity, while maintaining and even upgrading high levels of time and flexibility based performance (Rosenfeld and Bosworth, 1992).

Foremost in this second phase was the early decision not to directly copy the models shown to be successful in other states, but rather to learn from them and then develop a model well adapted to Québec's setting. Building this model, developing an intervention approach, and then teaching it to MICT industrial development agents, thus became a key start-up activity during the networking phase.

In order to develop the model and the intervention approach, and train its agents, the MICT established in 1992 a partnership with a research team composed of the three authors of this chapter, working at Université Laval. This team's cross-disciplinary and innovative nature, strong engagement in networking related research, and extended interest in collaborative research with industry, have been stated by the MICT to be key to its decision to engage in the partnership. Through the first six months of 1993, the team met extensively with the supervisory committee put together by MICT, as well as with the many stakeholders of this program.

At the time of this writing, both the model and the intervention approach have now been completed and approved. They will be thereafter be referred to as the network enterprise model and the network enterprise approach, respectively. A pilot test training program was successfully completed during the summer of 1993. The experience gained through the pilot training process and further field study led to various adjustments of the training program and the overall network enterprise approach. Large scale training was begun later that year, when half of the MICT agents attended the lead-off course. Training its network of agents is paramount to MICT's strategy implementation, as knowledge and learning are considered critical to networking. Those firms which already exploit networking can gain from a comprehensive vision and methodology to master the process, clarifying their intuition in solving specific problems or dealing with new challenges and opportunities. For many firms which are currently not actively engaged in networks because they prefer to remain autonomous, there is a need for a paradigm change from the "castle enterprise" to the "network enterprise."

In December 1993, the Québec government announced a series of financial incentives to catalyze the networking movement. Reporting the specifics of these incentives is beyond the intended scope of this chapter. But in general, the direct incentives are split into three categories: Incentives to support networking opportunity studies, incentives to support more elaborate network planning studies, and incentives to support network services centers. These three types of incentives are built on a matching funds basis, the latter being on a decreasing share basis leading to self-sustainability. The government's financial involvements are kept small in order to be felt by businesses more like a sparking catalyst than a financial incentive by itself.[2]

5.4 Linking the Network Enterprise Approach with the Industrial Strategy

Very early in the process of designing the approach, it became clear that the approach had to be anchored firmly within the government's general industrial strategy. It was judged to be of foremost importance to clarify its relationships with both facets of the industrial strategy. Therefore, before describing the approach in detail, it is useful to analyze its links with the industrial strategy.

First, using the network approach, a company seeks to develop its competitiveness through improvement of its major success variables (see Figure 5.1). These variables are directly used by the MICT in its enterprise facet of the industrial strategy. For a company, participating in a network should not be a goal in itself, but rather a means to develop a competitive advantage to help the firm thrive in the global market. The network approach also ensures that the potential impact of networking on competitiveness is not to be seen from a myopic cost minimizing perspective. This is achieved by listing a series of strategic criteria motivating a customer to purchase the company's products rather than those of its competitors. The list of criteria is taken from notes of the Commission on Industrial and Commercial Competitivity from the Faculty of Administration Sciences of Université Laval. These criteria include price, after-sales service, speed, reliability, market coverage, design flexibility, volume flexibility, product innovation, product performance, product mix, quality, as well as notoriety and image. The first objective of the Québec industrial strategy, namely developing worldwide competitive enterprises, is thus being achieved. At the same time, the approach also strengthens the industrial *grappes* themselves.

The potentials of networking should always be examined from as many broad perspectives as possible, including the mainstream industrial, technological, and geographic perspectives. Macrolevel perspectives bring to consider the synergies, interdependencies, and interactions between the companies and other economic actors. Geography is important in that there is a decreasing incentive in networking between firms as they shift from being in the same building to being in the same industrial park, town, county, province, country, continental region, continent, or world. An industrial and sector perspective offers insights as well, as enterprises within the same industrial sector, or larger industrial cluster or *grappe*, may gain from networking, be they in the same province or on oppo-

2 At the moment, the program is still in progress. Numerous projects have been developed and implemented in the field, but it is still too early to assess the degree of their success.

site sides of the planet. Incentives for networking also derive from technological considerations, as firms move into the new knowledge-based economy. Information technology, production technology, biotechnology, and materials technology have been identified as critical to Québec's industrial future.

The MICST structure reflects the intention of acting simultaneously at all three macro levels. The largest group spans Québec's territory with regional agents, each devoted to a specific region within Québec (geographic perspective). The second largest group spans Québec's industry with sectorial agents, each devoted to a specific industrial sector (industrial perspective). This includes nurturing high-technology enterprises as well as dealing with technology related projects within any enterprise, whether high-tech or not.

The development of world-class enterprises has a driving effect on the partners they collaborate with. Thus, networking results in the mutual reinforcement of the competitiveness of the firms and the industrial clusters they belong to. And in this way the networking approach integrates both facets of the Québec industrial strategy.

5.4.1 The Network Enterprise Model[3]

The network enterprise model is built around a series of basic concepts. Here we want to emphasize three dominant ones. First, we suggest that every enterprise in the world has always been and will always be dealing with networks, both internally within the firm and externally with other firms and organizations (Poulin, Montreuil, and Gauvin, 1994). The nodes of its internal network correspond to all the resources internalized to perform some activity within the value chain: internal logistics, production, external logistics, marketing and sales, after-sales service, supply/sourcing, human resources management, research and development, and infrastructure. This network may be very rigid and hierarchical, or very flexible and heterarchical. It may be structured based on customer-server market-like relationships, authoritarian relationships, or very fluid collaborative relationships.

Internal networks can be examined from multiple perspectives. For example, we speak of product development networks, production networks, order delivery process networks, and so on. Furthermore, networks are generally recursively defined in order to capture their complexity. The overall internal network of an enterprise may include a production node. This node can itself be decomposed into networks of finer grain with additional nodes such as nodes dedicated to producing a specific family of products or nodes grouping all processors of a given important type.

3 The following section is based on the work of Poulin, Montreuil, and Gauvin (1994), who conducted an exhaustive analysis of the literature on this topic.

The external network of an enterprise includes all firms and organizations with which the enterprise interacts. This includes suppliers, competitors, business partners, shareholders, public and semi-public organizations (including universities and research centers), unions, trade associations, etc. In the network-unaware enterprise, this external network is typically extremely underexploited. For example, the enterprise would have very limited sell-buy relationships with its suppliers, even with those major suppliers from which it obtains key inputs. By contrast, the network-aware enterprise consciously designs and exploits its external network connections, carefully selecting its partners and the type of relationships it wants to have, and nurturing these with each partner. External networks may be stable or dynamic, rigid or flexible, tactical or strategic, and they may take the form of a constellation around the enterprise, depending upon the context.[4] Firms may join networks involving many enterprises, as in consortia or in flexible interfirm collaboration networks. Describing the firm as a web of value-adding networks which drive its main processes, with emphasis on the interaction between the internal and external nodes of these networks, is a key modeling concept (Quinn, 1992).

A second concept revolves around the fact that *every* activity within the firm is subject to networking, from the most humble to the most strategic activity (Guilhon and Gianfoldini, 1990). For each activity, the firm must strategically select among the following alternatives: to do it, to have it done, to do it together, or not to do it (translation from the French: *faire, faire faire, faire ensemble, ne pas faire*) (Poulin, Montreuil, and Gauvin, 1994).

To do it implies using the internal network of the firm. *To have it done* implies exploiting the external network of the firm by outsourcing the activity to an external partner. *To do it together* implies exploiting the interrelationships between the internal and external networks by teaming up with external partners to jointly perform a given activity. *Not to do it* indicates the withdrawal of the firm from performing the activity. An example would be a firm deciding not to export to Asia. The choice between the four strategic options should be made from a holistic and pragmatic perspective dealing with the impact of key competitive criteria such as price, speed, flexibility, and quality. The choice has to be made for activities ranging from shipping and packaging, to precision machining, to head hunting and human resource evaluation, to research and development for a new generation of products, to accounting, to market studies, and so on all around the enterprise's value chain. The choice also has to be made at every level within the firm's overall network. For example, *to do it together* for a layout study of a major manufacturing unit may involve teaming up with other units from the same company (supplying unit, facilities engineering, materials management, staff consultants, etc.) as

4 For a complete typology of networks, see Poulin, Montreuil, and Gauvin (1994).

well as external partners (main customers, union, expert consultants, simulation company, etc.).

A third concept, integrating the first two concepts, is to put much more emphasis on the networking process rather than on promoting a specific form of network. It is important to know the various forms of networks, nodes, links, relationships and flows. It is important to be able to distinguish the forms which appear to produce interesting results, from the very light-weight fluid fast-paced networks, to the more stable strategic networks involving formal strategic alliances and even cross-ownership, and to the learning oriented flexible interfirm networks.

It is important to work on the paradigms of the decision makers within each firm, so that they begin to think of their firm in terms of its networks, and to think about the fit between its network and its ability to perform its core value-adding processes, exploit growth opportunities, or solve strategic problems. It is critical that every decision maker, engineer, planner, operator, etc., in a firm be conscious about the nature of the firm's networks and about the strategic choices for every activity related to his/her work. For example, every investment project should be required to present proposals based on each of the four alternatives and the strategic reasoning for selecting the proposition to be implemented.

When network thinking permeates the firm, and networking is clearly understood as a decision process, then innovative and lucrative networking decisions are bound to surface, and a variety of networks adapted to each setting are likely to be put together, activated, and maintained. The intelligent form of networking is to continuously attempt to achieve competitive excellence through economies of scale, economies of scope, speed, organizational flexibility, access to markets, and learning.

5.4.2 The Network Enterprise Approach

The network enterprise approach is composed of seven iterative steps, which amount to a practical synthesis of the numerous models described in the literature (Lyons, 1991; Forrest, 1992; Moss-Kanter, 1994). These steps include: (1) sensitizing managers; (2) diagnosing internal networks; (3) diagnosing external networks; (4) diagnosing untapped networking potentials; (5) evaluating network improvement potentials; (6) implementing prioritized networks; and (7) network monitoring (MICT, 1993b). Depending on the context, the approach may start with any of these steps and enact the steps in various orders.

Whenever an agent faces a situation where the firm's managers are not conscious of their networks and feels that the firm would benefit significantly from better networking, then his/her first task is to sensitize managers. Sensitizing may be accomplished in various ways. The key is for the agent to objectively make sure that the manager knows about the potentials offered by networking and how these can be obtained to support the firm's business objectives. Also, the agent must be prepared to list arguments in favor of networks and networking in general, and to answer major objections managers may have. In this respect, it is important to remember that sensitizing is very different in purpose from selling the latest fad in management techniques.

The second step is to diagnose the firm's internal network. This involves identifying the nodes and links of the internal network, stating the characteristics and capabilities of each node, and describing the relations and flows associated with each link between nodes. It also includes identifying the principal and support activities of the firm, as well as its fundamental operational processes. Once this is done, a careful analysis and diagnosis of the internal network is performed.

The third step is to diagnose the firm's external network. It starts by identifying all external nodes with which the firm is interacting. This involves classifying the suppliers and competitors as being major, commercial, or occasional, as well as understanding whether a competitor is a direct one or an indirect one. It also requires describing the business partners, the shareholders, the public and semi-public organizations, the unions, the trade associations, etc., with which the firm is interacting. Then the integration of external nodes with the company's activities and processes is to be studied. The desired outcome is a complete understanding of the firm's external network.

In the fourth step, the objective is to explore and diagnose as many untapped networking potentials as possible. This includes improvements of the internal network, refinement of links with existing external partners, as well as exploration of linking up with new external partners. As many perspectives as possible should be taken, including macrolevel geographic, industrial, and technological perspectives. All opportunities should be analyzed and diagnosed according to the firm's strategic objectives.

The fifth step deals with the evaluation of network improvement potentials. Whenever possible, it starts by performing a synthesis of the three diagnoses described above (steps 2 through 4). In general, the internal network may be improved by creating or acquiring internal nodes, improving internal nodes, removing internal nodes, creating internal links, improving internal links, and/or eliminating unnecessary internal links. Similarly, the external network may be improved by creating external nodes, improving external nodes, creating external nodes, creating external links, improving external links, eliminating external links, and activities-to-nodes assignments. These improvements are generally linked to better decisions concerning the *to do, to have done, to do together, and not to do* choices for key activities, and a better process and network architecture to achieve success given the decision (Poulin, Montreuil, and Gauvin, 1994).The end result of this step is an evaluation of each network improvement potential and a list of priorities for action. This is achieved in close collaboration between the firm's managers and the agent, with the decision being the responsibility of the firm's managers.

The sixth step involves the implementation of prioritized networks or network improvements. The nature of this step varies depending on whether the focus is on improving the internal network or the external network. At the external level, this involves selecting the type of structure and architecture to be privileged, selecting the type of relationships, searching and selecting the partner(s), negotiating cooperative agreements or alliances with all partners, and managing these agreements and alliances as well as the overall resulting network. At the internal level, it requires selecting the type of structure and architecture, and then to create or improve internal nodes and/or links, implementing the selected alternative, and managing this internal network.

The final and seventh step involves network monitoring. It requires the agent to regularly investigate the behavior and performance of the network(s), looping back to the previous steps as required, given the dynamic evolution of the firm's strategic orientations and environment.

Figure 5.3 shows that each step of the network enterprise approach is supported by an integrated set of tools and guides. Tools include forms to support the diagnosis of enterprise nodes, internal nodes and external nodes; forms to support graphical analysis of processes and networks; and forms to support the evaluation and prioritizing of network improvement proposals. A sample of the guides includes a guide to the overall approach, one guide for each form, another explaining the major networking concepts, and a guide to financial incentive programs.

Figure 5.3 also emphasizes the fact that in order to really succeed in applying the approach, an agent must use his/her own personal network as well as the firm's network. Networked entrepreneurs, managers of the firm, partners of the firm, speakers, consultants, universities, government agents, etc., should be constructively contacted throughout the process. Each MICST agent must work in close collaboration with other agents in the MICST network. For example, a regional agent may gain by interacting with other regional agents who are particularly knowledgeable about some phenomenon or about certain enterprises and organizations. The regional agent may also benefit from interacting with the sectoral agent who is dedicated to the sector in which the firm operates, and with technological agents whenever critical technology related issues surface.

5.5 Conclusion

The clustering strategy is already starting to produce dividends as it has generated a wealth of shared initiatives from groups of industrial firms in a common *grappe industrielle*. Direct competitors have learned that they have similar issues to deal with and that they can mutually gain from cooperating on these common issues, instead of dealing with them on their own (Jarillo, 1988). Actors at various levels of the value chain are recognizing their interrelationships. They are beginning to collaborate in critical processes, such as the product development

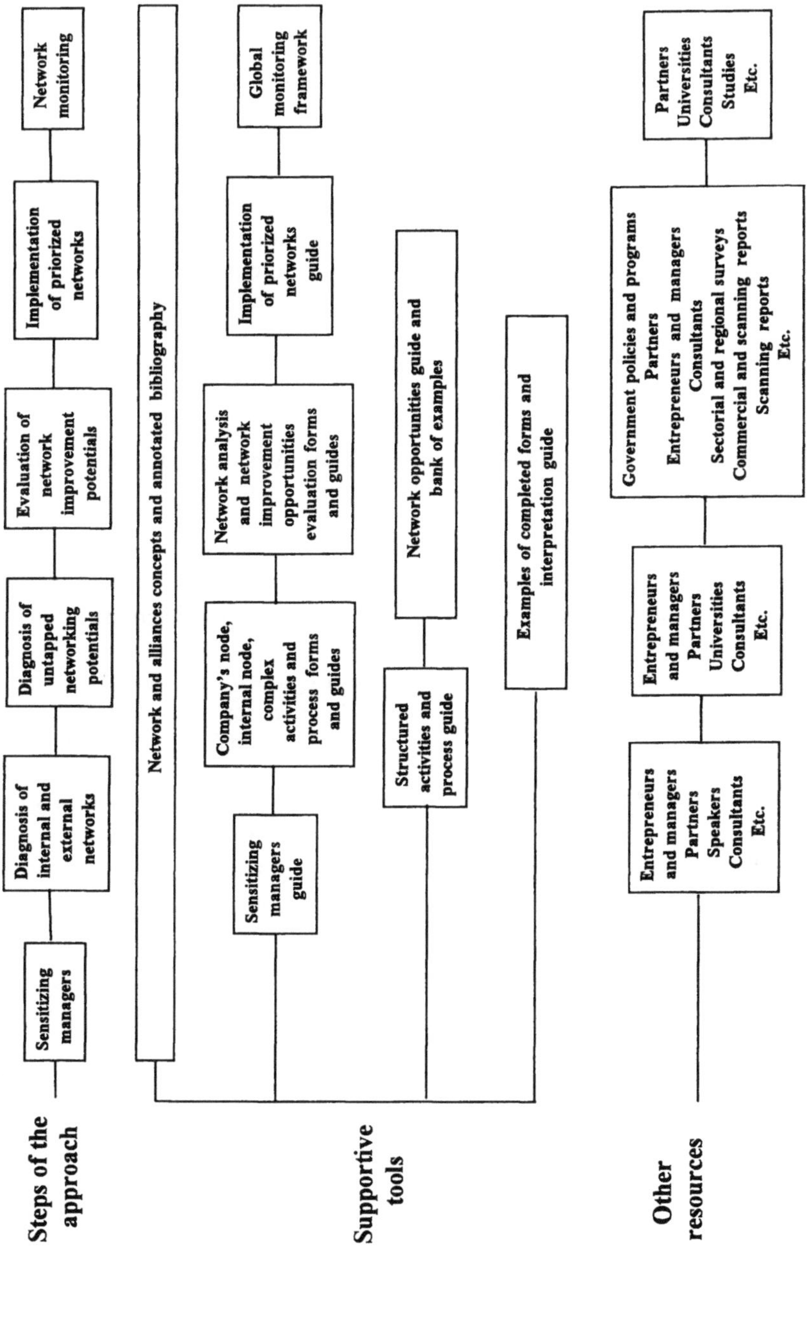

Figure 5.3 Global perspective of the network enterprise approach

process, and to synchronize their customer/server manufacturing processes. The future will demonstrate whether the clustering effort will have significant long-term structural impact on Québec's industrial fabric, as well as the competitiveness of its *grappes industrielles* and their constituent firms.

The validity and value of the networking strategy, and particularly that of the network enterprise approach, will be subject to critical testing during the next few years. Even though the approach appears conceptually solid and has been tested successfully in pilot studies, nothing is really proven until a significant number of participating industrial firms are really convinced that the process has benefitted themselves and has led them to innovate in ways they would otherwise not have considered. The impact at the macro level will be much more difficult to assess since there are many other environmental variables which concurrently influence the industrial fabric.

As the effects of the networking phase become more evident, an interesting challenge will be to evolve from a perceived dichotomy between top-down clustering and bottom-up networking toward a clear understanding and exploitation of their complementary nature. A black-and-white vision of clustering versus networking should be avoided, and should be replaced by a multicolor vision where industrial networks may be generated through bottom-up initiatives from groups of enterprises, but also as a natural implementation of concepts generated through the top-down clustering process.

Similarly, it is encouraging that some regions of Québec have already reorganized their regional agents from a purely geographic division of work to a *grappe* oriented division, where an agent gets to interact mostly with firms from a selected number of *grappes* in his region. While keeping an enterprise orientation, some agents are bound to come up with top-down networking initiatives which emerge from their deeper understanding of the sectoral needs of firms assigned to them, as well as their potential interactions with other firms in their *grappe* as captured through the agent's teamwork with appropriate sectoral agents.

6. The Industrial Resurgence of Southern California?

Allen J. Scott and David Bergman

6.1 Introduction

Since the late 1980s, the economy of Southern California has been subject to unprecedented losses of industrial capacity and jobs. Much of this problem can be ascribed to the long-term downturn in federal defense expenditures that has occurred as international détente has set in, resulting in massive erosion of the region's aerospace-electronics industrial complex. Much of the problem, too, is due to intensifying structural weaknesses in the region's manufacturing economy, as expressed in an accelerating slide into low-skill, low-wage sweatshop forms of production. In addition, local manufacturers have been facing increasing difficulties in meeting competition from foreign, high-quality producers on equal terms.

The seriousness of the current situation is hard to over-estimate. Los Angeles County attained its highest level of manufacturing employment in 1979, with a total of 924,900 jobs. In the entire region of Southern California (i.e., Los Angeles County plus the four neighboring counties of Orange, Riverside, San Bernardino, and Ventura) manufacturing employment reached a peak of 1,272,900 in 1988. Between 1988 and 1992, the region as a whole suffered an absolute loss of 218,600 manufacturing jobs, and the decline is still continuing. No doubt this situation will be ameliorated somewhat as the economic cycle in the US begins to improve. However, defense expenditures will almost certainly continue to shift downward over the rest of the decade, and the structural weaknesses alluded to above remain a worrisome feature. These concerns are compounded by the fact that over the last couple of decades some of Southern California's most daunting competitors (Germany and Japan in particular) have been putting into place a series of regional industrial policy initiatives that have unquestionably strengthened their competitive advantages and enhanced their performance on international markets. This has worked to the detriment of regions like Southern California, which to a significant degree are failing to provide adequate public support for local economic development. The failure is all the more striking in view of the extraordinarily successful (but now faltering) *de facto* industrial policies of the Department of Defense that helped to propel Southern California to high levels of economic growth and prosperity over much of the post World War II period.

The current conjuncture has prompted much reflection and debate in the region about these problems and how to address them. This concern became particularly intense in January 1992 when the Los Angeles County Transportation Commission (LACTC) [reorganized as the Los Angeles County Metropolitan Transportation Authority (MTA) in 1993] made a decision to buy 41 driverless trains for its new Metro Green Line from the Japanese supplier, Sumitomo-Nippon Sharyo. The decision raised a storm of protest in Southern California, especially as it appeared to favor a foreign producer over a lower-priced American competitor, and the contract with Sumitomo-Nippon Sharyo was later cancelled. The protest was intensified by the fact that large rail car procurement orders for the new Los Angeles transit system were being placed outside the region at a time when unemployment rates were soaring upward, and many questions were posed both inside and outside the LACTC regarding the feasibility of establishing a rail car manufacturing facility somewhere in Southern California. Running parallel to and intertwined with this set of issues are two further local outcomes that have raised aspirations about the possibilities of setting up a ground transportation equipment industry in the region. The first of these is a series of local economic development initiatives and entrepreneurial efforts that have been made since the late 1980s to create an electric vehicle and components industry in the region (Morales et al. 1991; Scott 1993c). The second is the establishment of Project California under the aegis of the California Council on Science and Technology, and which has been charged to report on the prospects for building an advanced ground transportation equipment industry in the state of California as a whole.

The present study attempts to shed some further light on these matters. Its particular point of emphasis consists in an effort to formulate an industrial development agenda for Southern California centered on advanced ground transportation equipment production. Our investigation proceeds on three main fronts. First, we provide a general analysis of regional economic development processes, and we attempt to draw out from this analysis some broad guidelines about how local industrial policy issues might be best approached in practice. We lay special stress here upon the dynamics of *spatially-agglomerated complexes of industry* and on the institutional and infrastructural arrangements that reinforce their competitive advantages. Next, we make a broadly ranging attempt to identify the prospects for establishing an advanced ground transportation equipment industry in Southern California, with special attention being devoted to (a) the current industrial base of the region and its capacity to sustain a ground transportation equipment industry, (b) the different forms that such an industry might take, and (c) the role of policy in creating a synergistic industrial agglomeration focused on ground transportation equipment manufacturing. Finally, we engage in a detailed discussion of some of the basic financial and public policy issues that are likely to be involved in any attempt to set up an advanced ground transportation equipment industry in Southern California. This latter part of the study looks at the local economic development possibilities of the MTA's $183 billion Thirty-Year Plan, and at the institution-building tasks that should be brought to the fore as the MTA (along with other local agencies) becomes more involved in efforts to foster new economic growth in the region.

We must stress that this study is presented more as a general framework of concepts and policy guidelines than as a series of detailed implementation plans leading directly to action. It is intended to aid policy-makers and analysts by directing attention towards certain strategic directions and away from others, but it can in no way be taken as an operational program to be put directly into effect.

6.2 A Brief Conceptual Overview of the Problem of Local Economic Development[1]

6.2.1 The Organization and Location of Industry

Modern industry is invariably organized in the form of a *social division of labor*. By this we mean that the production system is divided into different sectors, each of which specializes in a series of particular tasks. In turn, these sectors are typically linked to one another in networks of input-output transactions. Hence, the machine-tool sector consumes inputs from aluminum foundries, electronics components producers, and instrument makers; and its outputs become the inputs to sectors like automobiles and aerospace. There is no limit in principle to how finely we define the total set of sectors in the economy, and in the extreme case, we could think of every individual factory, or unit of production, as a row and a column in a huge input-output matrix of inter-unit transactions.

The precise form of the social division of labor in modern industry is both actually and potentially extremely variable. Thus, the machine-tool sector might at one point in time be characterized by producers who also fabricate their own printed circuit boards; in this case, we say that the two activities are *vertically-integrated*. At another moment in time, machine-tool manufacturers may find it more efficient to eliminate their in-house production of printed circuit boards and to purchase their needs from independent suppliers; in this case, we have two *vertically-disintegrated* sectors (but linked to one another in an input-output relationship). Obviously, if a particular set of sectors in the economy is undergoing vertical disintegration, then the social division of labor is by the same token deepening and widening.

Manufacturing systems marked by deep and wide social divisions of labor typically break down into industrial complexes, each of which is identifiable by the circumstance that its constituent sectors are tightly interconnected to one another through their mutual transactions. Such transactions are usually extremely het-

1 A more detailed view of the issues treated here can be found in Scott (1988b) and (1993a).

erogeneous in form and content. They may range, for example, from simple spot market exchanges of physical product to untraded interdependencies; they may embody (sometimes to the exclusion of all other content) complex and intangible bodies of information; and they can involve peculiar institutional arrangements like subcontracting, long-term contractual agreements, or quasi-vertical disintegration (in which one party actually owns elements of the production equipment of the other party).

Manufacturing activity, then, almost always proceeds in a series of staged operations linked together in a network of complex transactional interrelations. Sometimes such networks may be distributed over a widely-dispersed set of geographical locations; sometimes, the production units out of which they are composed – or a significant subset of these units – may be clustered or agglomerated together in one place. Whenever a given industrial complex is marked by a particularly transactions-intensive set of relations between individual producers, all else being equal, there will be some pressure on producers to locate in close proximity to one another in order to reduce the spatially-dependent costs of transacting. The inducement will be all the more forceful where inter-industrial transactions are (a) small in scale, so that they cannot take advantage of the increasing returns that invariably describe the cost characteristics of transfer functions, (b) variable and unpredictable in character, so that producers are unable to standardize transactional relations and are therefore continually faced with the expensive problem of finding and building new linkage partners, and (c) composed in significant degree of personalized information exchanges, so that the process of transacting must be mediated by face-to-face contacts. Thus, when a transactions-intensive industrial complex is marked dominantly by small-scale inter-establishment linkages which are susceptible to instability and involve frequent personal contact, we are likely to find that at least some elements of the complex coalesce out to form dense industrial districts or regions. When transactions have the opposite features, the complex is more likely to be locationally-dispersed.

These remarks must remain provisional for the moment. The analysis thus far has proceeded in *ceteris paribus* mode, and as we shall see, many additional factors come into play in determining patterns of agglomeration and dispersal in industrial complexes. That said, we will often, though not necessarily always, expect to find that place-bound or regional production systems are constituted by a core group of industries with strongly-developed inter-linkages. Such systems may occur within narrowly circumscribed bounds, as in the cases of the garment district of Los Angeles or the medical instruments complex of Orange County; or they may occur on a wider regional scale as in the cases of the Detroit car industry or the Southern Californian aerospace-defense complex (which itself is composed of a series of smaller high-technology industrial districts in places like Chatsworth-Canoga Park and northern Orange County). In all such agglomerations of industry, producers reap the advantages of *external economies* (specifically, *agglomeration economies*) by reason of their close proximity to large numbers and wide varieties of other producers with whom they share actual and potential transactional relations. Even within these tightly-knit clusters, many producers will nonetheless typically have connections to firms and markets on a wider national, indeed global, scale.

6.2.2 The Emergence and Growth of Industrial Regions

In the first instance, then, the geographical agglomeration of manufacturing activities is typically at least in part a consequence of the social division of labor and the associated transactional structure of production. If markets are growing, vertical disintegration will tend to occur over a wide front (Stigler, 1951), and agglomeration of the production system will intensify. At the same time, agglomeration is also a response to a number of other important factors, three of which are of particular interest in the present context. These other factors relate to issues of infrastructure, labor markets, and entrepreneurial/technological innovation.

Urban and regional infrastructure is typically made up of artifacts like city streets, expressways, airports, utility distribution networks, sewer systems, and so on. The innate unevenness, high fixed costs, and increasing returns that characterize physical infrastructure make it a primary source of agglomeration economies. Manufacturers, along with other social and economic groups, depend for their survival on this type of general infrastructure. They depend, too, upon very specialized sorts of infrastructural inputs whose agglomerative effects are confined to particular sectors. Examples of the latter phenomenon might be a crash-testing site shared in common by a group of car producers, a wind-tunnel facility for aerospace manufacturers, or a publicly-funded electronics research laboratory offering subsidized technical assistance to firms in the local area. Manufacturers also often benefit from land development projects in the form of industrial or science parks in which easy access to other manufacturers and the ability to draw upon common specialized services yield benefits to all parties.

Regional production systems consist not just of complexes of interdependent producers and an appropriate stock of infrastructure; they are also, and of necessity, intertwined with dense local labor markets. These labor markets are important repositories of information and the sites of intensive search processes. At any one time, a proportion of the labor force will be seeking out job openings, and various employers will be looking for individuals to fill vacancies. Agglomeration economies are almost always called into play here, for the greater the localized concentrated of job-seekers and job-vacancies, the less costly it is to acquire, process, and act upon relevant information. Perhaps more importantly is the circumstance that workers in any agglomeration will tend to acquire agglomeration-specific skills and aptitudes which enable them to move with comparative ease between different sorts of firms in the local area. The job-hopping patterns of qualified personnel in the semiconductor and computer complex of Silicon Valley, or in the film-music-TV complex of Hollywood exemplify this point well. Even so, there is a tendency for workers to under-invest in the acquisition of skills (because they can never be sure that their skills will be fully marketable), just as there is a parallel tendency for firms to under-invest in worker training (because they can always expect to lose some of the workers that they train to other firms). Thus, in the absence of publicly-funded worker training programs, there will often be problems of short supply of requisite skills in particular industrial agglomerations.

In addition, because industrial agglomerations exist in part as networks of interlinked producers, they also represent structures of innovative opportunities. In other words, individual managers and workers within any agglomeration are optimally positioned to perceive and to take advantage of new business opportunities whether through vertical (or horizontal) disintegration or through process and product innovations of various kinds. The tangible expression of this phenomenon is the endemic spin-off process observable in dense industrial agglomerations, as represented most clearly by dominant patterns of growth in Silicon Valley over the last few decades.

This network structure of industrial agglomerations also sustains important processes of technological learning. Many kinds of technological knowledge, of course, are highly proprietary and are purely internal to the firm. Other kinds exist as a sort of tangled skein of capabilities which are only truly mobilized when they are pooled together in various ways. From this perspective, technology is always in some important senses a feature of the regional collectivity of producers as a whole, and it often exists (like workers' forms of socialization and habituation) as an agglomeration-specific attribute, identifiable as a sort of "culture" or "atmosphere". Thus, we commonly think of places like Detroit (cars), Los Angeles (aerospace and movies), or the Swiss Jura (watches) as being not just physical centers of production, but also as places where it is possible to tap into the minutiae of peculiar kinds of technological and product design sensitivities (Sternberg, 1991). Because of this possibility, their competitive advantages are much enhanced. A number of studies have shown, moreover, that the detailed day-to-day interactions between producers in localized production complexes can be a potent source of technological dynamism. As firms go about their business, they often constantly exchange information with one another about their input needs and output possibilities, and in this manner they open themselves up to external stimuli that sometimes prompt small, but cumulatively important, innovations. Russo (1985) has demonstrated the power of this process in a study of the relations between tile-makers and machinery producers in the ceramics industrial complex of Sassuolo, Italy. Here, the interplay between these two groups of producers has over time resulted in a steady stream of process and product improvements, any one of which may be unobtrusive, but all of which taken together help to heighten Sassuolo's productive capabilities and reputation. This dynamic of innovation is further boosted in cases where producers interact with one another in high-trust environments in which information sharing and the occasional pooling of resources may also occur, so that the potential synergies of groups of firms are more effectively released. Friedmann (1993) has recently argued that these sorts of high-trust cooperative relations help to explain much of the technological and commercial success of Japanese production systems.

In light of all of the above, we can now see that at least some of the ingredients for regional economic success revolve around a capacity to put together vertically-disintegrated clusters of industry, to underpin them with rich endowments of infrastructure, to establish smoothly-operating local labor markets, and to encourage a structured propensity for innovative change and technological learning. Regions that have some or all of these attributes stand a good chance of becoming significant articulations of value-adding activity within the national economy as a whole. Moreover, because the logic of agglomeration economies leads to a virtuous circle of increasing returns, growth of any cluster at one point in time becomes a stimulus to further growth later on (Romer, 1986).

Unfortunately, this scenario of events cannot always be easily and unproblematically accomplished in practice. Even where all of these ingredients for success are present, regional industrial growth and development may still falter for any number of reasons. In particular, in any industrial agglomeration there are always endemic problems of market failure and system coordination, and any regional industrial complex that lacks the *institutional and political competence* to deal with such issues may on occasions find the virtuous circle of growth described above sharply curtailed.

6.2.3 Markets and Institutions in Regional Economic Development

The operation of market forces is an essential condition for the achievement of allocative efficiency in regional economic complexes of the sort under investigation here. But this essential condition of static efficiency is not always sufficient condition of development and growth. There are, in fact, many facets of regional economic systems that do not perform adequately under market conditions, either because of technical failures (e.g., in the case of infrastructure provision), or because market conditions actually undercut other desirable features of the system (e.g., pure competition in labor markets tends to depress the supply of labor skills). Equally, as the earlier discussion has already made clear, many economic benefits can be obtained by non-market (untraded) forms of association and cooperation between producers. These benefits range from enhanced technological innovativeness to the institutionalization of capacities for overall strategic decision-making and choice. Three main points now need to be made.

First, many firms, particularly small vertically-disintegrated firms caught up in flexible transactional networks, are often not able efficiently to provide many kinds of services for themselves in-house. These services, such as accounting, payroll preparation, personnel recruitment, and so on, can often be bought on the open market in the form of subcontract services. In other cases, especially where critical (e.g., proprietary or information-sensitive) relations between firms, service providers, and the wider regional community are at stake, other forms of provision may be more suitable and efficient. Such cases may consist, for example, of export marketing organizations, R&D alliances, design centers, and so on. Here, the institutional bases of supply might be either an association of producers, a private-public partnership, or a local government agency charged with a specific mission.

Second, there may be failures in the regional economy to provide certain critical and system-wide functions, and in whose absence local competitive advantages would begin to decay. Labor-training and skills provision represent just such a function, and accordingly there is in practice a pervasive tendency for public intervention to fill the breach. Another example can be cited in the area of technology research, for the leakiness of technological knowledge encourages firms to perform below socially optimal levels in this regard. Two examples of extra-market attempts to deal with this species of problem in Southern California are the CALSTART electric car consortium in Burbank, which has successfully produced a prototype vehicle by bringing many different components manufacturers together into a research and manufacturing partnership, and the CONNECT biotechnology program in San Diego, linking together university researchers and local firms. The provision of risk capital for startup firms, and the effective management of information in local labor markets, are other domains in which extra-market initiatives can often improve overall performance.

Third, regional economies evolve along pathways of development that are characterized by many different alternative branching points and historical possibilities. Accordingly, regional economies in which decision-making is confined to completely decentralized market operations are blind to possible superior developmental options that can only be attained if some suitable institution of collective strategic choice is in place. To highlight the point, we may ask, what if the boosters in Southern California at the beginning of the present century had not by-passed the inertia of markets and brought abundant supplies of water to the region, and later, helped to establish the bases of a fledgling aircraft industry? What if Stanford University in the 1950s had not played such an activist role in industrial development in what has now become Silicon Valley? What if Southern California in the 1970s and 1980s had had the institutional capacity to foresee and plan for the problems that were to come in the early 1990s from its lopsided dependence on defense spending? These questions all point in the direction of the importance of strategic planning in regional economic systems. The point here is that well-designed and prudently-managed coordinating institutions can be crucial assets in promoting regional economic efficiency and in the effort to foresee, deal with, and resolve local crises.

6.2.4 Local Economic Development in Practice

In the above discussion we have tried to outline a conceptually-rich and disciplined framework for thinking about local economic development in general, and for investigating regional industrial policy issues in particular. The discussion reveals that there are, in principle and practice, many significant areas in which local economic policy can not only be effective but is, indeed, imperative. There are, in particular, important tasks of institution-building to be carried out if agglomeration economies are to be preserved and competitive advantages enhanced in regional industrial systems. These tasks are all the more important in the new global economy where competition comes ever more strongly from those regions that have already effectively constructed public responses to problems of local economic development.

By the same token, the analysis laid out above contains a strong implicit critique of the position that is currently being widely advocated by many different groups in California, to the effect that the roots of local economic problems can be discovered in a deteriorating "business climate". Specifically, there have been widespread claims that a negative business climate has been created in the state as a consequence of sundry environmental controls, minimum wage legislation, workers' compensation rules, state and local taxes and other regulatory arrangements (California Council on Competitiveness, 1992). Of course, there can be little doubt that regulations like these *do* increase the costs of production for many industries, and they do tend to drive away many forms of manufacturing, particularly those that are not able to compete unless they can operate under Third World environmental and labor market conditions. However, there is in any case little to be gained from such manufacturing activities except low-quality jobs and a general deterioration the entire urban and institutional fabric of production. If Southern California is to re-direct its industrial economy along the road to long-term prosperity, it needs policies that can help to build and rebuild cultures of innovative high-skill and high-quality manufacturing. This sort of manufacturing is not going to be fatally discouraged by legislation that ensures a high level of environmental quality and decent conditions for workers; on the contrary, it is likely to thrive on such safeguards. The most successful regional economies today are those that compete not so much by means of rudimentary cost-cutting, but by constantly increasing product quality *relative* to cost. Such economies are able to play the game in this manner because they are rich in the sorts of institutional infrastructures that sustain their overall levels of industrial performance.

A further corollary of the argument developed here is that regions need not be passive subjects of wider national and global trends, but can indeed tangibly alter the course of their own development. However, it must be added at once that there are also many constraining conditions that limit the degree of success that can be expected from any given set of development policies. For example, it will often be extremely unwise for regional authorities to attempt to launch a new industry if some other region has already acquired and is thriving on a similar kind of production activities. This is because the *first mover advantages* and acquired agglomeration economies of early starters give them a competitive edge that late arrivals will find difficult to match (unless they command some decisive and idiosyncratic advantage). The lessons of this simple insight are writ large in the many failed experiments in different parts of the world over the last couple of decades by local economic development agencies to promote new foci of high-technology industrial growth (Castells and Hall, 1994). Regions that seek to embark on ambitious development programs must first take careful stock of the state of development in other regions.

An early start is hence one of the ingredients of eventual success in regional development programs. Another resides in the local potential to construct collective action agendas of the sort described earlier. These two moments of the development process intersect with one another in critical and decisive ways. The early stage of industrial growth, when an infant industry is struggling to establish itself, is particularly fraught with hazards. At this stage, process and product configurations are usually very unstable, markets are unpredictable, and the risks of business failure high. In certain cases direct public support of the infant industry may be justified, especially where a region is seeking to acquire first mover advantages and to leverage this early start into an instrument of long-term growth. The public efforts that have attended the birth of the electric vehicle industry in Southern California over the late 1980s and early 1990s are an exemplary case of these kinds of interventions, and (thus far) they appear to have been largely successful (Scott 1993c).

More generally, regional economic development programs need to focus on those forms of support for localized transactions-intensive industrial complexes that underpin and complement normal market forces. In one way or another, this prescription is likely to translate out into a series of programs that deal with such issues as the physical infrastructure of production, labor training, technological innovation, and the creation of a network of institutional services that enhance trust, inter-industry cooperation, and regional capacities for strategic choice. The object is to initiate and to sustain a virtuous dynamic of growth, self-transformation, and competitive success.

6.3 The Advanced Ground Transportation Equipment Industry: Specifications of a Regional Industrial Complex for Southern California

6.3.1 Southern California's Current Industrial Assets

In spite of the severe economic problems that it faces at the present time, Southern California remains one of the world's great manufacturing regions with an impressive array of production capabilities in sectors ranging from apparel and films to aircraft and space equipment.

Obviously not all of the region's existing industries are relevant to an eventual advanced ground transportation equipment industry, whereas others are extremely so, either because they are capable of providing important inputs to the industry, or because they are already in fact producing various kinds of transportation equipment. Tables 6.1 and 6.2 display data on employment and number of establishments, respectively, in a series of three-digit industrial sectors that would seem to constitute a particularly important foundation for any eventual advanced ground transportation equipment industry in the region. These sectors are likely to become sources of important inputs to the industry, for their main products consist of basic intermediate goods like rubber and plastics, metallurgical products, machinery, electronics, and instruments. A significant number of the industries arrayed in Tables 6.1 and 6.2 are already linked to the massive aerospace-defense manufacturing system of the region, and as this system declines, they are faced with either redeployment or extinction. These industries employ a total of 416,691 workers (i.e., 33.0 per cent of all manufacturing employment in the region), and they are represented by 9,966 establishments (i.e., 33.8 per cent of all manufacturing establishments). The average size of these establishments is just 41.8 employees, and as previous studies have shown, they tend to be functionally organized within an extensive series of flexible transactional networks (Scott 1993a). In regard to producers of intermediate machinery/electronics outputs, no other region of comparable geographic extent in any other part of the country can claim to be endowed with such an abundant assemblage of manufacturing capabilities as Southern California.

Southern California, too, is a major center of certain kinds of service sectors that would provide important back-up to any eventual ground transportation equipment industry. As shown in Tables 6.3 and 6.4, the region has a large complement of engineering, research, and testing firms, many of which are already fully capable of providing critical services to advanced ground transportation equipment manufacturers. This group of firms includes large numbers of mechanical and civil engineering consultants, transportation and urban planners, and private laboratories offering a wide range of scientific testing services. There is also a notably rich infrastructure of not-for-profit research organizations and universi-

Table 6.1 Employment in three-digit industries in Southern California providing (actually and potentially) important inputs to the advanced ground transportation equipment industry, 1990

Standard industrial category	Los Angeles County	Orange County	Riverside County	San Bernardino County	Ventura County	Total
301 Tires and inner tubes	175	0	0	60	0	235
305 Hose, belting, gaskets	1,755	502	79	483	0	2,819
306 Fabricated rubber, nec.	4,912	1,681	81	549	0	7,223
308 Miscellaneous plastics, nec.	27,312	15,016	3,010	3,767	1,908	51,013
332 Iron and steel foundries	3,631	736	0	175	348	4,890
334 Secondary nonferrous metals	887	60	60	411	0	1,418
335 Nonferrous rolling etc.	5,638	690	375	175	0	6,876
336 Nonferrous foundries	5,455	604	275	208	0	6,542
339 Miscellaneous primary metal	1,699	171	0	60	0	1,930
344 Fabricated structural metal	16,653	4,101	1,556	2,469	439	25,218
345 Screw machine products	8,790	4,335	255	519	60	13,959
346 Metal forgings and stampings	7,613	2,896	80	731	60	11,380
347 Metal services nec.	10,559	2,947	0	731	109	14,346
349 Misc. fabricated metal prods.	10,924	3,459	779	1,621	493	17,276
351 Engines and turbines	3,888	175	0	175	60	4,298
354 Metalworking machinery	8,372	2,587	281	414	380	12,034
355 Special industry machinery	4,105	2,278	0	162	764	7,309
356 General industry machinery	6,568	2,381	375	425	856	10,605
357 Computer and office machinery	6,534	12,389	0	0	896	19,819
359 Industrial machinery nec.	19,447	7,741	828	1,265	750	30,031
361 Electric distribution equ.	2,287	276	0	175	60	2,798
362 Electrical industrial app.	5,289	2,548	0	0	375	8,212
364 Electric lighting, wiring	8,890	1,443	0	791	754	11,968
367 Electronic components	22,531	18,595	2,805	418	3,131	47,480
369 Misc. electrical equ.	5,806	5,927	74	389	1,482	13,678
381 Search and navigation equ.	36,792	21,935	0	0	1,530	60,257
382 Measuring, controlling dev.	14,865	5,731	182	712	1,587	3,077
Total	251,465	121,204	11,095	16,885	16,042	416,691

Source: United States Department of Commerce, Bureau of the Census, *County Business Patterns*. (Nb.: In order to protect confidentiality, this source of information sometimes provides only an upper and lower range of values for employment; where this is the case, the median value has been inserted in the table above.)

Table 6.2 Establishments in three-digit industries in Southern California providing (actually and potentially) important inputs to the advanced ground transportation equipment industry, 1990

Standard industrial category	Los Angeles County	Orange County	Riverside County	San Bernardino County	Ventura County	Total
301 Tires and inner tubes	3	0	0	1	0	4
305 Hose, belting, gaskets	39	9	5	5	0	58
306 Fabricated rubber, nec.	90	28	6	11	0	35
308 Miscellaneous plastics, nec.	623	296	59	93	40	1,111
332 Iron and steel foundries	37	7	0	2	4	50
334 Secondary nonferrous metals	19	5	3	7	0	34
335 Nonferrous rolling etc.	50	15	3	4	0	72
336 Nonferrous foundries	131	19	5	9	0	164
339 Miscellaneous primary metal	60	8	0	1	0	69
344 Fabricated structural metal	565	157	45	85	19	871
345 Screw machine products	142	52	11	12	2	219
346 Metal forgings and stampings	193	77	7	28	10	315
347 Metal services nec.	414	110	0	24	8	556
349 Misc. fabricated metal prods.	390	131	31	50	18	620
351 Engines and turbines	16	7	0	3	1	27
354 Metalworking machinery	463	175	39	53	14	744
355 Special industry machinery	159	68	0	14	16	257
356 General industry machinery	158	57	5	19	10	249
357 Computer and office machinery	109	116	0	0	15	240
359 Industrial machinery nec.	1,401	551	92	115	78	2,237
361 Electric distribution equ.	32	8	0	3	1	44
362 Electrical industrial app.	97	49	0	0	8	154
364 Electric lighting, wiring	183	46	0	12	8	249
367 Electronic components	400	299	32	27	68	826
369 Misc. electrical equ.	117	57	5	7	9	195
381 Search and navigation equ.	65	26	0	0	7	98
382 Measuring, controlling dev.	184	129	12	17	26	368
Total	6,140	2,502	360	602	362	9,966

Source: United States Department of Commerce, Bureau of the Census, *County Business Patterns*.

Table 6.3 Employment in selected service sectors in Southern California, 1990

Standard industrial category	Los Angeles County	Orange County	Riverside County	San Bernardino County	Ventura County	Total
8711 Engineering services	22,622	18,647	2,560	2,136	2,409	48,374
873 Research and testing services	19,461	3,051	364	262	1,225	24,363
8731 Commercial physical research	7,608	991	102	71	950	9,722
8732 Commercial nonphysical research	4,710	762	0	0	55	5,527
8733 Noncommercial research organizations	3,545	374	175	0	81	4,175
8734 Testing laboratories	3,292	917	60	128	139	4,563
Total	42,083	21,698	2,924	3,361	3,634	72,737

Source: United States Department of Commerce, Bureau of the Census, *County Business Patterns*. (Nb.: In order to protect confidentiality, this source of information sometimes provides only an upper and lower range of values for employment; where this is the case, the median value has been inserted in the table above).

Table 6.4 Number of establishments in selected service sectors in Southern California, 1990

Standard industrial category	Los Angeles County	Orange County	Riverside County	San Bernardino County	Ventura County	Total
8711 Engineering services	1,343	730	140	146	148	2,507
873 Research and testing services	632	242	24	36	53	987
8731 Commercial physical research	156	64	8	10	23	261
8732 Commercial nonphysical research	243	81	0	0	10	334
8733 Noncommercial research organizations	102	21	3	0	7	133
8734 Testing laboratories	128	71	6	13	12	231
Total	1,975	972	164	182	201	3,494

Source: United States Department of Commerce, Bureau of the Census, *County Business Patterns*.

ties and colleges in the region providing an essential background of scientific and technological expertise.

In addition to these actual and potential input industries, Southern California has an existing transportation equipment industry of major proportions, though most of it is concerned with producing air-borne defense matériel. There is also a small and miscellaneous group of sectors focused on ground transportation equipment as such, ranging from SIC 3534 (elevators and moving stairways) to SIC 375 (motorcycles, bicycles, and parts). The transportation equipment industry as a whole in Southern California is identified in Tables 6.5 and 6.6 in terms of a series of three-digit and four-digit sectors. Obviously, this is a generous and not entirely satisfactory definition of the industry. All of these sectors, however, overlap significantly with a prospective industry devoted to the production of ground transportation equipment proper, either because they are already making products that must be included in any wider and viable conception of this industry, or because they have especially strong latent synergistic relations with the industry. Current employment in these sectors stands at about a quarter of a million, and they are represented by over one thousand individual establishments. They are dominated by SIC 372 (aircraft and parts) and SIC 376 (guided missiles, space vehicles, and parts), with SIC 371 (motor vehicles and equipment) coming a distant third. Most of SIC 371 in Southern California is devoted to the production of after-market parts and accessories, and it could conceivably play a quite meaningful role in a future re-oriented transportation industry. This is then followed by SIC 366 (communication equipment), which breaks down into sub-sectors focussed on telephone and telegraph apparatus, radio and TV communcation equipment, and other miscellaneous communication equipment (such as traffic signals, railroad signalling devices, and intercom equipment). Finally, there is an extremely small group of industries concerned with the production of specialty ground vehicles (SICs 3534 to 3537), railroad equipment, and motorcycles and bicycles. As small and marginal as it may be at the present time, this latter collection of industries has much potential for future development, and as it currently stands, it includes a number of innovative firms, particularly a small group of producers of battery-powered industrial vehicles such as Badsey Design of Capistrano Beach, Nordskog Electric Vehicles of Redlands, Taylor-Dunn of Anaheim, and Trans Lectric of Gardena. This group overlaps with a handful of startup electric bus manufacturers such as Bus Manufacturing of Goleta and Specialty Manufacturing Corporation of Downey.

Not specifically mentioned in the Standard Industrial Classification, and hence not reported in official statistics, is a small but critical group of employment activities focused on automobile design. Southern California is today the home of what is probably the largest concentration of automobile design studios and consultants in the world. Many of the world's major car producers maintain a studio in the region, and there are also several independent design firms that work on a subcontract basis. This established design capability in the region is sure to be a major factor in any future advanced ground transportation equipment industry, for it constitutes a major source of innovative ideas. It also overlaps significantly with (and is able to draw upon the energies of) the dynamic fashion and cultural

Table 6.5 Employment in the transportation equipment industry in Southern California, 1990

Standard industrial category	Los Angeles County	Orange County	Riverside County	San Bernardino County	Ventura County	Total
3534 Elevators and moving stairways	121	0	0	0	0	121
3535 Conveyors and conveying equipment	450	82	0	115	0	647
3536 Hoists, cranes, and monorails	77	60	0	0	60	197
3537 Industrial trucks and tractors	473	580	0	0	0	981
366 Communication equipment	9,473	3,315	375	349	750	14,262
3661 Telephone and telegraph apparatus	572	581	175	0	375	1,703
3663 Radio and TV communication equipment	7,908	2,336	0	0	375	10,619
3669 Communications equipment, nec.	944	393	200	375	0	1,912
371 Motor vehicles and equipment	18,281	1,897	2,156	2,782	175	25,291
3711 Motor vehicles and car bodies	3,750	280	0	375	0	4,405
3713 Truck and bus bodies	1,507	190	0	606	0	2,303
3714 Motor vehicle parts and accessories	11,039	1,373	724	1,220	174	14,530
3715 Truck trailers	1,027	0	60	175	0	1,262
3716 Motor homes	750	0	1,364	175	0	2,289
372 Aircraft and parts	112,650	6,810	3,750	3,750	3,379	130,339
3721 Aircraft	77,489	0	60	1,750	375	79,674
3724 Aircraft engines and engine parts	3,092	750	0	750	60	4,652
3728 Aircraft parts and equipment, nec.	31,981	7,500	3,690	175	3,750	47,096
374 Railroad equipment	60	0	0	0	0	60
375 Motorcycles, bicycles and parts	514	375	175	60	0	1,124
376 Guided missiles, space vehicles	51,152	7,500	0	3,750	375	62,777
3761 Guided missiles and space vehicles	37,500	7,325	0	3,750	375	48,950
3764 Space propulsion units and parts	7,500	0	0	0	0	7,500
3769 Space vehicle equipment, nec.	989	175	0	175	0	1,339
Total	193,251	20,547	6,456	10,806	4,739	235,799

Source: United States Department of Commerce, Bureau of the Census, *County Business Patterns*. (Nb.: In order to protect confidentiality, this source of information sometimes provides only an upper and lower range of values for employment; where this is the case, the median value has been inserted in the table above.)

Table 6.6 Number of establishments in the transportation equipment industry in Southern California, 1990

Standard industrial category	Los Angeles County	Orange County	Riverside County	San Bernardino County	Ventura County	Total
3534 Elevators and moving stairways	7	0	0	0	0	7
3535 Conveyors and conveying equipment	19	6	0	4	0	29
3536 Hoists, cranes, and monorails	7	3	0	0	1	11
3537 Industrial trucks and tractors	19	10	0	0	0	29
366 Communication equipment	78	46	6	8	13	151
3661 Telephone and telegraph apparatus	14	11	2	0	3	30
3663 Radio and TV communication equipment	31	19	0	0	7	57
3669 Communications equipment, nec.	23	11	2	4	0	40
371 Motor vehicles and equipment	254	65	27	52	12	410
3711 Motor vehicles and car bodies	14	14	0	7	0	35
3713 Truck and bus bodies	36	7	0	14	0	57
3714 Motor vehicle parts and accessories	186	40	14	24	8	272
3715 Truck trailers	9	0	1	2	0	12
3716 Motor homes	4	0	7	3	0	14
372 Aircraft and parts	222	62	7	15	15	321
3721 Aircraft	17	0	2	5	1	25
3724 Aircraft engines and engine parts	34	6	0	1	1	42
3728 Aircraft parts and equipment, nec.	161	52	4	9	11	237
374 Railroad equipment	3	0	0	0	0	3
375 Motorcycles, bicycles and parts	36	15	4	2	0	57
376 Guided missiles, space vehicles	29	6	0	2	1	38
3761 Guided missiles and space vehicles	9	3	0	1	1	14
3764 Space propulsion units and parts	7	0	0	0	0	7
3769 Space vehicle equipment, nec.	13	3	0	1	0	17
Total	674	213	44	83	42	1,056

Source: United States Department of Commerce, Bureau of the Census, *County Business Patterns*.

products industry of Southern California as represented by film-making, television, music, clothing manufacture, furniture, jewelry, and so on.

6.3.2 Broad Outlines of a Prospective Advanced Ground Transportation Equipment Industry

At the outset, we should indicate that any attempt to define the detailed configuration of a prospective ground transportation equipment industry is an extremely hazardous manoeuver. This is because the industry is endemically open to major and unforeseeable mutations due to changes in technologies, government policies, consumer preferences and habits, and so on. Yet there are sufficiently strong emerging trends to make it possible to advance a number of remarks about some of the industry's likely future outlines, and to speculate on at least a few of its possible trajectories of development.

To begin with, we may in broad outline conceive of the structure of any multifaceted ground transportation equipment industry as shown in Figure 6.1. Here, the basic products of the industry are divided into four main categories, namely:

- Rail vehicles (e.g., long-distance, commuter, metro rail, light rail).
- Road vehicles (e.g., automobiles, buses, fleet vehicles, and specialty vehicles).
- Rail and road vehicle components and sub-assemblies.
- A disparate group of products identified here under the rubric of infrastructure, peripherals, and accessories (e.g., pertaining to public transportation systems, roadways and private vehicles, and telecommunications processes).

Production of these four main categories of products calls for inputs of goods and services as represented (in part) by the sectors designated in Tables 6.1 to 6.6. Each category of products draws upon a diversity of technologies, which it embodies either directly or indirectly through its input sectors. For the purposes of Figure 6.1, we may make a distinction between *technology*, meaning something that is represented by blueprints and ideas, and the actual *artifacts* that physically incorporate any given technology. A complete catalogue of actual and foreseeable technologies related to ground transportation processes would be almost interminable. However, a brief listing of some of the more obvious technologies that can be confidently calculated to play a specific future role will give some idea of the enormous range and complexity of what is at stake here. Thus, we may mention propulsion systems, new materials, electric batteries, fuel cells, flywheel batteries, sensors, superconductors, magnetic levitation, infra-red technologies, fiber optics, communication satellite technologies, artifical intelligence, geographic information systems. These and a bewildering variety of other technologies are all actually and potentially prominent inputs (directly and indirectly) to an advanced ground transportation industry.

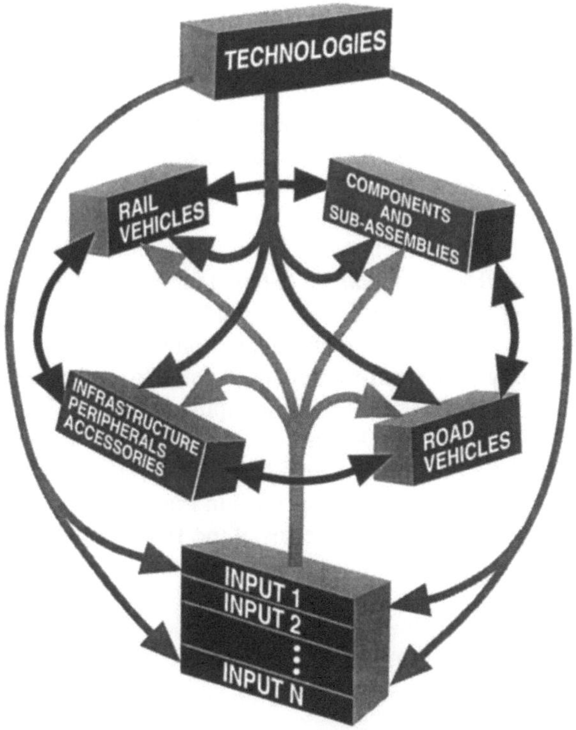

Figure 6.1 Schematic representation of a core system of advanced transportation equipment manufacturing

To summarize Figure 6.1, the core ground transportation equipment manufacturing system consists in principle and practice of a set of final products industries, linked to an intricate input supply mechanism, and in the best of all possible worlds, endowed with a capacity (institutionalized in firms, public agencies, and activity systems) to constantly create and commercialize superior new technologies. Southern California is currently underdeveloped as a center of ground transportation products industries, but it is, as we have seen, extraordinarily well endowed with potential input industries, and it is also a major repository of just the sorts of technologies and technological competencies that would be called massively into play should the region begin to move decisively into advanced ground transportation equipment manufacturing. The bases of this stock of technological resources are located primarily in Southern California's aerospace-defense industry and its suppliers, as well as in the laboratories, research institutes and universities that abound throughout the region. And then again, if Southern California has only a weakly-developed ground transportation equipment industry at the present time, no other region (with the exception of a few dense automobile-producing agglomerations in North America, Europe, and Asia) has emerged as a major center either, though there are individual firms in different parts of the world that are certainly on the leading edges of the industry. This means that first-mover advantages may well be capturable by the region or regions that manage to make an early start in building a viable complex of ground transportation equipment industries in response to new market trends and technologies.

With the above comments in mind, we may ask, just how functionally integrated is the ground transportation industry *as it currently exists* in the United States? We can investigate this issue in part by looking at the detailed input requirements of each of the sectors enumerated in Tables 6.5 and 6.6, and then trying to determine the degree to which these sectors are rooted in common upstream structures of production. We accordingly took input-output coefficients from the 1982 US input-output table for the 541 industries that provide inputs to each of these transportation equipment output sectors (US Department of Commerce, Bureau of Economic Analysis, 1991), and we then performed a cluster analysis on the resulting data matrix. The results of this analysis are set forth in Figure 6.2, where, it should be noted, industrial sectors are defined in terms of the 1972 (rather than the 1987) Standard Industrial Classification.

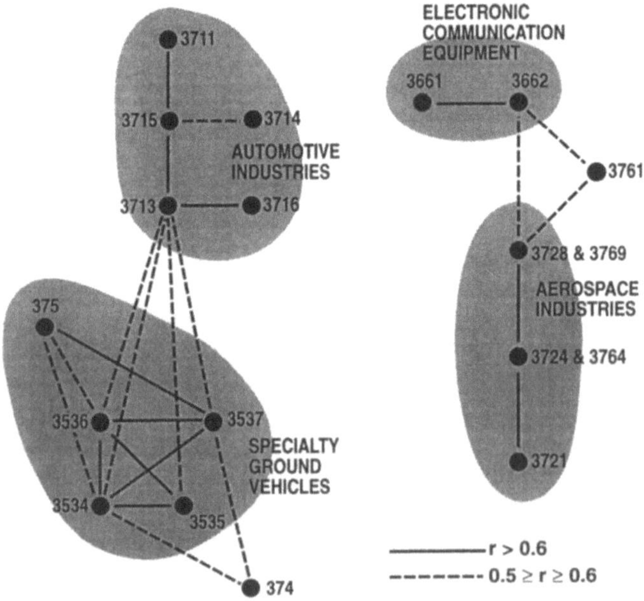

Figure 6.2 Cluster analysis of U.S. transportation equipment industries.

Cluster analysis involves computing the simple correlation coefficients for all pairs of variables under investigation, and then grouping together those variables that have high positive levels of statistical inter-association. In the present instance, each variable comprises a set of input coefficients for a particular ground transportation equipment output sector. Grouping of variables was performed by selectively focusing on correlation coefficients with a value of 0.5 and above; and this operation resulted in four very distinctive clusters. These are represented by (a) an automotive industries group, (b) a specialty ground vehicles group, (c) an electronic communication equipment group, and (d) an aerospace industries group.

While there are certainly some interconnections between these groups – notably between groups *a* and *b*, and between groups *c* and *d* – the analysis reveals that they are nonetheless remarkably distinct from one another in functional terms. This suggests that from the point of view of a standard industrial complex analysis, there are rather limited synergies between the main transportation equipment production industries of the United States as things now stand. One inference from this observation is that policies seeking to foster localized agglomerations of these industries in the future will in all likelihood need to pay close attention to the question of inter-industrial relations in order to promote positive synergies and to tie producers as closely as possible into a single regional complex. It would seem that the low-technology and high-technology ends of the transportation equipment production spectrum are particularly far from each other in this regard at the present time.

6.3.3 The Detailed Structure of a Possible Ground Transportation Equipment Industry in Southern California

How, though, might these industries be structured in the future, and is there an emerging set of synergies that might bind them more tightly together into a single functional complex? It is possible to put together a sort of cognitive map of the advanced ground transportation equipment industries of the immediate future, though there can be no claims about the completeness of the following list of industries:

A. *Rail vehicles* (locomotives, passenger cars and freight cars)
   (a) Long distance rail vehicles, including high speed trains like the French TGV, the Japanese bullet train, and the German Inter-City Express
   (b) Commuter rail vehicles
   (c) Metro rail vehicles
   (d) Light rail vehicles
   (e) Other vehicles, including monorail trains, central city people movers, and innovative systems such as experimental magnetic levitation vehicles, or the French VAL system (voiture automatique légère)

B. *Road vehicles*

(a) Automobiles
   (i) Conventional internal combustion engine vehicles
   (ii) Alternative-fuel vehicles
      – Methanol-powered cars
      – Electric cars
      – Compressed natural gas cars
      – Hybrid cars
(b) Buses
   (i) Conventional buses
   (ii) Methanol-powered buses
   (iii) Electric buses
      – Battery-powered
      – Trolley buses
   (iv) Compressed natural gas buses
(c) Fleet vehicles, such as trucks, vans, and minivans (internal and alternative-fuel driven)
(d) Specialty vehicles, such as recreational vehicles, park service vehicles, airport personnel and freight carriers, robotized trucks, and so on.

C. Rail and road vehicle components and sub-assemblies (propulsion systems; bogeys; drive trains; inverters; heating, ventilation and air-conditioning systems; etc.)

D. Infrastructure, peripherals, accessories
(a) Public transportation
   (i) Tracks and guideways (automated guideways, magnetic levitation, and so on)
   (ii) Command and control systems (central control mechanisms, in-vehicle receivers/transmitters, driverless trains, etc.)
   (iii) Passenger information systems (in vehicles, at stations, at information centers)
   (iv) Revenue collection devices
      – Fare boxes
      – Electronically-coded debit/credit cards
      – Registering devices
(b) Roadways and private vehicles
   (i) Intelligent vehicle and highway systems (IVHS)
      – Advanced traffic management
      – Advanced traveller information
      – Fleet management and control
      – Advanced vehicle control
   (ii) Electronic road pricing systems
   (iii) Signs and signals

(iv) Alternative-fuel vehicle charging and recharging infrastructures (e.g., battery exchangestations, powered roadways, outlets and wiring for electric vehicle recharging)

(c) Telecommunications (cellular phones, call processing equipment, fax, video, remote imaging, etc.)

The above list is constructed on the basis of the primary four-fold categorization of transportation equipment arrayed in Figure 6.1. Each item shown actually or potentially represents a significant sector of employment, though it is highly unlikely that Southern California could be an equally attractive location for all of them. For example, various firms in Europe, Japan, and other parts of North America already have a decisive competitive edge in the production of rail vehicles of all kinds. Southern California will soon acquire a branch plant of Siemens Duewag (to fabricate rail car shells for the region's new Green Line), and there is much local technological expertise in some of the more advanced rail transportation technologies (such as magnetic levitation or command and control systems), but the region has far to go before it could ever compete commercially on equal terms with rail vehicle producers elsewhere. In the matter of road vehicles, too, Southern California's prospects are cloudy in a number of respects. What little was left of the conventional automobile assembly industry in the region in the 1980s had disappeared entirely by the beginning of the 1990s, and clearly, there are minimal chances of the industry ever being resuscitated in any significant way in the future. Conventional bus and fleet vehicle manufacturing similarly would seem to have only limited promise. By contrast, several kinds of innovative road vehicle sectors may well begin to take off in the region in the not too distant future. Among these, electric cars, vans, and buses (and their components), as well as a number of different kinds of specialty vehicle sectors appear to have strong potential. In addition, the infrastructure, peripherals, and accessories sector assuredly has outstanding prospects in Southern California, and it is already present in nascent form throughout the high-technology industrial base of the region.

We may note that Project California (1992) has estimated that the advanced ground transportation industry is likely to generate 208,850 direct *and indirect* manufacturing jobs in the state of California as a whole by the year 2010 (where the indirect element includes both intermediate input producers and R&D work on new technologies). It should be added that the growth of any advanced transportation equipment industry in Southern California is likely also to stimulate growth in the emerging environmental controls and devices industry, in part because of some strong technological overlaps (e.g., in the areas of energy conversion, recycling, or pollution controls), and in part because transportation activities are themselves a major source of environmental pollution and hence a focus of possible solutions. The latter point is exemplified dramatically by the budding electric car industry.

In fact, for exactly the same reasons that make it difficult to predict the overall structure of the ground transportation industry over the next couple of decades, any attempt to forecast future employment in the industry is almost certain to turn out in reality to be far from the mark. What is evident, however, is that there are (a) some significant prospects for Southern California to make an early start in developing a number of important new industries, (b) concrete possibilities for creating growth-enhancing synergies between these industries, (c) many and varied existing industries that offer an unparalleled basis for new rounds of development, (d) rapidly-growing markets for ground transportation equipment, especially as many major metropolitan areas throughout the world begin to renew their aging infrastructures, and (e) a major window of opportunity for creating a new dynamic system of technological innovation and job growth in Southern California. Should such an industry indeed eventually begin to grow substantially in the region, there are good grounds for presuming that it will take off for the most part on the basis of alternative-fuel vehicles (mainly electric cars) and their components, specialty vehicles (such as recreational vehicles or electric school buses), and above all, a wide range of infrastructures, peripherals, and accessories (including telecommunications, which already has a significant presence in the region). To this main group of industries we should no doubt append such adjunct but important activities as research and development, and transportation planning and consulting. It may also be the case that Southern California will ultimately acquire some production capacity in rail vehicles of various kinds, particularly if current political pressures in the region to force higher levels of local job creation by means of public transit development funds continue. However, the region's competitive advantages in the latter area are distinctly less potent than they are in the former.

In general, if there is to be a viable advanced transportation equipment industry in Southern California, we can expect it to make its geographic and historic appearance on the basis of the region's existing strengths, which reside above all in its unique potentialities to create outputs that combine mechanical and electronic capabilities in complex systems in the context of a deeply-rooted and multifaceted high-technology industrial culture. These potentialities may in part be realized by reconversion of existing aerospace-defence firms, though most such firms evidently find it difficult to move successfully into commercial markets. We are no doubt more likely to witness the emergence of large numbers of new ground transportation equipment producers without any significant history of aerospace-defense contract work, though with considerable openness to the possibility of utilizing technologies and skills previously developed in the military sector.

6.3.4 A System of Regional Synergies

We are now in a position to provide a synthetic overview of much of the theoretical and empirical discussion that has been laid out thus far in this study. Figure 6.3 presents this overview in schematic form.[2]

A fundamental condition for growth and development to occur in any region is that there be accessible and contestable markets for local products and that these markets themselves be expanding. As shown in Figure 6.3, there are two major market segments for advanced transportation equipment, namely, one constituted by public agency demands, and the other by private consumer demands. Public agency demands may be expected to grow considerably over the next several years, both locally and nationally. Consumer demands are also likely to grow with great rapidity for selected outputs, as for example, in the cases of specialty vehicles, certain kinds of IVHS products (i.e., intelligent vehicle and highway systems such as route-finding systems or accident-avoidance devices), telecommunication devices, and alternative-fuel vehicles, particularly if the latter should start to become feasible substitutes for internal combustion vehicles.

Such demands sustain production in a variety of industrial sectors, and a large regional production complex could conceivably emerge in cases where these sectors, or a selected set of them, engender agglomeration economies on a significant scale. In the preceding discussion, it was argued that an advanced ground transportation industry may well materialize in Southern California on the basis of a core group of technology-intensive sectors capable of combining modern electronics with advanced mechanical platforms, with a possible secondary tier of industries focused on the production of more conventional rail and road vehicles. Figure 6.3 makes explicit reference, too, to a series of critical input suppliers and subcontractors, and many different kinds of service providers, from venture capitalists to urban and transportation planners. These sectors represent a crucial element of Southern California's industrial base and an imporant source of local agglomeration economies.

In Figure 6.3 we also present a roster of *manufacturing organizations* that are either already in varying degree present as elements of the manufacturing system of Southern California (e.g., joint venture activities, industry associations, labor unions), or that are currently under-developed but likely to be important in the future (e.g., collaborative manufacturing systems and just-in-time processing networks). These organizations all lie, partially or wholly, outside the sphere of market relations, and all of them pose puzzling questions about the (necessary) forms of governance that would be most appropriate for them: all-out public regulation? self-government? private-public agreements? etc. To judge from the experience

2 Smilor et al. (1988) develop a "technopolis wheel" that has certain resemblances to Figure 3.

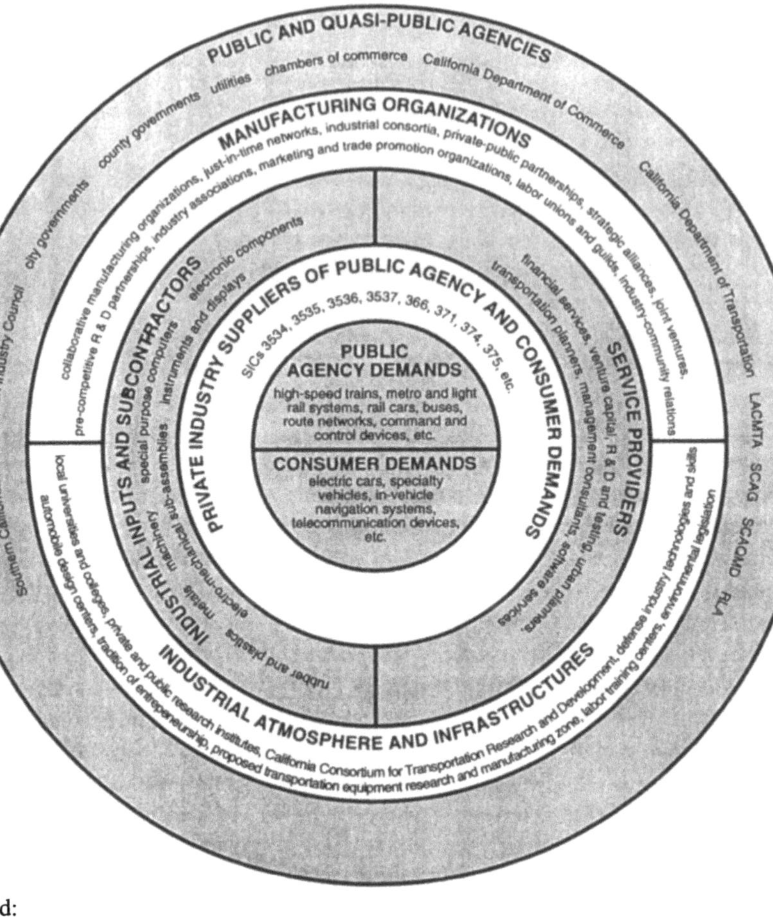

Legend:
LACMTA – Los Angeles County Metropolityn Transportation Authority
RLA – Rebuild Los Angeles Committee
SCAG – Southern California Association of Governments
SCAQMD – South Coast Air Quality Management District

Figure 6.3 Schematic outline of a system of regional synergies for the advanced transportation equipment industry in Southern California

of countries like Germany, Italy, and Japan, para-market organizations like these, particularly where they engender increased levels of inter-firm trust and collaboration, can be major factors in the construction of regional competitive advantages.

At the same time, we display in Figure 6.3 a catalogue of heterogeneous factors collectively designated here *industrial atmosphere and infrastructures*. These factors are all key constituents of regional manufacturing systems. They represent either fundamental services that are susceptible to market failure, and thus call for public intervention if they are to be supplied at socially-rational levels (e.g., technological research or labor training), or externalities which are likely to have large impacts on local economic prospects (e.g., in the case of Southern California, defense industry technologies and skills). Two important items here have a somewhat anticipatory character. One is a California Consortium for Transportation Research and Development which is now being established by the Community Development Department of the City of Los Angeles as a not-for-profit think-tank for investigating transportation processes and technologies (with particular reference to large metropolitan areas), and for transferring selected research findings to the commercial domain. Eventually, the Consortium might be capable of capturing part or all of the funds that the California Department of Transportation is planning to allocate to a proposed Western National Transportation Research and Development Center (cf. California Assembly Bill 3096, November, 1992). The other item is a proposed transportation equipment research and manufacturing zone, or industrial park, devoted to core R&D, design, prototyping, and advanced manufacturing activities. The proposed manufacturing zone would help to anchor an emerging ground transportation equipment industry in the region by creating a strong localized nexus of agglomeration economies.

Lastly, the effectiveness and competitiveness of any regional system of production can be greatly enhanced where it is bolstered by a system of locally-based agencies and institutions that variously help to resolve coordination problems, to ensure effective resource deployment, and to intensify agglomeration economies. In the outermost circle of Figure 3 (under the rubric of *public and quasi-public agencies*) a great many different examples of such instruments of collective action are cited; some of these represent agencies and institutions that actually exist in the region, whereas others only have a hypothetical status at the present time. Among those that currently function are the Los Angeles County Metropolitan Transportation Authority, whose role over the next several years will certainly be of great importance. We also list a "Southern California Transportation Industry Council," a body that does not actually exist, but whose establishment is much to be recommended should an advanced ground transportation equipment industry begin to take off in the region. In this particular instance, we are thinking of an institution something like the regional economic councils that are to be found in German *Länder*, and that bring together representatives of local government, banks, employers, and labor unions in an attempt to forge broadly-based agreements about local economic development strategies. A Southern California Transportation Industry Council, in short, would constitute a forum of stakeholders for monitoring the industry's prospects and problems and for coordinating remedial action when it is called for.

In sum, the complex system of regional synergies sketched out in Figure 6.3 can be seen as a generalized blueprint of a latently powerful engine of regional growth and development (cf. Scott and Paul, 1990). Not every item mentioned in the figure needs to be physically present for ultimate success to be achieved. We suggest, however, that the details set forth in Figure 6.3 capture at least some of the facets of a type of regional economic organization that can be a foundation for industrial success in the new global economy at the dawn of the twenty-first century. The details displayed in the figure represent a preliminary guide to policy-makers in Southern California, i.e., a means of identifying and contextualizing the many difficult decisions that lie ahead as the region begins to deal with the problem of creating and promoting a dynamic agglomeration of advanced ground transportation equipment industries. The application of this sort of approach to the fostering of an infant electric vehicle industry in the region has already begun to produce tangible results, and we believe that it can also be applied successfully to the other newly emerging transportation equipment industries in the region, ranging from IVHS to high-technology rail cars (see Scott and Bergman, 1993, for greater detail on this point).

6.4 Practical Policy Issues

6.4.1 The MTA's Thirty-Year Plan

Early in 1992, the Los Angeles County Transportation Commission (later, the MTA) released a thirty-year integrated transportation plan for the county (Los Angeles County Transportation Commission, 1992). The Plan as it now stands calls for the expenditure of a total of $183 billion over the next thirty years (i.e., an average of $6.1 billion a year) on a variety of rail, highway, bus, and demand management programs. Some sense of the magnitude of the sums involved may be gained by noting that in 1990 federal Department of Defense prime contract awards in Los Angeles County (by far the largest recipient of such awards in the country) amounted to $8.88 billion. The authors of the plan recognize that many unforeseeable events may intervene at any stage over the next thirty years, thus making their projections increasingly less probable with the passage of time. Indeed, the prolonged economic recession in Southern California is already exerting heavy pressure on the plan as it is currently formulated.

The bulk of this money (i.e., 74.3 per cent) will come from purely local sources. It consists mainly of funds made available by electoral approval of Propositions A and C. Proposition A was passed by the voters of Los Angeles County in 1980; it added one half cent to the local sales tax for the purposes of transportation funding. Proposition C was passed in 1990 and added a yet further one half cent to the sales tax for transportation funding. Farebox revenues, commitments from other local agencies, and debt offerings account for the balance of the local funding sources. An additional 17.1 per cent will come from the federal government, much of it from provisions enacted by the 1991 Intermodal Surface Transportation Efficiency Act (ISTEA), with a further 8.3 per cent from the state, and just 0.3 per cent from private sources. Table 6.7 indicates the proposed disposition of these funds in terms of major programs, and Table 6.8 lists the detailed components of each program. Among the more important of these are a major effort of urban and commuter rail construction, considerable new expenditure on buses and trolley-buses, and a massive deployment of IVHS, command-and-control, and systems management technologies. In addition, one-hundred new buses will be added to the fleet over each of the first six years of the plan, and a total of four-hundred trolley-buses will be added too. It is planned to convert all buses in Los Angeles to clean fuel propulsion systems by the year 2004.

Table 6.7 Proposed allocation of funds to major programs in the MTA's Thirty-Year Plan, in billions of dollars

	Capital expenditures	Operating and maintenance expenditures	Total
Rail	55.6	22.6	78.2
Highway	26.3	—[a]	26.3
Bus	14.3	58.6	72.9
Transportation demand management	4.1	1.4	5.5
	100.3	82.6	182.9

[a] Capital and operating costs for freeways, streets, and roads not subject to MTA authority are estimated at $58 billion.

Source: Los Angeles County Transportation Commission, *LACTC Proposed 30-Year Integrated Transportation Plan*, Los Angeles, 1992.

Booz-Allen and Hamilton Inc. (1992) have calculated that MTA's procurements as specified in the thirty-year plan will generate as many as 66,000 new jobs in Southern California. It is predicted that most of these jobs will occur in non-manufacturing sectors, notably in the construction industry, the transportation and public utilities sector, and in services. The Booz-Allen Hamilton report estimates that job creation in manufacturing in Southern California will account for only 7 per cent or 8 per cent of the 66,000 jobs. The major reason for this estimated relatively mild impact of the plan on manufacturing in Southern California, is that the report takes the economic structure of the region as given by its current configuration. Thus, it is calculated (no doubt correctly under this assumption) that as much as 40 per cent of all capital equipment expenditures will be directed outside the region – a reflection of the circumstance that major transit equipment producers at the present time are all located in other parts of the country and other parts of the world. Clearly, the kinds of economic development scenarios proposed in the

Table 6.8 Detailed components of major programs in the MTA's Thirty-Year Plan

Major Program	Component Elements
Rail	Four hundred miles of total rail
	– Two-hundred miles of urban rail and high capacity improvements
	– Two-hundred miles of commuter rail
	– over three-hundred miles operational in next six years
	Enhanced rail line security
Highway	Freeway service patrol
	Freeway system management
	Freeway incident management
	Signal synchronization and other transportation systems management improvements
	Three-hundred miles of car-pool lanes on major freeways
	Freeway gap closures
	Park and ride lots
	Bikeways
	Soundwalls
Bus	Over one-hundred buses added over first six years of Plan
	1400 additional peak buses up to the year 2010
	Bus fleet 100% clean fuel
	Four-hundred high-capacity trolley buses
	Three-hundred miles of electrified bus routes
	New express bus service on carpool lanes with stations
	Relief of congested corridors
	Expanded bus feeder service to rail
	Implementation of Americans with Disabilities Act
	Bus security
Transportation demand management	Reduce work-trips by 2.4 million by the year 2010
	Ride-sharing (carpools and vanpools)
	Flexible work hours
	Telecommuting
	Incentive pricing strategies

Source: Los Angeles County Transportation Commission, *LACTC Proposed 30-Year Integrated Transportation Plan*, Los Angeles, 1992.

present study are capable of transforming, perhaps quite drastically, the parameters of this calculation.

6.4.2 Institution-Building and Political Mobilization: Some Proposals

In addition to the procurement policies that the MTA and other governmental agencies in Southern California can fashion to promote local economic development, there is an important set of specific tasks to be accomplished in the domain of institution-building and the mobilization of interests and resources. In this regard, cross-agency cooperation is a prime ingredient for success. Collaboration with the four counties surrounding Los Angeles county, as well as with other transportation agencies in the state (such as BART, the San Diego Metropolitan Transit Development Board, and Caltrans) is also apt to pay dividends, especially where this facilitates the achievement of scale economies in organizational effort, engineering and R&D programs, procurement, and so on. And close liaison with the many community organizations in the region concerned with economic development issues – including groups like the RLA Committee, Community Build, the Coalition of Neighborhood Developers, and the recently-formed Urban League Business Development and Entrepreneur Center – is of major importance; these groups can play a critical role in helping to match broad top-down development efforts with detailed needs and constraints on the ground, and, above all, with the increasingly urgent imperative of economic revitalization in Los Angeles' most deprived neighborhoods.

With these preliminaries in mind, and in light of our earlier analyses six important tasks calling for concrete collective action are now briefly reviewed.

(1) Promotion of transportation technology research

We have already indicated that basic technological research, of whatever kind, is typically subject to severe market failures. This means that some form of public support is usually necessary and desirable in order to create and consolidate a durable technological advantage in particular sectors of industry. There is, in particular, a major need for a central transportation research institute in Southern California to carry out and to coordinate work on transportation technologies and processes, with a particular emphasis on commercialization and diffusion of results to local industry. We therefore advocate vigorous public and private support for the efforts now under way in the City of Los Angeles to establish a *California Consortium for Transportation Research and Development.*

(2) Provision of high-risk capital investment funds

It is notoriously difficult for small innovative startup companies to gain adequate investment backing, even from venture capital sources, and all the more so when they are seeking to develop unconventional and little-understood ideas. It is therefore imperative in any economic development program that seeks to build a dynamic and multifaceted regional complex of production activities to find some way of supplementing normal market-driven lending agencies with other, and especially more patient, sources of investment capital. Accordingly, we recommend the formation of a *Southern California Transportation Equipment Industry Venture Capital Fund.*

(3) Creating an appropriate skills base

Worker education and training represent another domain of activity that is susceptible to severe market failure. In fact, the MTA has already made an excellent start in coming to terms with this kind of problem by now requiring, as its official policy, that all of its contractors set aside three per cent of their labor costs for job development and job training purposes. Of equal importance is the proposal that has recently been made by the School of Engineering and Applied Science at the University of California, Los Angeles, to establish an Integrated Manufacturing Engineering Program with a primary focus on the teaching of manufacturing processes and procedures for advanced transportation systems.

(4) Industry consortia and collaborative manufacturing

As we argued earlier, within any system of market competition there are significant gains to be made from certain forms of inter-industrial collaboration. The CALSTART consortium has demonstrated in practice the realizability of such advances through its collaborative showcase electric vehicle program, and more recently, its electric bus program. Careful study now needs to be made of opportunities for, and the limits on, further collaborative ventures in the advanced ground transportation industry in Southern California, and of the institutional forms most appropriate for them. One promising proposal is for a Fuel Cell Commercialization Alliance that would bring together private industry, utilities, governmental agencies, and universities in Southern California in order to accelerate industrial development of this promising new technology (Economic Roundtable, 1992; and Edgar, Dunn and Co., 1992).

(5) Proposal for a Transportation Equipment Research and Manufacturing Zone in Southern California

We urge that local authorities in Los Angeles and the state of California begin to investigate the prospects for establishing a *Transportation Equipment Research and Manufacturing Zone* somewhere in the region as a way of anchoring and stimulating a wider series of industrial developments throughout the region. The goal, ideally, would be to construct a zone that housed a mix of activities, such as advanced prototype and high-technology manufacturers, selected adjunct service providers, transportation industry consortia like CALSTART, testing facilities, a labor-training center, and in the best of all possible worlds, the new California Consortium for Transportation Research and Development.

(6) Overall steering and coordination

Our final major recommendation is that a *Southern California Transportation Industry Council* be established as a forum for bringing together relevant parties in an effort to construct broad agreements about solutions to industry problems and to head off free-rider problems. Such a council might be constituted as a special committee or task force within the wider regional economic council whose possible outlines are now being studied by the Southern California Association of Governments (SCAG, 1993).

6.4.3 The Wider Political Context

A series of organizational and infrastructural initiatives along these lines, combined with judicious deployment of MTA's procurement efforts, could do much to generate a tissue of dynamic new industries in Southern California and to reinforce the region's competitive advantages on national and global markets. However, the activist policies suggested by this agenda may well in different ways encounter resistance from other regions elsewhere in the state, and particularly the Bay Area, that also have ambitions to share in the benefits to be obtained from serving emerging markets in high-technology ground transportation equipment. At the same time, it is important to ensure that public resources are not wasted either by unnecessary duplication of efforts in different parts of the state, or by self-defeating competition among local government agencies. It is essential, in this respect, that state-wide coordination of local economic development efforts focused on the advanced ground transportation industry be undertaken, and that clear understandings be hammered out about what each major region is prepared to do and not do. In this context, regional alliance-building and joint-venture activities around issues of economic development may prove to be a viable way forward, not just within the state, but also between Southern California and regions in other parts of the country. It has recently been suggested, for example, that a prospective Southern California-Michigan alliance would be well worth exploring, bringing together the high-technology assets of the former region and the mechanical-automotive capabilities of the latter (Slifko, 1993).

The policies deployed over the coming years by the MTA and other local agencies in Southern California can help the region to make an early start and thus to gain first-mover advantages in the development of an advanced ground transportation equipment industry, and they can mold in decisive ways intra-regional agglomeration economies and inter-regional competition and cooperation. These policies should not focus indiscriminately on the (relatively simple) task of building new physical production capacity in the region, but rather on setting in motion a dynamic complex of flexible, transactions-intensive industries capable of attaining high levels of technological innovation, skill-creation, and product quality. The ultimate goal is to create a continuously innovative advanced ground transportation equipment production system in the region that can eventually rise to a position of leadership in national and international markets. We suggest that the right kinds of financial and institution-building policies on the part of the MTA and other local and state agencies can stimulate a great leap forward in this direction.

6.5 Conclusion

Southern California is today at a critical cross-roads in its history, much as it was at the beginning of the century and in the years immediately following the Second World War. A great many uncertainties hang over its economic future, and there are some grounds for the assessment that in the normal course of events (and abstracting away from the ups and downs of the business cycle), the region may well be facing an extended period of economic difficulties. Since 1988, it has most certainly suffered a severe erosion of much of its industrial base. The normal course of events, however, (i.e., inaction), is not engraved indelibly in the region's destiny. There are several disciplined and theoretically-informed lines of action that policy-makers can take in an effort to prevent further deterioration of the region's industrial base; and we have argued that the future development of an advanced ground transportation equipment industry represents one of Southern California's best options for continued growth and prosperity.

As we have shown, regions as such can be potent articulations of value-adding activity. This is particularly the case where regional economies are organized as transactions-intensive industrial agglomerations complemented by a rich framework of institutions which ensure that certain basic coordination tasks are performed, market failures corrected, and efficiency-enhancing forms of inter-industrial cooperation encouraged. Throughout the modern world, manufacturing regions that are characterized by at least some elements of this ramifying complex of relationships frequently, though not necessarily always, command strong competitive advantages on national and international markets for their products, (Porter 1990; Scott 1988b; Storper 1991). We have outlined some of the actions that policy-makers can take to try to move economically flagging or underdeveloped regions into a virtuous circle of continuous growth and development. To be sure, the task is not easy or clear-cut, and it assuredly cannot be successfully achieved in all places and at all times. What makes Southern California a particularly compelling candidate for development as a major center of advanced ground transportation equipment manufacturing is that it has already laid the foundations for a convincing early start, and it has an existing industrial base that is pregnant with innovative possibilities. The problem in Southern California is less, perhaps, the technicalities of putting a physical production apparatus into place than it is of accomplishing the political tasks that are needed to underpin such an effort with an effective institutional base.

The Southern Californian economy as it now stands is caught in a sort of double bind. On the one side the high-technology defense contracting business is steadily winding down; on the other side, the low-wage sweatshop sector continues to absorb large and increasing numbers of unskilled workers. The great need in the region at this point is not simply for quantitative employment growth, but more especially for growth of high-skill, high-wage jobs in production sectors that are able continually to climb the product quality/price curve. The advanced ground transportation equipment industry is a sector that is potentially capable of filling this role. Indeed, given the right kinds of public policy initiatives, Southern California has at least as great a chance as any other industrial region in any other part of the world of becoming a significant national and international hub for the industry. Should this come about, we would expect to see it expressed in the geographic form of a sort of Silicon Valley (or, rather, a series of Silicon Valleys) of ground transportation equipment manufacturing activities in the region. As local policy-makers begin to grapple with the complex issues raised by this agenda, the experience gained will provide a crucial lesson and reference point for other local economic development initiatives across the nation.

7. Strategic Economic Cooperation and Employment Relations Issues

Basu Sharma, Anil Verma, and Sarosh Kuruvilla

7.1 Introduction

National industrialization strategies indicate a balance of roles played by markets and governments. Markets traditionally played a predominant role in the industrialization process of most of today's mature industrialized countries, whereas governments have played a dominant role in the industrialization of East Asian and Southeast Asian countries. In fact, the so-called Asian model of industrialization is based upon an interaction between government guidance and market competition where companies compete vigorously to meet the goal set by government (Fallows, 1995:445). Terms such as "Japan Inc.," "Singapore Inc.," and "Korea, Inc." essentially convey closeness of the relationship between business and governments for coordinating economic activities for the greater good of society. The application of this model at a supranational level is manifested in the establishment of various strategic cooperation arrangements among groups of countries. Formation of an economic growth triangle is one of the prevalent methods of such arrangements, and embedded in the concept of economic growth triangle is a complex of relationships evolving among and between various business firms and national governments.

Strategic economic cooperation arrangements in Southeast and East Asian countries have taken many different forms such as twinning, creation of growth triangles, and formation of an integrated economic area. All of the fastest growing dynamic economies of Asia (Singapore, Taiwan, Hong Kong, Indonesia, Malaysia, Thailand, and China) have been parties to one or another form of economic cooperation arrangement. One of the earlier cases which promoted the concept of the economic growth triangle involved Singapore, the Johor Bahru of Malaysia, and the Riau islands of Indonesia. It is commonly known as *SIJORI*. The main objective in forming this triangle was to realize economic growth "out of proportion to the size of its local economy" (Stewart and Png, 1993:1). This is a sub-regional strategic cooperative arrangement among three countries, and each country is expected to benefit from a complementarity of resources and capabilities.

The regional cooperation arrangements such as the Association of Southeast Asian Nations (ASEAN) and the South Asian Regional Cooperation (SAARC) have professed to promote political stability and trade within the region. The subregional arrangements, such as the economic growth triangle and the Chinese Economic Area, are premised on promoting investment and production activities (Guilloute, 1990; Pillai, 1992; Jones et al., 1993). These arrangements for strategic economic cooperation have implications for labour and employment relations, as an interface of international capital and local labour is the most visible characteristic of these borderless (in a political sense), sub-regional economic nodes. However, while trade and investment aspects related to these arrangements have been debated and discussed in literature, employment relations issues pertaining to these new developments have not received much attention. Our objective in this paper is to reflect on these issues, and discuss their implications for debates on changing employment relations in Asia and abroad.

This chapter is divided into four sections. As a background to inform the debate, we begin with a brief description of economic growth triangles. This discussion is grounded in the broader context of global competitiveness concern of firms and the rapid industrialization objective of national governments which give rise to commodity chains and regional division of labour. We then identify likely employment relations issues related to economic growth triangles with specific reference to SIJORI (Singapore, Johor Bahru, and Riau). This is followed by a discussion of the consequences of these employment relations issues for some strands of current theoretical debates. These include the new international division of labour hypothesis (Frobel et al., 1980), strategic choice paradigm (Kochan et al., 1986), and flexible specialization thesis (Piore and Sabel, 1984). In the subsequent section of the chapter, we summarize the main issues raised and point out the need for research to study evolving employment relations in the economic growth triangles.

7.2 Strategic Economic Cooperation in Asia

A concern with competitiveness of firms and nations pervades throughout most of the developed and developing world at present. Political boundaries become less important when nations are confronted by an economic logic of competitive advantage (Ohmae, 1993). That is to say, these days economics is linking countries faster than politics. This is evident from developments such as the formation of the European Economic Community (EEC), the ASEAN Free Trade Agreement (AFTA), and the North American Free Trade Agreement (NAFTA). The focus of these arrangements is regional integration predominantly through trade. Traditional textbook models of regional integration include free trade areas, custom unions, common markets, and economic unions. Free trade areas imply elimination of trade barriers among member countries, whereas custom unions imply creation of free trade areas and the adoption of common tariffs against third countries. Common market arrangements allow for free movement of goods, services and factors of production, whereas economic unions go even further with full co-ordination and harmonization of economic policies. These are the ideal-typical forms. New forms of economic cooperation arrangements have begun to appear for investment and production activities across borders which fall somewhere between free trade areas and common market arrangements. Southeast and East Asian countries have been leading the way in this respect.

The Chinese Economic Area (CEA) which links Southern China (Guangdong and Fujan provinces), Hong Kong and Taiwan is one of the earlier examples of strategic economic cooperation. This area is generally known as the *South China growth triangle*, and came into existence in the early 1980s. It has succeeded to achieve its original objective of generating a high rate of economic growth through use of complementary resources at the disposal of participating countries (Ash and Kueh, 1993; Jones, King, and Klein, 1992). In Southeast Asia, the dominant mode of this process of economic integration in recent years has been the formation of economic growth triangles. Examples abound. The SIJORI triangle – also known as *southern triangle* – came into being in 1989. There has been a proposal for a growth triangle linking parts of Mindanao in the Philippines with Sulawesi in Indonesia and Borneo in Malaysia (*The Economist*, September 25, 1993, pp. 41-42). This goes by the name of *eastern triangle*. The governments of Indonesia, Malaysia, and Thailand have recently agreed in principle to form a growth triangle linking five provinces in southern Thailand (including Phuket), four states in northern Malaysia (including Penang and Medan), and northern Sumatra in Indonesia. It is known as *northern growth triangle*. This area has over 21 million people at present and had a combined output of $12.4 billion in 1988 (Vatikiotis, 1993). Another proposed triangle includes Sarawak in eastern Malaysia, East Kalimantan in Indonesia and Brunei. Under the Tumen River Area Development Project, there is a proposal to establish a *Tumen River growth triangle* involving parts of Jilian province of China, Siberia, and North Korea. This project is considered as "one of the most far reaching strategic economic ventures ever proposed for Northeast Asia" (Marton, McGee and Paterson, 1995:9). Figure 7.1 helps to visualize these growth triangle arrangements sprawling in Asia.

The most potent case of an economic growth triangle in Southeast Asia is the SIJORI triangle. It was initially promoted by the government of Singapore as "the concept of borderless economic zones with coherent and integrated divisions of labour that transcend formal national political boundaries" (Rodan, 1993:223). The triangle links Singapore, Johor Bahru of Malaysia, and Batam, Bintan and other Riau Islands of Indonesia. Figure 7.2 facilitates a visual inspection of the SIJORI growth triangle.

The SIJORI economic growth triangle is an arrangement based on the notion of complementarity of resources, and thus an aspect of the industrialization strategies pursued by the governments of Singapore, Malaysia, and Indonesia. Singapore is a newly industrialized country which has developed state-of-the-art transportation and communication facilities, as well as a significant pool of scientific, professional and technical human resources. However, Singapore lacks not only

Figure 7.1 Growth triangles in Asia

raw materials and space, but also suffers from a shortage of labour. On the other hand, Johor is the largest state in the Malaysian Federation with 8,941 square kilometres of space and a population of about 2.2 million. It supplies water to Singapore, and is directly linked to it by the Causeway. It has plenty of land and relatively skilled labour. On the Indonesian side, the Riau archipelago has several islands. Of these, Batam island, with an area of 415 square kilometres with a population of only about 100,000, was chosen first as a Free Trade Zone. Bintan

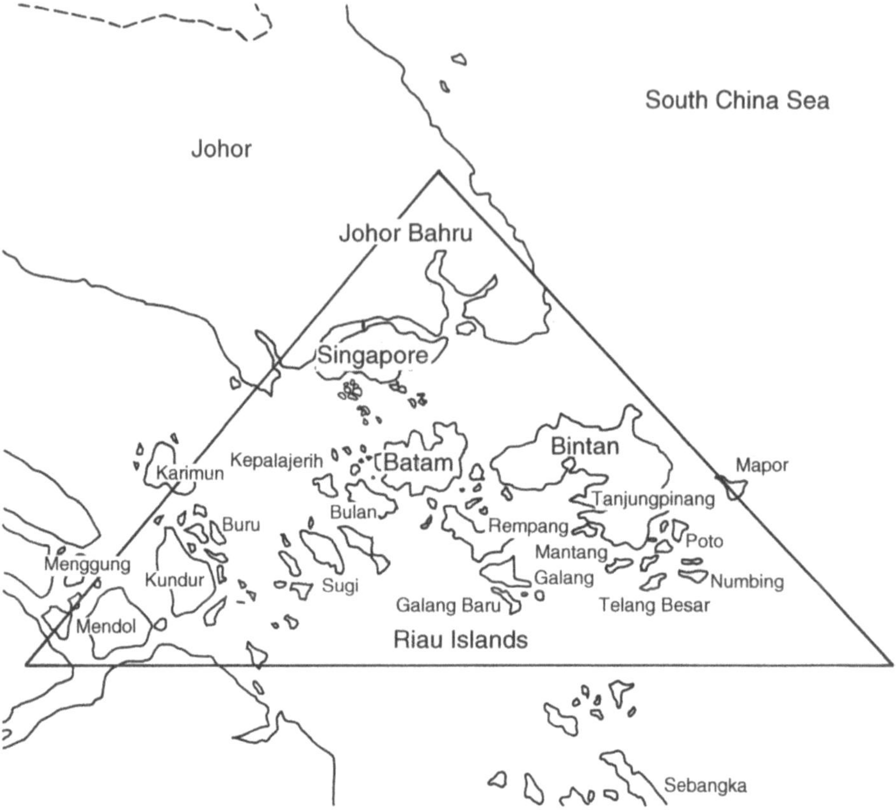

Figure 7.2 The SIJORI growth triangle

and Kurimun were added later. Since these islands are closer to other islands in the Riau archipelago and Sumatra, they offer a further source of additional space and labour. Both Malaysia and Indonesia have plenty of physical space and raw materials, but Indonesia has also plenty of "cheap" labour (Guillouet, 1990). In fact, with nearly 2.5 million people entering the work force every year, a major problem for the Indonesian government is job creation. The Indonesian government expects the triangle to be helpful in solving this problem. Thus Singapore is strategically located to take advantage of these resources, while Johor and Riau can benefit from Singapore's technological capacity and transportation and communication infrastructures.

Development of industrial estates, construction of housing units and an airport are the projects in progress in Batam. The Batamindo industrial complex is a Singapore-Indonesia joint venture established in January 1970. It is owned by PT BATAMINDO Investment Corporation. The Indonesian partners own 60 per cent and the Singapore partners the remaining 40 per cent. The Indonesian partners are organized in a group called Herwido Rintis, comprising one of the major business groups known as the Salim Group, together with Bimantara and Timmy Habibie. The Singapore shareholders are comprised of Singapore Technologies Industrial Corporation, and Jurong Environmental Engineering. The Batamindo industrial complex is a 500-hectare integrated industrial estate. It is significant that it was officially inaugurated by the Indonesian President Suharto and Singapore's Prime Minister Goh Chok Tong in April 1992. Batam has already begun to produce results. Leading multinational corporations (MNCs) such as Telemecanique and Thomson of France, AT&T and Seagate of US, Sumitomo and Sanyo of Japan, and Philips of the Netherlands have established assembly plants in the facilities at Batamindo. "Most of these companies have operations in Singapore and are using Batam as an assembly site" (*Far Eastern Economic Review*, 20 May 1993, p. 62). Nevertheless, it is reported that this complex has already generated millions of dollars in revenue and created more than 20,000 new jobs (*Indonesia Development News Quarterly* (Autumn 1993/Winter 1994). Table 1 presents some statistics on the inflows of foreign direct investment (FDI) in Batam and Johor.

As it can be seen from Table 1, Singapore is the largest investor in Batam, whereas it is just behind Japan in Johor. Singapore firms invested over M$1.5 billion between 1990 and 1993, and they were responsible for creating more than 37,000 jobs in Johor. Taiwan is also a major player insofar as foreign direct investment in Johor is concerned. The FDI inflows have been increasing spectacularly, especially in Batam. According to a recent report, "about 154 companies and $4.5 billion (US) of investment have poured into this free-trade island, where labour and land, at least by Singapore standards, are cheap and plentiful" (*Globe and Mail*, May 24, 1994, p. B1).

While the showpiece of the SIJORI triangle is Batam, a 500-hectare free port industrial zone with $ 6 billion expenditure for construction, due for completion in 2006, Bintan has become the focus of the latest attention in the SIJORI triangle (*Institutional Investor* (April 1994), p. 37). Construction of an industrial estate is in progress. As in the case of the Batamindo industrial complex, Indonesia's Salim Group and Singapore's Jurong Environmental Engineering and Singapore Technologies Industrial Corporation are jointly participating in its development. Several Japanese investors have also already made commitments for investment. Bintan, an island, with over 11 miles of pristine beach, is to be developed as a resort to benefit from international tourists coming to Singapore. There is a plan to build about 20 hotels with nearly 8000 rooms, 30 villa clusters, 10 condominium complexes, and 10 golf courses (Stewart and Png, 1993). At a cost of 3.5 billion, this development is supposed to span a period of 20 years (*The Straits Times*, July 23, 1994, pp. 1 and 20).

Since the growth triangle is not a common market, there is no harmonization of tax and investment codes. Each country implements its own regulations, and each provides incentives to foreign investors in line with its industrialization policies.

Table 7.1 Foreign Direct Investment in Johor and Batam

	Johor (cumulative, 1987–1991)	Batam (cumulative, end of 1991)
Total FDI	M$ 5,178.9 million	US$ 1,054.8 million
	Per cent distribution	
ASEAN	20.3	51.7
Indonesia	1.0	—
Malaysia	—	0.3
Philippines	0.3	—
Singapore	18.9	50.5
Thailand	0.2	0.9
NIEs-3	28.6	10.6
Hong Kong	3.9	8.4
Korea, Rep.	8.2	0.4
Taiwan	16.6	1.8
Japan	21.3	11.4
United States	6.3	15.3
Europe	6.4	10.0
Others	17.1	1.1

Source: Chia Siow Yue (1993), Table 9.

Singapore provides incentives for pioneer status, expansion, research and development, and for making Singapore the operational headquarter. These incentives either imply no tax for a specified period of time, or a relief through a reduced rate for a period of time. Singapore does not have any restrictions on equity ownership except for a few industries and sectors considered strategic and of national importance. It also does not have restrictions on the employment of expatriates. Malaysia also provides incentives for pioneer status, export, research and development, training of workers, and for establishing overseas operational headquarters in Malaysia. Again, these incentives take various forms such as tax holidays and an accelerated capital cost allowance. In Malaysia, equity ownership is tied to the *bumiputras* policy of the government and exports. In cases where foreign equity is less than 100 per cent, up to 30 per cent is to be held by *bumiputras*. The *bumiputras* are indigenous people receiving preferential treatment as a result of the government's new economic policy in place since 1969. Unlike in Singapore, employment of expatriate staff is also tied to the capitalization of a company and the *bumiputras* policy. According to this policy, Malaysians should be trained to take up the position of an expatriate at least after 10 years. Incentives provided by Indonesia to foreign investors include provisions such as generous depreciation and amortization rates for capital goods, exemption from or concessions on imports duty, and exports credit. Investors investing in the triangle segment can have 100 per cent ownership for the first 5 years and 95 per cent thereafter, 30 years leases, and status as a duty free zone. Indonesia also has a *prebhumi* policy which requires some participation by indigenous people.

Even though the concept of triangle implies trilateralism, in practice both bilateral and trilateral arrangements have been used. The Riau Accord is a case of bilateral arrangement. It was signed between Singapore and Indonesia in August 1990. It covers areas such as joint development of industrial estates, tourist resorts, and water catchment areas in Batam and Bintan. The planned development of a 600 hectare technology park in Skudai, Johor is a case of trilateral arrangements. This park is to be developed through cooperative arrangements among authorities in Singapore, Batam, and Johor. Upon completion, it is to become the largest technology park in the region.

Strategic economic cooperation arrangements in the form of growth triangles differ significantly from other forms such as the ASEAN Free Trade Agreement (AFTA), the North American Free Trade Agreement (NAFTA), the Association of Southeast Asian Nations (ASEAN), the European Community (EC), and the Asia Pacific Economic Caucus (APEC). The main objective of the latter type is to promote "free movement of goods and factors of production to members' mutual advantage" (Ash and Kueh, 1993:742). However, the triangle arrangements are based on joint production and international division of labour with a view to serving the global market. These arrangements are also different from existing production arrangements elsewhere, such as maquiladoras, in that the "triangle" concept is based on complementarities of capital, labour, and managerial know-how for regional economic growth. The "maquiladora" phenomenon, on the other hand, is primarily aimed at taking advantage of low-cost Mexican labour rather than promoting local economic development. Furthermore, it is important to note that where complementarities are weak or absent, the triangles are unlikely to serve as a vehicle for regional industrial growth.

In sum, the underlying rationale for the strategic economic cooperation arrangements is based on stage-specific competitive advantages of each individual country, and the political will to create synergy out of this cooperation. The southern growth triangle was conceptualized along this line. In fact, the SIJORI triangle is already a $40 billion subregional economy with 5 million people. In Batam, more than 50,000 jobs have been created since the formation of the growth triangle. The total shipment from Batam in 1993 reached $925 million. Nevertheless, labour and technology are the two crucial factors in the process of linking up countries and regions at different stages of development. Some people consider this a low-cost assembly site for MNCs based in Singapore. Hence a few words on commodity chains and regional divisions of labour are in order.

7.3 Commodity Chains and Regional Divisions of Labour

Growth triangles in Asia, particularly Southeast Asia, are the result of governments' regionalization and restructuring drives. Put differently, they are a part of broader industrialization programmes. In Southeast Asia and East Asia, there are three groups of countries – newly industrialized countries (NICs), new NICs (NNICs) and other industrializing countries. In the group of ASEAN, Singapore is a NIC whereas Malaysia and Thailand are the NNICs. Indonesia, the Philippines and Brunei are other industrializing countries. Based on stages of industrialization, countries in each group have emphasized different types of industrialization policies. For example, Indonesia prefers more labour-intensive industries while Malaysia goes for more capital-intensive industries. Singapore is a NIC, and it prefers skill-intensive, high value-added production activities. It has also the ambition of becoming a knowledge centre for the regions. These differences allow for promotion of a regional division of labour as well as the creation of commodity chains.

Abundance of cheap labour in Indonesia, low land costs in Malaysia, and a high technological infrastructure in Singapore were the forces leading to the development of the SIJORI triangle. The idea was to move labour-intensive production away from Singapore to Johor and Batam, while encouraging research and development activities and the production of high value-added goods and services to stay behind (Frenkel, 1993:26). This follows the logic of commodity chains and regional divisions of labour. It has been occurring already. Stewart and Png (1993:2) have noted the example of Sumitomo Electric which has expanded "its wire harness manufacturing operations in Batam and Johor, while maintaining technical support facilities in Singapore." Similarly, Louis Kraar (1992) has reported that the Thomson Consumer Electronics of France makes components for TV sets in Malaysia and Indonesia and assembles them in its highly automated plant in Singapore. AT&T has recently formed a unit in Singapore to act as a regional centre for manufacturing research and development. Mitsubishi has been using the Singapore plant for international procurement operations, research and development, and technical support for other Mitsubishi plants in the Southeast Asian region (Teal, 1995). Such examples abound. The ones cited here are only to illustrate that labour-intensive production activities take place in Riau, skill-intensive activities in Johor, and research and development activities in Singapore.

Even though the concept of the growth triangle was initially proposed by the Singapore government and later endorsed officially by the governments of all three countries, it has always been depicted as a market-driven phenomenon. The official *Memorandum of Understanding* for cooperation among the governments of three countries was signed only recently on December 17, 1994. But cooperation through business networks and alliances have been taking place for a long time. In fact, private enterprises have had a considerable degree of involvement in intra-regional trade and investment prior to the establishment of growth triangle. But what is remarkable is that business has moved faster than bureaucracy in the aftermath of the formation of the economic growth triangle. Nevertheless, the regional division of labour was not so well defined earlier. In the new commodity chain arrangements supported by the regional division of labour, research and development, human resources, finance and marketing functions are to be located in Singapore and manufacturing operations are to be relocated elsewhere in the region. The other nodes of the growth triangle – Johor and Riau – are the logical places for the latter.

The regional division of labour specifies a pattern of vertical relationship in the commodity chains. It organically links the industrial expansion of neighbouring countries while helping Singapore to reduce its dependence on external markets and multinational corporations. However, it should be emphasized that the thrust of the growth triangle is based upon cooperation. If participating governments begin to evaluate costs and benefits in terms of economic nationalism, and national pride overtakes the agreed upon arrangements, then there is a danger of undermining the usefulness of the cooperative arrangements. Since each of the participating countries has ambition to eventually catch up with developed countries, arrangements based upon the regional division of labour may soon be questioned. In fact, Indonesia has recently raised the possibility of developing Batam as a high-tech centre rather than a place for labour-intensive, low value-added activities. This might have sent a warning signal to Singapore. It comes as no surprise that Singapore has already begun to promote the concept of regional diversification. In fact, Singapore firms are touted by the government for not going to far-away lands such as India and Vietnam at a faster pace.

7.4 Growth Triangles and Employment Relations

Nation-states have mostly provided an institutional framework for employment relations. However, the concept of the Growth Triangle rejects the idea of a nation-state (Rodan, 1993:237). As Ohmae (1993:78) has stated, "The nation state has become an unnatural, even dysfunctional, unit for organizing human activity and managing economic endeavour in a borderless world." A fundamental question now arises – what are the employment relations issues that arise from commodity chains and a regional division of labour in reference to the economic growth triangle? Since a particular node of the triangle is an enclave of the national economy, particularly in the cases of Malaysia and Indonesia, one could ask whether the evolving system of employment relations is insulated from the broader national patterns.

Relatively speaking, the nodes of a growth triangle will be the high-tech, high-value added, high-wage segments of the national economies. Also, since MNCs are the dominant players, each faces the pressures of the international marketplace insofar as the quality of products and flexibility in labour and product markets are concerned. Four potential strategies for labour market flexibility discussed in the literature are numerical flexibility, functional flexibility, pay flexibility, and working time flexibility. Numerical flexibility is the ability to respond to changes in demand and output by altering labour inputs. Mechanisms for altering labour inputs include part-time, temporary and short-term contract, as well as casual employment. Functional flexibility involves the broadening of tasks performed and skills deployed by employees. Pay flexibility means moving away from a strict time-based pay system to a productivity or performance-based pay system. Working time flexibility is mainly concerned with altering the traditional distribution of time. One could then hypothesize that the greater the extent of direct foreign investment by MNCs, the greater the extent of labour market flexibility characterized by the use of subcontracting and atypical forms of employment such as home-work, casual work, and part-time work to promote flexibility. One could also expect that the greater the inflows of foreign direct investment, the greater the pressure on a government to provide mechanisms for skill formation and skill development. If there is evidence to support these hypotheses, then a question arises whether flexibility has come at the cost of employment security.

The concept of the economic growth triangle was predicated on a trilateral government agreement for institutionalizing the cooperation arrangements. Following the downturn in the Singapore economy resulting in a negative growth rate of the gross domestic product in 1985, the Singapore government in 1986 mooted that because of limited domestic opportunities Singapore should invest to exploit opportunities in neighbouring countries. In line with this policy of regionalization, the triangle was first suggested by current Singapore Prime Minister Goh Chok Tong in 1989 as a way of providing a complete operating area for foreign investors that would allow each nation to benefit from development. However, this has not yet fully materialized. In fact, some observers have noted that the Malaysian government does not seem to be that interested in institutionalizing these arrangements. The state of Johor is the de facto party for negotiation regarding growth triangle arrangements. However, employment relations matter come explicitly under the federal jurisdiction in Malaysia. What then, should be the nature of public policies regarding employment relations in this special economic area? While businesses and governments have participated, formally or informally, in the formation of the triangle, labour is left to its own national jurisdiction. Its interest is therefore not represented at the regional level. Moreover, Indonesia and Malaysia are emerging as new NICs, whereas Singapore is already a NIC. Broadly speaking, industrial relations approaches of these two groups of countries differ, with the conflictual pattern being the predominant mode in the former and cooptation in the latter (Sharma, 1991). Will there be a more conflictual employment relations in firms operating in the Malaysian and Indonesian nodes of the economic growth triangle vis-a-vis firms operating in Singapore? The logic of complementarity of resources and capabilities implies that participating countries will have reached varying stages of industrialization. If different stages of industrialization lead to different patterns of industrial relations, what will be the dominant pattern in strategic economic cooperative zones such as the growth triangle, given that there is no attempt made towards harmonization of public labour policies? This will have significant bearing on the convergence-divergence debate. This debate concerns whether national systems will converge into one specific model, or diverge as the systems across countries are embedded in cultural, historical, and national idiosyncracies.

In the island of Karimun, which is targeted for development of a heavy-industrial centre by Singapore's Semgawang group and Indonesia's Salim group, there is already a shortage of skilled labour. As FDI continues to increase, there will be an acute shortage of workers in Batam, Bintan, and Johor Bahru as well. How have firms addressed the problem of skill shortage? Have they preempted local firms? Or, have they introduced their own training system? This shortage can be met by bringing migrant workers from Medan and other nearby areas. In fact, workers from other regions of Indonesia have begun to be attracted by the rapid development of Batam. With migrant workers come problems as well as opportunities. While there is the prospect of easying the pressure of a tight labour market on the one hand, there is a danger of having some undesirable social developments on the other. Migrant labour may contribute to the development of a segmented labour market. In the SIJORI triangle, this segmentation is also gender-based. For example, construction workers are largely male whereas domestics and factory workers are mostly female. Also, in view of the rather transitory nature of migrant labour, firms may put less emphasis on employee skill development at the plant level. If so, what are the consequences for skill development and flexibility?

The SIJORI area has enjoyed a very high rate of economic growth over the years, which has created distributional problems at various levels. At the national level, costs of living in the triangle segments of Malaysia and Indonesia have been increasing quite rapidly. Consequently, wages have also been increasing at high rates. For example, the minimum daily wage in Batam are already over 200 per cent of the national average minimum. This development has exacerbated the interprovincial migration problem, creating a "crowding-in" effect, often leading to the growth of shanty towns in some areas (Ahmad, 1993). In addition, a high level of foreign direct investment activities and associated labour market developments have led to growth of prostitution, degradation of the environment, and a lack of social development (*New Straight Times*, June 2, 1994:33), especially in Batam. The welfare of local people and their lifestyle have often been threatened. So far, such negative social externalities have gone almost unnoticed by policy makers.

The objective in making arrangements for strategic economic cooperation through growth triangles is to realize economic growth "out of proportion to the size of its local economy." Foreign direct investment is to play a key role in achieving this goal. As discussed earlier, several multinational corporations from various countries have already begun to participate in the growth triangle area. Have global corporations become the change agent in the triangle for employment practices? What kinds of firms practices, trade unions strategies (if there are trade unions at all), and public policies are necessary? How have employment relations been transformed in the triangle? What are the distributional issues associated with very high rates of economic growth within a particular segment of the national economy? These and other related issues need to be explored for an understanding of the nature of evolving labour and employment relations in the economic growth triangle. These labour issues are not trivial as they have important theoretical and policy implications.

7.5 Consequences for Theoretical Debates

There are debates regarding continuities and changes in employment relations throughout the world. Even though ambiguities abound (Hyman, 1994), these themes have recently been debated and analyzed in the tradition of three major theoretical strands: the new international division of labour (NIDL), the strategic choice framework (SCF), and the flexible specialization (FS). Employment issues related to the economic growth triangle need to be related to these debates if we are to gain insights into economic development.

In a world system characterized by a classical international division of labour, developed countries export finished goods to underdeveloped countries which supply raw materials, minerals, and agricultural commodities. However, with the globalization of production, a new international division of labour (NIDL) has evolved. Its major characteristics are: concentration and monopoly associated with the strategies of global corporations, export-oriented industrialization, collaboration of capital and state, and production switching to low-wage areas in response to a falling profit rate. The effect of the NIDL on employment relations include segmentation of workforces, repression of the working class, marginalization of employees, and the failure of a political response by trade unions to the actions of employers and governments (Southall, 1988). In this tradition, internationalization is one of the outcomes of the crisis of competitive capitalism. International firms establish their operations in low wage countries to take advantage of cheap labour and to avoid effective trade unionism so that the problem associated with falling rates of profits can be solved. Nevertheless, this contention of the NIDL school has been challenged as MNCs are known to shun poorer developing or least-developed countries (Kiely, 1994). Thus the interaction of international capital and local labour gives rise to the question whether there have been cases of compromise on security and protection of workers to serve the interest of capital alone. In this context, the question is whether Batam and Bintan become the havens for low-skill, low-wage sweatshops. Furthermore, as Hill (1989:184) has pointed out, "Global production systems cross-cut economic sectors and mesh discrete enterprises into larger systems. Contrary to conventional wisdom, comparative advantage is based less upon the activities of individual firms than upon the structure of whole production system." Hence the NIDL hypothesis proposes that there will be a vertical integration of production systems throughout the globe, with significant correspondence between production sites and product components. If this prediction of the NIDL hypothesis is correct, what strategic choices will labour have vis-a-vis governments and global corporations for promoting and protecting its interest?

Literature on production organization by international corporations draws a distinction between vertical and horizontal strategies (Porter, 1986; Gilpin, 1987). The NIDL is a case of vertical strategies, whereas the flexible specialization is a case of horizontal strategies. In the latter case, innovation and efficiencies are achieved through spatial agglomeration, and capacities to respond to market uncertainties created through continually reshaping the production process. Given the discussion of commodity chains and regional divisions of labour presented earlier, the growth triangle arrangement comes close to a strategy of low-cost production arrangement for global competitiveness in line with a vertical integration of production system where production activities are distributed among the three nodes. The strategy followed is a mixture of a high-value added and low-cost approach. This will also have implications for the flexible specialization thesis which foresees an end to mass production, and the beginning of a system of production based on flexible specialization supported by a horizontal integration of the production system (Piore and Sabel, 1984). Is there a case to be made, then, that a post-Fordist regime of employment relations is in the making in the more industrialized countries, while Fordism still dominates employment relations in less industrialized countries? Has globalization reinforced segmented employment relations? What are the prospects for convergence? In this context, the popularity and proliferation of economic growth triangles based upon complementarities among countries with varying levels of industrialization compel us to rethink the scope of the flexible specialization thesis itself.

The strategic choice framework (SCF), as proposed by Kochan, Katz and McKersie (1986), proposes at its core that (1) industrial relations decisions are made at three levels: business, collective bargaining and the workplace, (2) effective strategies are those that act in concert at all three levels, and (3) parties face a number of choices in adopting a suitable strategy. Thus the SCF captures the actions that each party may engage in to further its objectives through concerted action over a period of time. Such behaviour is termed strategic by its authors. Verma and Sharma (1992) have argued that if this framework is applied to the case of developing economies in an export-driven growth context, the implications are that the parties to industrial relations must act strategically. This would suggest that workplace changes must center towards policies such as training, employee involvement, sharing plans and flexible work organizations, with governments realigning their macro-level policies to adjust to the micro level changes demanded by markets. Are evolving employment relations consistent with the demands of global market place? What is the extent of this realignment in the context of economic growth triangles? These questions need empirically grounded answers, calling for appropriate research strategies.

In any case, the implications of industrialization strategies such as the one described here for theories of employment relations are far reaching. At least two things are clear. First, economic activities that are organized across national boundaries require a new conceptualization of employment relations (Castells and Aoyama, 1994). Secondly, policy makers need information and analysis of employment relations in a subregional economic area to arrive at sound policy decisions. However, a dearth of information on employment relations practices in certain nodes of growth triangle precludes them from doing so. At the same time, researchers do not seem to have raised their sights to develop new models of employment relations in relation to employment practices in the growth triangles.

7.6 Concluding Remarks

The dynamic economies of Asia successfully mobilized resources for different sectors to bring about rapid structural changes. This involved movement out of agriculture and into manufacturing – firstly, labour-intensive and then capital-intensive – activities. More recently, business and governments have come up with more sophisticated methods of resource mobilization for sustaining the process of rapid industrialization and for countering the pressure of global competitiveness. The growth triangle is one of such methods, and has thus become an important part of a larger argument for rapid industrialization in Asia.

The SIJORI growth triangle, as discussed in this paper, is an exercise in the economics of interdependence. Looking another way, this is a case of a Pan ASEAN international division of labour. Even though it was largely initiated by Singapore, it is embedded in broader industrialization strategies of participating countries very much along the line of strategic alliances formed by global corporations. This is because the concept is based on notions of complementarities and cooperation, and business networks have played a very crucial role in the development of the growth triangle. The economic growth strategy, as embedded in the concept of growth triangle, has become so popular in Southeast Asia that the second-tier NICs are beginning to take initiatives to look beyond their shores. One example of such a development is the "Makavi" triangle mooted by Malaysia. This triangle is supposed to link Malaysia with Cambodia and Vietnam. More recently, the concept of growth triangle has expanded to encompass more than three countries, leading to the formation of economic growth quadrangles. The example is the proposed golden quadrangle which includes parts of Burma, Laos, China, and Thailand (see Figure 7.1). The Philippines has been pushing for a growth quadrangle as well – the *East ASEAN Growth Area*, constituted of parts of the Philippines, Malaysia, Indonesia and Brunei. Even though they have been initiated by governments of respective countries, these arrangements are driven by markets and private sector businesses. While there is some discussion of the importance of this development for Asian industrialization, there is virtually no information regarding industrial relations and human resource practices of firms operating in growth triangles. However, the emphasis on developing an economic infrastructure for industry needs to be tempered with the need to develop an appropriate social infrastructure for the workforce.

Most of our models of employment relations are predicated around the argument that the regulatory framework for interest aggregation among stakeholders is nationally bounded. As politically defined national boundaries give away to economically integrated region states, like in Southeast Asia, old institutional mechanisms face a new challenge as well. Our quest must be to find out the nature of this challenge. In this quest, the SIJORI growth triangle has the potential to serve as a microcosm of newly evolving employment relations regimes in the emerging strategic economic areas in Asia. Given the importance of such arrangements for global competitiveness and community welfare, there is a need to further our understanding of this phenomenon.

8. The Social Embeddedness of Industrial District Networks

Udo Staber

8.1 Introduction

The ideal-typical industrial district describes agglomerations of mostly small and medium-sized firms working in close proximity (Piore and Sabel, 1984). The firms are highly specialized and they compete fiercely on price, service, and quality. But competition in industrial districts has a distinctively social flavor, in that firms are deeply embedded in a local social milieu. This milieu reflects cultural values and beliefs about the form and pattern of economic exchange. The firms in a district are expected to balance their commitment to collective purposes with their own, more specialized objectives. Producers are motivated to cooperate in the exchange of information relevant to risk-taking and continuous learning about new techniques and opportunities. Given these characteristics, the district model views cooperative networks of specialized firms as a viable alternative to mass production, with competitive consequences for the regions in which they are embedded (Piore and Sabel, 1984; Best, 1990).

The embeddedness of firms in a distinctive local social fabric is a key feature of the industrial district model. Social embeddedness encourages risk-taking and innovation, and enhances business success under conditions of uncertainty. If business owners fail, their experience is not lost, but can be applied elsewhere in the district. If they succeed, the district as a whole benefits, as innovations are diffused throughout the system. What the district model does not address, however, is how the actors in this system arrive at a particular pattern of competition and cooperation and how they interpret their position in the district network. The model does not explore the series of events and actions that shape and transform the underlying social fabric in the first place. Without an explanation of the processes by which actors come to see themselves as network participants the district concept of social embeddedness remains theoretically empty. In short, the idea of social embeddedness leads to important questions about how actors build an account of the network that forms the basis for behaving cooperatively and innovatively. Actors do not build such accounts in isolation. Sense-making takes place at the collective level, in that actors may or may not arrive at *shared* assumptions about the identity of their partners and the rules for coordinating individual decisions. Inter-firm networks in industrial districts are *socially* constructed, reflecting *collective* beliefs about economic exchange. But the district model, as it stands now, presents a static image of pre-existing social structures, and in doing so it reifies network relations. I propose to infuse the idea of social embeddedness with a greater concern for human agency, but not in the narrow terms of calculative rationality that is typical of standard economic approaches.

Institutional theory in sociology, as it is currently used, helps to explain the social construction of interfirm networks in industrial districts in a way that standard economic approaches cannot. Neo-classical economists, including those working within a transaction cost perspective (Williamson, 1985), have generally taken a rationalist and instrumentalist approach to designing institutional governance systems, such as interfirm networks. They argue that actors view the choice among institutional arrangements as part of an overall optimization problem, subject to efficiency pressures and information-processing limitations (Masten, 1986). By contrast, a sociologically informed institutional analysis focuses more on the cognitive and normative frameworks which give meaning and legitimacy to choices (Powell and DiMaggio, 1991; Zucker, 1987). From an institutional perspective, efficiency may not be a key motive in the design of industrial districts. Outcomes may be driven more by non-economic considerations, such as concerns for legitimacy, social justice, or political conformity. To account for the emergence, development, and transformation of district relations, it is thus important to understand the meaning that participation in networks has for the actors involved. Policy makers interested in regional economic development usually assume that district structures can be designed rationally and that these designs are transferable across industries and regions. But they tend to overlook the possibility that meaning systems are variable, nonrational, or unstable, and thus may have unexpected consequences for the form and stability of district relations. Institutional processes, which define such meaning systems, can be important sources of indeterminacy in the outcomes of strategic intervention.

Neo-institutional theory in sociology exists in several variants, but they all agree on the idea that organizations are embedded in a wider socio-political context.[1] Some approaches focus on institutional processes, but at different levels of analysis (an individual organization, organizational community, or society at large). Other approaches differ in terms of the particular institutional mechanisms and processes they emphasize. The district model applies to the organizational community level, but makes no distinction between types of institutions, nor is it explicit about the carriers of institutional processes. Indeed, most writers on industrial districts are not even explicit about the theoretical perspective they follow. When questions are asked about district structures and outcomes, the source of these questions are usually other theories, such as management and organization theories. District analysts generally do not ask how their perspective handles

1 For a comparison of traditional and neo-institutional theories in sociology, see Powell and DiMaggio (1991) and W. Scott (1995).

a particular theoretical problem, and so it is not clear what theoretical contribution the district model makes.[2] My objective in this chapter is to put the district model on a firmer theoretical footing by clarifying how it can be informed by concepts and propositions from institutional theory in sociology.

This chapter is structured as follows. First, I discuss balancing cooperation and competition as a core objective of institutional interventions in industrial districts. Next, I outline the social embeddedness approach to the study of business networks, contrasting it with standard economic approaches. I then place the idea of social embeddedness within an institutional-sociological framework, focusing on institutional elements, mechanisms, and carriers. Finally, I discuss the policy implications of this institutional view, and conclude with some comments about directions for further research.

8.2 Balancing Cooperation and Competition for Continuous Learning

Firms in the ideal-typical industrial district are mostly small or medium-sized, they each specialize in particular tasks, and are linked both horizontally and vertically through various forms of cooperation. Firms are integrated in a wider net of exchange relationships which may extend far beyond industry boundaries, although it is usually focused on a particular industry and is concentrated territorially.[3] The district brings together organizations that, in the aggregate, "constitute a recognized area of institutional life" (DiMaggio and Powell, 1983: 148) within a relatively narrow geographical space: producers, research institutes, trade associations, consultants, labor unions, development agencies, and other specialized service providers. Districts thus include not only producers, traditionally defined; they also include organizations which would normally not be considered part of the industry, but which are functionally interdependent with producers and among themselves. Functional interdependence (through the exchange of

2 Given this ambiguity it is somewhat questionable if the district approach has the status of a theoretical model. It may be more appropriate to consider it a broad conceptual framework for thinking about certain spatial relationships. We are given several concepts (such as continuous learning and social embeddedness) and some loose propositions (such as cooperation enhances permanent innovation), but no testable hypotheses. Without precise operational definitions of concepts, and without clear specifications of relationships between concepts, the "model" of industrial districts, as it stands now, is not falsifiable. With this caveat in mind, I will refer to the district approach as a model throughout the remainder of this chapter.

3 Examples of industry-focused districts include the fur district in Montreal (Canada), the knitwear district in Albstadt (Germany), the ceramic tile district in Sassuolo (Italy), and the tufted carpet district in Dalton (United States).

advice, technological know-how, personnel, money, political support, and so on) implies that the fate of an individual actor is tied to the performance of the district as a whole. As a result, producers and other organizations have a vested interest in local development and stable relations. By sourcing within the local area they contribute to endogenous economic development and to the region's economic self-sufficiency and political identity. Of course, interdependence and territorial concentration do not necessarily mean that all organizations will benefit equally. First-movers, for example, may be harmed by the ability of others to copy them. But the point of clustering is that managers may not know which organization will first innovate, so that all firms will be better off when locating together. This holds true especially in industries where innovations are unpredictable and scattered, and knowledge is mostly tacit.

That interfirm linkages are integrated locally does not necessarily mean they are rigid. On the contrary, integration creates opportunities for risk-taking and experimentation. According to the district model, embeddedness in the local social fabric fosters trust and facilitates social compromise and change in times of stress. Knowing that network partners can be relied upon to make available their resources (such as specialized expertise, personnel, and equipment), if needed, encourages firms to build highly specialized competencies, while accepting the dependencies that are associated with specialization. In networks of highly specialized firms, asset specificity (skills or equipment) raises the costs of exit, while interdependence strengthens actors' commitment to the network (Jarillo, 1988). When interdependence is high and information flows freely, opportunistic intentions of any one member of the network become known quickly. Interdependence thus discourages opportunism, even without normative pressures, but where norms of cooperation prevail opportunism is virtually ruled out.

Network forms of exchange seem especially appropriate when the value of transactions is difficult to measure and knowledge of production capabilities is mostly tacit and thus not easily tradable through markets or accessible by hierarchical fiat (Powell, 1990). In industries that demand rapid organizational and technological change, firms with problem-solving capability have innovative potential and thus have an advantage over those that merely imitate the leaders (Best, 1990). Cooperative network relations support problem solving by giving all actors access to new knowledge as it becomes available. As a result, the risks of innovation are not borne by specific producers, but are socialized across a variety of organizations. Districts that have such networks are flexible because each task (in research, production, marketing, and so on) can be organized with a different mix of specialized producers, depending on market conditions. District flexibility thus depends to a significant degree on interfirm cooperation.

But the district model favors cooperation only insofar as collaboration has competitive consequences. Successful industrial districts are characterized by intense competition along all dimensions of price, quality, and service. District members compete vigorously, but they define their self-interest collectively within the social context of the district. Porter (1990) describes how rivalry among local competitors pressures firms into developing skilled human resources, new technologies, and market-specific knowledge. Rivalry is very personal in the districts that Porter cites, pushing firms to engage in continuous innovation.[4] But he also notes the willingness of firms to collectivize knowledge and to contribute to common pools of expertise, following a particular understanding of collective needs in the district. When "the exchange and flow of information about the needs, techniques, and technology among buyers, suppliers, and related industries ... occurs at the same time that active rivalry is maintained in each separate industry, the conditions for competitive advantage are most fertile" (Porter, 1990: 152). Thus, successful industrial districts feature a dynamic balance of competition and cooperation which gives producers in such systems an advantage over those that pursue either externalization (market) or internalization (organizational hierarchy) strategies. Successful districts are driven by a "learning dynamic," in that firms are constantly modifying their behavior and developing new solutions in reaction to the moves of district partners (Maillat, 1995).

The appropriate balance, according to the district model, is best achieved if actors are spatially concentrated. Geographic proximity promotes mutual trust and partnership, but it also encourages continuous innovation through direct rivalry. This view is in stark contrast to the standard agglomeration theory on business networks. The agglomeration approach treats spatial proximity as a necessary condition for obtaining external scale economies. By clustering territorially, small firms can minimize the transaction costs associated with transportation, communication, labor recruitment, and so on. But from a social embeddedness perspective, co-location implies an additional quality, of a sort that gives firms the incentive to interact in a trustworthy manner. Geographic proximity is the basis for intense interpersonal interaction which controls the flow of attention to the actions of network players. The presence of strong social bonds distinguishes industrial districts from other, more instrumentally oriented production agglomerations, where co-location is valued mostly for the realization of external scale economies and where producers see themselves as independent competitors.

In summary, the industrial district model views social embeddedness as the key to what would normally be considered a contradictory combination of competition and cooperation. Of course, most other perspectives on business networking, including standard agglomeration theory, would agree that most firms (especially the smaller ones) are embedded in their local environment, certainly in compari-

4 In their study of competitive relations among Scottish knitwear producers, Porac et al. (1995: 224) show that the definition of these relations takes place at a very personal level. The form and extent of rivalry is socially constructed in the minds of managers. "While markets are arenas for economic transactions, at their core are routinized thought patterns and interlocked networks of managerial attention."

son to absentee-owned branch plants (Bade, 1983). But the district model posits a very strong form of embedding, capable of reproducing sustained cooperation in a dynamic production system. The concept of social embeddedness (Granovetter, 1985) cautions researchers that it is not always possible to decouple the economic process of innovation from its social structural and local institutional base. District-type entrepreneurs, for example, fit the Schumpeterian image only insofar as they are the originators and movers of novel ideas. But whether their energies are promoted or stifled by the economic context in which they operate depends largely, from the district perspective, on the social connections that provide access to new information in the first place. Building and maintaining those connections involves institutional processes, as discussed further below.

8.3 The Social Embeddedness Approach to Networking

Sociologists take as axiomatic the proposition that economic action, including business behavior in industrial districts, is embedded in interpersonal networks (Friedland and Robertson, 1990; Swedberg, 1990). In their struggle to create and maintain a place for themselves in industrial districts, social networks are crucial assets for business owners.[5] Networking allows them to enlarge their scope of action, economize on time, and gain access to resources and opportunities otherwise unavailable (Staber and Aldrich, 1995). But what kinds of networks do owners construct, given the district environment in which they are embedded?

The standard neo-classical economic answer to this question is that owners build and transform their networks pragmatically, without much attention to habit or convention. The standard economic model describes business owners as individuals who fearlessly enter unfamiliar territory and seek advice and resources from whomever might be willing to provide them. Social networks are viewed as a means of obtaining access to resources with exchange value: they may be used to enhance upward mobility, to maximize economic gain, or to obtain technological knowhow. Business owners view information as a commodity and networks as the marketplace in which information is traded. Because owners, as individual gain-maximizers, are interested in making the best deals possible, they pick members of their network on an efficiency basis, acquiring and discarding network mem-

5 Because industrial districts are agglomerations of mostly *small* firms one would expect their owners to be directly involved in enterprise management. Hence, it is appropriate to couch the analysis of district networks in terms of the *interpersonal* relations that owners (and managers) have with others in the district. Of course, this is equally true for other business networks as well. Organizations are linked through relations among "boundary spanners," and in that sense all interorganizational networks are *social* networks.

bers as needed, given evolving circumstances. Strong ties, such as those built on intimate friendship and long-standing relations, are viewed as clouding people's vision and constraining their abilities to make pragmatic business decisions. Social ties that are infused with non-economic notions such as equity, loyalty, and tradition are viewed, from the standard economic perspective, as *constraints* on efficient exchange.[6]

This reasoning is consistent with transaction cost theory in economics (Williamson and Ouchi, 1981; Williamson, 1985). To cooperate, owners must develop contractual rules to govern their exchange relationships. The costs of creating the rules for negotiating, monitoring, and enforcing incurred in this contracting process are called transaction costs. These may be particularly problematic in environments that place a premium on innovation and risk-taking, as in the ideal-typical industrial district. Under conditions of environmental uncertainty (which limits predictability of exchange and disrupts mutual expectations) and actors' bounded rationality, the risk of opportunism (which is assumed to be ever present) limits the stability of cooperative behavior and motivates the search for other, more efficient, forms of exchange. Thus, one would expect network relations to be of short duration, as the actors fear being exploited by people motivated by short-term gain. Business owners, from this perspective, will rely on social networks only to the extent that they minimize transaction costs. Evidence supporting this view of business networking comes from research on the high dissolution rates of R&D consortia in the United States (Aldrich and Sasaki, 1995b), joint ventures in US manufacturing industries (Harrigan, 1988; Kogut, 1988), and marketing cooperatives in Canada (Staber, 1992). Kogut (1988: 184) argued that many of the disbanded joint ventures he studied are the result of a "fundamental instability in governance," indicative of actors behaving opportunistically under conditions of uncertainty.

These studies, however, are of interfirm cooperation outside the context of industrial districts. District relations are expected to be more stable, because they are embedded in a social milieu which rewards cooperation. Transaction cost theory has been criticized for downplaying the wider social context in which economic transactions are embedded (Granovetter, 1985). Transaction cost reasoning tends to be best at explaining relations between pairs of actors (as, for example, in narrowly focused joint ventures), given its individual unit of analysis and a focal organization perspective, but it is less successful at explaining the structure and development of cooperation in networks that are deeply embedded in a social and

6 Neo-classical approaches have paid surprisingly little attention to business networking. They assume that networks appear whenever opportunities arise. Hence, my outline of the neo-classical model of networking is based on an extrapolation from what such theorists have said about other forms of economic behavior (see also Granovetter, 1985).

historical context. Industrial districts with a long history of business cooperation furnish such a context.

Transaction cost reasoning emphasizes efficiency and competition, and downplays the ties that bind actors together and enable collective action, but as Granovetter (1993: 16) noted, "human nature is not isolated from the rest of social structures, interactions, and institutions." From the standard economic perspective, information is exchanged in networks as a commodity. However, from an embeddedness perspective, information can also be seen as a product of social relations which provide access to information in the first place and which give it meaning. An economic analysis of business networking cannot be separated from an understanding of the social context in which business relations are embedded. From an embeddedness perspective, business owners behave rationally and instrumentally if they conduct their activities through social networks, because all economic action is infused with social motives and because economic actors are never wholly atomized in economic life. Embeddedness in social structures may explain why network arrangements may persist in situations where, at first glance, other forms of governance (such as open markets) may appear more efficient.

The idea of social embeddedness figures prominently in neo-institutional theories of organizational behavior (Zucker, 1988). Whereas standard economic theory neglects the power of close ties in attenuating opportunism in economic exchange, institutional theories highlight the socio-political context in which business strategies, including network strategies, are enacted. Mutual trust, social expectations, and the force of tradition and history may be powerful mechanisms for blunting opportunistic motives and preventing the breakdown of cooperative relations.

The significance of trust for economic exchange in an industrial district is that it removes the fear of taking risks when interacting with partners who might behave opportunistically. Believing in the reliability and commitment of other actors encourages business owners to make risky investments, to pass on novel ideas, to exchange valued personnel, and so on. Trust is important in all economic exchange (Axelrod, 1984; Granovetter, 1985), especially when business activities involve uncertainty, resources are scarce, and information is limited. In dynamic networks of specialized firms, as in industrial districts, trust may be considered a lubricant that encourages and facilitates the mutual adjustment of strategies and competencies. In that sense, trust is a key resource for holding district networks together. District actors conform to rules of network conduct not because it serves their individual interests (narrowly defined as calculative rationality), but because it is expected of them. They are socially obliged to trust their partners.

Trust does not come naturally to most business owners and managers, including those who are embedded in district networks. Trust has to be learned, and such learning takes time. While a minimum degree of trust may be constitutive of all economic exchange (Sabel, 1992), it can never be taken for granted but has to be reproduced constantly. This is especially true in networks that reward innovation and change, as those in industrial districts. Trust is facilitated by actors' personal reputations and histories as reliable and committed network partners. Some people have such reputations, others do not. But trust can also be learned, under certain conditions. Recurring transactions, for example, or even the belief that transactions will be repeated, set expectations and create opportunities for discovering a potential partner's integrity and willingness to invest in long term relations. In time, recurring exchanges become increasingly structured and implict rules for continued cooperation may emerge (Larson, 1992). The eventual outcome may be a network of individuals who are prepared to forego opportunities to abuse the trust bestowed upon them. Standard economic theory cannot easily account for such outcomes.

From a social embeddedness perspective, trust is a property of the relationship, rather than the person. Ongoing economic relationships have social content that leads to expectations for further dealings, independent of network members' personal attributes. Trust-building is usually difficult to achieve over long distances because of the need for face-to-face interaction (Lipparini and Sobrero, 1994). Personal contacts encourage the informal communication of ideas and ensure that technical and market information is diffused rapidly among "customers, suppliers, and competitors with the region, continually paving the way for new opportunities and enterprises," as Saxenian (1990: 97) found in her case study of Silicon Valley small business networks.

Transaction cost theorists might consider geographic proximity as facilitating efficient exchange, independent of actors' belief in the legitimacy of the exchange. But efficiency may only be a secondary issue, if actors question the fairness of what is to be learned. Proximity alone does not explain why economic actors should trust one another and engage in sustained exchange, even if they share a belief in efficiency as a basis for compliance. The question is, why should potential trusting parties trust a business person's claim that a relationship "will work out," given that this person may be no more than a fool looking for opportunities where none exist (Aldrich and Fiol, 1994)? Trust may also have unintended consequences. Close connections with business partners and other resource persons may lead to trust which may create opportunities for malfeasance and manipulation (Granovetter, 1992). Persons who are strongly embedded in tight-knit communities may be quite vulnerable to "being taken for a ride" by others in whom they place trust. How widely and quickly malfeasance spreads in the community depends partly on the social structure of the wider network, especially its density and connectivity. One may imagine a close-knit business network in which, say, new business founders find it easy to raise capital, attract workers, and contract with suppliers not because there is general trust but because trust is enforceable through the ability of network members to confer unique rewards (Portes and Sensenbrenner, 1993). The group's sanctioning capacity may be used either to legitimize malfeasance (as in corruption schemes and insider trading arrangements), or it may be used to police unacceptable behavior. The same social structures that support innovative business behavior can also divert it from its original objectives.

In either case, one would expect socially embedded networks to be fairly resistant to change. Because business ownership is always fraught with a certain degree of risk, especially in industries that place a premium on innovation and change, one would expect owners to rely on networks with a core of close personal relations, built on ties of reciprocal interdependence, and a periphery of weaker ties assembled on a more ad hoc basis. At the center of business networks will be people owners have known for years: friends, family, school mates, and former co-workers. These intimate connections provide the social support needed to weather crises and economic hardship, as in those Italian industrial districts that have a significant "informal sector" (Murray, 1987). Many small businesses in Italian districts are connected by a sense of "familism" which defines the terms of competition and cooperation (Orru, 1991). The persistence of networks based on kinship relations is difficult to explain with standard economic theory.

In summary, the concept of social embeddedness offers a corrective to standard agglomeration theory and neo-classical economic theory by treating social relations, rather than individual actors, as the unit of analysis. Yet, the concept remains theoretically vague because it is silent on the *content* of social relations. Without knowing the meaning (i.e., the interpretations, beliefs, and motives which evolve in a particular institutional context) that actors attach to their participation in a network it is impossible to predict their behavior in relation to network partners. The content of social relations gives meaning to the word trust. The concept of social embeddedness is also silent on the *mechanisms* by which social structures constrain or facilitate economic action. It is also not clear what the *carriers* are through which social expectations exert their influence on network actors.

The concept of social embeddedness merely highlights the idea that all economic behavior is overlaid with social content which gives each network and district its particular shape and dynamic, but it does not explain how the actors construct relations and how they interpret the meaning of relations. In the end, the embeddedness concept is as static and rational-individualist as standard economic approaches to the role of territory and proximity in collective learning and development. Many case studies of industrial districts end with the conclusion that districts have evolved along *unique* trajectories because of each district's social and cultural distinctiveness. Some writers argue that, despite unique developmental trajectories, it is possible to identify a "common underlying system of structural dynamics," revolving around a social division of labor or the formation of external economies in geographic proximity (A. Scott, 1988a: 181). But the mechanisms by which such dynamics unfold, and the carriers of these mechanisms, are usually left unexplored. Neo-institutional theory in sociology offers some insights and helps put the concept of social embeddedness on a stronger theoretical footing. In doing so, it also guides further research on the institutional structures and processes of industrial districts.

8.4 Institutional Structures and Processes in District Relations

Table 8.1 summarizes the key elements of an institutional perspective on business networks in the ideal-typical district and contrasts these with the standard market approach to networking. These two models of the social organization of networks may be gleaned from the general distinction between markets and networks as principal modes (in addition to internal organizational hierarchies) of governing economic exchange. This distinction is so well known (for a summary, see Powell, 1990) that I can pass over these modes quickly. The central idea in this chapter is that business networks in industrial districts have a particular *social* quality which is distinct from the social content of market relations and which is best explained from an institutional perspective.

Table 8.1 Stylized comparison of an institutionalist and a market perspective on business networks

Key Features	Market View	Institutionalist View
Key actors	Firms,entrepreneurs	Communities, clans, families, professions
Principal motives	Material benefits, private gain	Collective identity, collective gain
Normative foundation	Property rights, constitutional rights	Customary practices, cultural correctness
Basis of compliance	Expedience, efficiency	Social obligation
Guiding principle of coordination	Dispersed competition	Solidarity, local cooperation
Ideational resources	Calculative rationality	Trust

What distinguishes the ideal-typical district from standard business agglomerations and networks is its "social atmosphere" (Marshall, 1890), evident in culture and tradition, as opposed to the competitive allocation of resources in market-driven networks. The guiding principles of market and institutional approaches are often not rendered explicit and tend to get lost in abstract descriptions of districts having a unique balance of cooperation and competition. At the core of the different assumptions about actors, resources, mechanisms, and normative foundations lie the central and controversial questions of what motivates actors to participate in networks and what makes them accept the collective outcomes of their economic efforts. In the ideal-typical district, actors seek a sense of belonging to the community and are interested in building a distinctive collective identity. Participation in networks is both a source and outcome of these motives. In the ideal-typical market-driven network, by contrast, actors seek to maximize their individual profits and other material benefits arising from competition. Neither of these orders is intrinsically harmonious or conflict-free. Market-driven networks have to cope with the basic conflict of interest between buyers and sellers, and have to settle the conflicting claims of constituency groups. District-type networks have the general problem of deciding what behaviors are to be considered "culturally correct" and how social obligations are to be formulated and enforced. Both types of networks have to deal with questions of regulation: what are the appropriate regulative processes for rule-setting, monitoring, and sanctioning behaviors?

The concept of institution has been used and interpreted by social theorists in a number of ways, which makes it difficult to speak of *the* institutional theory, as if it were an intellectually integrated enterprise. In summarizing the literature, W. Scott (1994; 1995) distinguishes between three components and three carriers of institutions. Both, components and carriers, are evident in industrial districts, although district analysts have generally not made the relevant distinctions explicit. This inattentiveness to institutional variations accounts for some of the theoretical vagueness of the so-called district model. I first discuss institutional elements with respect to the mechanisms by which they exert their influence on district relations. I then turn to the carriers of these elements.

8.4.1 Institutional Elements and Mechanisms of Control

"Institutions consist of cognitive, normative, and regulative structures and activities that provide stability and meaning to social behavior" (W. Scott, 1995: 33). In practice, these elements are often interwoven, although their individual weight may vary in different contexts. Each element is also associated with a distinct mechanism of control (DiMaggio and Powell, 1983).

The *regulative* element of institutions constrains behavior so that it conforms to expected rules of conduct. This is perhaps the institutional element with which economists are most comfortable, and which tends to be stressed in most discussions of district design. On the assumption that individuals are instrumentally motivated and make choices on a cost-benefit basis, economists are interested in explaining how individuals can be brought to obey rules. A stable district, from this perspective, is one whose rules are backed by a system of rewards and penalties. The question of interest then is, what type of system and agencies (e.g., public or private, individual entrepreneurs or collective groups) can most expediently enforce the rules.

Sociologists interested in the regulative aspects of institutions are also attentive to issues of fairness and justice. Enforcement mechanisms are effective not only if backed by sanctioning power, but also if they are supported by a belief in the legitimacy of rules and sanctions. That is, regulative institutions are effective if they are *endorsed* by subordinates, because they accept rules as fair or reasonable. The question of interest then is, what conditions lead to the emergence of regulative institutions that will support a stable and endorsed order in industrial districts.

In a situation where endorsement from below cannot be counted upon or where actors behave instrumentally, in a narrow calculative sense, regulation implies some degree of *coercion*. Coercive pressures may lead business owners in districts to affiliate with others because they are compelled to do so. Pressures may be formal or informal. Network affiliations may be mandated by government bodies, as in the case of businesses having to affiliate with their local chamber of commerce. Or, businesses may be forced to comply with practices or "strategic visions" determined by headquarters, as in the case of local owners of franchises connected to distant parent companies. Or, pressures to conform to institutional expectations may be felt as persuasion, as when association leaders appeal to their members' sense of solidarity. In each case, coercive forces ensure that business owners accommodate their preferences to external demands. To the extent that these demands are similar or are controlled by an elite of rule makers, coercive pressures may lead to a fairly homogeneous network in terms of the content of collective action. But group solidarity, if achieved coercively, is not an outcome of shared sentiments, loyalty, or moral obligation. Rather, solidarity results from the group's, or an external agent's, sanctioning capacity. Trust, thus generated, is tied to the ability of the community to confer on its members unique rewards or punishments. Actor orientations, in this case, are primarily utilitarian, motivated not so much by value convictions, but by the anticipation of obtaining rewards associated with "good standing" in the community (Portes and Sensenbrenner, 1993). Rewards and sanctions may be nonmaterial (e.g., reputation, public honor, and shame), but they may also have material consequences (e.g., opportunities to develop new competences or to discover new markets).

The *normative* aspects of districts define the objectives of network relations (e.g., sharing available resources in times of economic stress), as well as the means of pursuing these objectives (e.g., absorbing some of the partner firms' redundant workforce). The normative system introduces a prescriptive, evaluative, and obligatory dimension into the life of industrial districts, which is usually missing in standard economic accounts. Normative rules are important because they act as constraints on behavior, but they can also be seen as facilitating action. Not only do they structure choices, they also enable choices, as in some Danish districts where any kind of entrepreneurial activity is viewed with admiration (Kristensen, 1994). Preexisting normative systems can empower business owners to try out new relations, to improvise, and to venture into unknown market territory. A question of interest is how such norms arise in the first place and, once they exist, how actors can be brought to conform to them or to make use of them.

DiMaggio and Powell (1983) refer to the mechanisms by which normative systems are diffused as normative, to distinguish them from the coercive powers of regulative institutions. In industrial districts, normative processes are evident, for example, in the role of labor market flexibility and personnel exchange. Districts include dynamic networks of businesses and service providers who employ and depend upon mobile workforces, with skills that are industry (or district) rather than firm specific. The literature on Italian districts indicates that firms make extensive use of workforce flexibility by sharing personnel or by outsourcing personnel as the need arises. In this way, labor mobility and flexibility facilitates the diffusion of norms and technical know-how. Personnel movement serves as a filtering device, diffusing similar business strategies, organizational procedures, worker competencies, and understandings of normative rules. The circulation of personnel thus ensures that the local culture is reproduced and transformed to fit evolving circumstances.

Finally, some institutionalist theorists emphasize the *cognitive* aspects of institutions, which constitute the "meat" of social relations. A cognitive conception of institutions stresses the meaning that network connections have for the actors involved. The usual approach in the district literature is to *infer* from the observed pattern of connections the meaning that these ties have for the individuals involved. But this practice can lead to a misunderstanding of the origins and transformations of structural relationships (DiMaggio, 1992). Without an understanding of the motives and cognitions that underly structures, the structural outcomes of networking can easily be misinterpreted as indicating strategic intentions when many other outcomes are equally probable. The cognitive aspects of network structures are important especially when the relations to be explained are transformational, network boundaries are fluid, and information is limited. Under conditions of uncertainty, network structures are not fixed for long and rules of conduct are never fully institutionalized or taken for granted. They are the subject of constant negotiation and renegotiation. These are the conditions of industrial districts, where cooperative strategies are mixed with competitive pressures. Ideal-typical district structures are dynamic, and strategies are fluid.

A purely structural analysis of district relations risks losing sight of the human agents who interpret meanings, modify rules, and articulate preferences (W. Scott, 1994). The question is, why do normative expectations not always lead to active cooperation? Why do some understandings become institutionalized, and why do others get abandoned? Why do different normative rules and regulative powers in different contexts sometimes lead to similar outcomes, and vice versa? Why do particular practices diffuse throughout a district in ways not predicted by the role and structure of organizations adopting them? Empirical research on industrial districts has not addressed these questions directly. What we do know from case studies is that each district represents a "unique configuration of social and political life, which means that each is also caught up in a unique developmental trajectory" (A. Scott, 1988a: 181). But how these configurations become institutionalized and, possibly, deinstitutionalized is usually not explored.[7]

7 Orru's (1991) study of small firm networks in Italy and Taiwan is a useful step in this direction. His account points to factors (political, cultural, financial, and economic) which

The mechanisms by which cognitive elements of institutions are diffused throughout an organizational community are referred to as *mimetic* (DiMaggio and Powell, 1983). Mimetic processes exist when actors imitate other actors. Business owners are especially likely to copy models under conditions of uncertainty. When technologies are poorly understood, when markets are new, or when preferences are unclear, modelling may be a viable solution. In an information vacuum, business owners will look for direction outside of their organizational boundaries and may find themselves pursuing options that have little to do with technical efficiency. They will tend to imitate businesses in their area that they perceive to be successful, as Galaskiewicz and Wasserman (1989) found in their study of corporate donations in a community of non-profit organizations. The question is, how do owners know which organizations are worth imitating. Most likely, they will rely on existing network connections, but there is no guarantee that these connections are the most useful ones if actors rely only on those partners they trust.

Models may be diffused in a variety of ways. Business associations set standards for their members; trade fairs provide a forum for information exchange; employees are transferred to another firm in the network; or former employees set up their own business. Movement of personnel, discussed above as a normative device, also ensures that individuals become exposed to different organizational settings, where they can meet individuals with different identities and competencies. If such movement cuts across all organizations in the district it creates opportunities for the emergence of a larger collective sentiment, permeating the entire district and giving it a distinct identity. But if industrial districts include an array of highly specialized organizations, the number of available models may be quite low *within* any particular functional area. Thus, for any given activity – say, marketing a particular service, rather than marketing in general – one would expect that the organizations engaged in that activity are fairly homogeneous in their blueprints for action and that these blueprints are not easily copied by other organizational forms.

To summarize, an institutional explanation of governance systems in industrial districts calls for greater attention to the *processual* aspects of creating structures in a context of bounded rationality and constant change. Individual actors do not simply conform to external structures. Although they may feel the pressure of social obligations and regulative constraints, they also resist and manipulate. Or, they may differ in opinion about the form and intensity of networking, despite general consensus on the benefits of networking, as Sydow (in this volume) found in his study of network formation in a community of insurance brokers. Network structures constrain choices and steer interests, but they are also

have led to similar outcomes in both countries, although they varied in their specific combinations. The analysis also indicates the flaws of models which build on discrete variables and assume unidirectional influences and predictable outcomes.

transformed through action. Actors are continually involved in interpreting, transmitting, and modifying meanings (Geertz, 1973). For practitioners, this institutional view opens up possibilities for strategic action, permitting multiple paths of district development. For theorists, it curbs the tendency to propose deterministic explanations for evolutionary trajectories (W. Scott, 1994).

8.4.2 Carriers of Institutional Processes

The regulative, normative, and cognitive elements of institutions are borne by a number of carriers. W. Scott (1995) focuses on three carriers, social structure, culture, and routines (see also Jepperson, 1991, for a somewhat different formulation), and suggests that they can be found with each of the three institutional elements.

Social structure reflects the fact that expectations (whether they are regulative, normative, or cognitive) are patterned, rather than distributed randomly. Structures are the medium through which expectations are enacted. Thus, they both constrain and facilitate action (Giddens, 1987). Network structures determine, for example, if every actor can be reached by everyone else, if some actors can reach more than others, or if a subgroup of actors interact only among each other. With knowledge of structural patterns one can infer other phenomena, such as the sharing of cognitive interpretations and the similarity of business strategies. Stylized accounts of Italian districts tend to infuse the idea of geographic proximity with social-structural meaning. For example, Becattini's (1989b: 132) analysis of what makes districts "tick" refers to a "*tangled web* ... of historical and cultural vestiges, which envelops both inter-firm and interpersonal relationships [emphasis mine]." But the structure of such webs, such as their density, centrality, and connectivity, is usually not explored.

The structure of a district's institutional context can be understood in terms of the foci around which business owners organize their relations with partners. This approach borrows from Simmel's (1955) idea of society consisting of loosely connected social circles of relationships. A district can be viewed as a set of circles and individual actors, where each actor is related to others within the same circle and the circles intersect to some degree. Any given circle is likely to include actors who are affiliated with other circles, and these connections serve to link circles. Feld (1981) discusses circles with reference to particular foci of interest. He defines a focus as any entity (such as social, legal, and physical) around which joint activities are organized. One may also define a focus institutionally, in terms of the weight given to regulative, normative, and cognitive elements. Each focus is the basis of clustered behavior, connecting individuals with joint interests. But to the extent that individuals have several affiliations, networks cannot be understood without attention to an individual's relations to extra-network foci. In the case of industrial districts, this requires analysis of all organizations in the region that serve as foci around which business ties are formed.

In his study of new business ventures and entrepreneurial networks in the Boston Route 128 high-technology cluster, Nohria (1992) identified a number of organizations that serve as focus groups. They include business clubs, professional associations, universities, and venture funds. Some of these organizations have over time spun off new foci, creating new business circles and thus shaping the evolution of the region's business networks. Today, this technology cluster includes a large number of highly specialized actors. In other districts, different types of institutions serve as prominent foci. In Baden-Württemberg, Germany, it is primarily chambers of commerce, trade associations, and educational organizations which bring firms together. Chambers of commerce (IHKs) represent all firms at the local level, collect trade statistics, set industry norms and standards, and administer training programs (Boelcke, 1987). Regional trade associations serve similar functions. The chambers' and associations' broad scope places them in a strategic position as overlapping foci. There are also a large number and variety of educational organizations in Baden-Württemberg which act as foci for the exchange of information, personnel, and technical know-how (Cooke and Morgan, 1993). In Italian districts, it is political associations and local government bodies that serve as important focus groups (Trigilia, 1986). In New Hampshire, discussion forums have been conducted as focus groups to bring together public officials, enterprise managers, and representatives from the educational sector (Gittell et al., in this volume). In Southern California, institution-building to promote an advanced ground transportation production complex involves a number of community organizations and technology research centers (Scott and Bergman, in this volume).

While organizations of various sorts can serve an important structural function, by bringing together actors from different circles, they do not necessarily create the kind of "community spirit" that is said, from the district perspective, to "bind" the actors socially. Structuralist theorists focus on the pattern of interfirm relations, but downplay the cultural content and meaning of the connections which give rise to focus organizations in the first place and which define the "logics" of particular foci and relations. Institutionalist theorists, by contrast, are interested mainly in the interpretive schemes which inform structural patterns.

Interpretive schemes are reflected in the belief systems, or *cultures*, within which network relations are embedded. These belief systems, which tend to be customary in character, provide the meaning that participation has for network actors. Some accounts of industrial districts describe small firm districts as "milieus" and emphasize their spontaneous and emergent qualities (Maillat and Lecoq, 1992). Porter (1990: 225) talks about clusters of firms having a particular "subculture" with "organic" qualities which, because they are hard to replicate, create sustainable advantages. Local cultures, as carriers of institutions, provide the foundation for ongoing business relationships and give meaning to the idea of trust.[8]

One may imagine a variety of "meaning systems" (W. Scott, 1994) which support cooperative exchange. Some of these have been identified, typically in passing only, by district analysts. For example, in his study of labor market segmentation in Italian apparel districts, Taplin (1989: 418) refers to "familism ... [as] a significant normative (and structuring) principle of industrial organization." There may be a significant amount of self-exploitation in family firms (with people working long hours for low pay), but accepted conventions of mutual assistance also provide a cushion in times of economic stress. In the case of Baden-Württemberg, it is often argued that this state's economic success after World War II has much to do with a particular brand of pietism, evident in small business owners' and workers' industriousness, reliability, commitment to quality, and cooperative work ethos. These values interact with another set of values revolving around individualism and autonomy. Baden-Württemberg has a long tradition of political liberalism which emphasizes local self-government, state decentralization, and private self-government through interest associations (Sedatis, 1979). Combined with a long history of artisanship (which in this case means technical ingenuity, quality, and attention to detail), political institutions and religious belief systems are said to produce the particular mix of cooperation and competition that has propelled Baden-Württemberg to become one of the leading economic regions in Europe (Boelcke, 1986). Religion also figures prominently in some Italian small firm districts, where deeply-rooted Catholic subcultures provide a basis for social compromise and economic flexibility. Religious ties, according to some accounts, sustain community values which span social classes and thus play an integrative role in dynamic districts (Trigilia, 1986). Similar arguments have been put forth concerning the effects of "Catholic milieus" on interfirm networking in the Le Choletais region in France (Hardill et al., 1995). The difference, however, is that in the Third Italy religious belief systems are tempered by a secular "civic culture" (Putnam, 1993: 88), which is not the case in Le Choletais.

Kinship relations, religious beliefs, and political traditions are not the only possible meaning systems supporting business cooperation. A study of employment

8 At a time of market globalization, strategies that seek competitive advantages in *local* social relations and traditions seem to be curiously out of place. But some interpretations of "modernism" and globalization emphasize important discontinuities in the development of modern society, leaving room for local deviations from global trends. Giddens (1987), for example, argues that modernism permits ambivalence, including the possibility of returning to earlier forms of space-time relations. His idea of "re-embedding" is consistent with what some observers have termed a "renaissance" of regional economies (Sabel, 1989). Whether current trends are in the direction of localization or globalization, and what the prospects are for industrial districts in modern societies, has been the subject of considerable debate (Amin, 1993).

systems in the New England fishing industry, for example, found that in certain communities economic decisions about who gets hired and how available work is assigned are embedded in the ethnic character of boat ownership and crew membership (Doeringer et al., 1986). Ethnicity informs collective arrangements, with competitive outcomes for vessel owners, workers, and communities by encouraging a level of effort, commitment, and flexibility that is hard to obtain under more individualistic forms of organization. In other districts, it is professional norms which are believed to give meaning to economic exchange. In her description of social cohesion among Silicon Valley entrepreneurs Saxenian (1990) refers to shared professional experiences, loyalties, friendships, and respect. These elements are sustained over time as individuals move between firms and industries within the region. The professional culture, Saxenian argues, has created a distinct language which would not be understood by counterparts in other high-tech districts.

Kristensen (1994) explains the unique development of particular districts in Denmark with reference to the influence of "spectator communities" which provide the meaning context within which entrepreneurial activities are interpreted and legitimized. Such communities can have powerful effects on the direction of entrepreneurship and network evolution in particular locales, even in a country as small as Denmark whose national institutions and political strategies would normally be expected to produce general patterns throughout the country. In some communities, entrepreneurial activity is regarded with suspicion, and business failure is interpreted as confirmation that not everyone can succeed. In other communities, entrepreneurial efforts are viewed with admiration. Business founders are celebrated and those who fail are encouraged to make their experiences available to other potential founders.

Historical accounts of industrial districts turn up diverse cultural sources of social ties, including religious beliefs, artisanship, ethnicity, and professionalism. "Cultural correctness" (Table 8.1) can have many faces and can be shaped in many different ways. "Under the right circumstances, it would appear, almost any set of common experiences can form the basis of a common culture" (Zeitlin, 1992: 287). There are a variety of meaning systems that can support cooperative exchange and stabilize network relations. It is exactly this variety which has led many researchers to view industrial districts as unique historical structures which cannot be replicated elsewhere. Exceptional cultures can give the region a sustainable competitive advantage because such cultures are difficult to emulate. But the question is, if interfirm cooperation is an important problem to be solved, and if there are various possible institutional solutions, then why *this* particular solution, and not another? Why do different districts generate different solutions? Institutional solutions do not emerge routinely. Rather, institutional responses to particular problems arise in a context of constrained choices, ambiguous preferences, and imperfect information. But district analysts have generally ignored such complications.

The third carrier of institutions are *routines*, which W. Scott (1995: 54) defines as "patterned actions that reflect the tacit knowledge of actors -deeply ingrained habits and procedures based on inarticulated knowledge and beliefs." The management of business networks involves a number of routine procedures, especially as they relate to the regulative aspects of relations, such as the application of computer-based management information systems and the administration of technical standards in production. In industrial districts, routines contribute to reliable performance, and are thus valued by most stakeholders. But routines may also lead to rigidities which limit the network's adaptability to changing circumstances. There may be too much trust and too many ingrained habits which are never questioned, and relationships may over time become so cozy that they lead to a cognitive "grid lock."

The idea of social embeddedness suggests an image of a small community of business owners and managers where everyone knows everyone else. In structural terms, relations of trust and habit are strong ties. In dense business networks, information known to one person is rapidly diffused to other network members, but because all participants know each other well no new information is learned. Research on job search has shown that strong ties put people at a disadvantage in labor markets, especially if there is little diversity among network members in terms of resources, information, skills, commitments, and the like. Similarly, people with few weak ties "will be deprived of information from distant parts of the social system and will be confined to the provincial news and views of their close friends" (Granovetter, 1982: 106). By contrast, people who have large sets of overlapping ties will have access to a wider range of information and resources, as Aldrich (1989) noted for entrepreneurial networks. Dense networks, with limited diversity, may become too ingrown and isolated, and thus deprive business owners of information with potentially adaptive value. Thus, the same dense and homogeneous network structures that facilitate trust-building may also suppress innovation, if they become a force for defending old ways (Harrison, 1994: 101).

Grabher's (1989) study of interfirm relations in the coal and steel districts in the Ruhr region in Germany uncovered tightly-coupled structures. The system worked well for small firms, as long as market conditions were relatively stable. Small suppliers learned to survive under the umbrella of their large customers, and the large corporations benefitted from long-standing relations with small sets of suppliers. But strong interdependencies and tight relations, enacted routinely, also robbed them of the capacity to respond adaptively to changing circumstances, with disasterous consequences for the entire sector in turbulent environments. Glasmeier (1993) found a similar problem of rigidity in her study of interfirm networks in the Jura region of Switzerland. With the onslaught of foreign competition businesses in this region found it difficult to conceptualize new products and create new technologies because of their longstanding dependence on a single industry (watchmaking). Network relations were so tight and structures were so entrenched that even significant public investments in research centers and educational facilities could not shake up old habits and routines. Consequently, government development policy in this region has favored firms and industries with a proven record of success, rather than supporting the business community in general with broad infrastructural projects, with the effect of maintaining the status quo. Such conservative, risk-minimizing public strategies may limit the capacity of a region's business community to respond to uncertain future changes. Harrison's (1994) survey of recent studies of Italian districts also suggests that dense network structures can stifle innovation. The benefit of density is that information spreads rapidly, and routines ensure that conventions are not constantly being challenged. But, if some actors treat information as proprietary and act on competitive instincts, they will hold on to it, rather than share it, or they will attempt to impose their own routines on the weaker actors in the network.

8.5 Policy Implications

The social embeddedness and place specificity of district networks raises the question of "whether the districts are capable of being the objects of a more general application or replication, or whether they are simply the products of historically or geographically specific processes" (Pyke and Sengenberger, 1990: 4). If it is true that districts are culturally unique and historically sedimented artefacts, as historical accounts of district development suggest, then opportunities for political intervention to *create* district structures appear limited. It may be relatively easy to set up arrangements for formal networking, depending on available funds and political will, by offering financial incentives, organizing focus groups, creating formal enforcement mechanisms and appeal systems, and the like. But there is no guarantee that businesses will take advantage of these opportunities in ways that conform to the district model.

Industrial districts include infrastructural arrangements that provide collective services, such as consulting, export promotion, and research facilities. Because these services have a public good character, their provision requires institutions which are capable of internalizing costs and benefits (Gittell at al., in this volume). It is not known, however, if certain institutions are more suitable than others for certain kinds of services. The carriers of institutional solutions range from specific organizations such as local governments acting alone or with private partners, to interest groups such as trade associations and development consortia, to generalized belief systems operating at various levels. The main question may not be how specialized businesses can be assembled in clusters, but how a cluster of autonomous firms can be transformed into a community of trusting partners, willing to share scarce information in pursuit of innovative projects. So far, no systematic comparative research has been conducted to identify the conditions under which, say, private consulting firms are more successful at building the right mix of cooperation and competition than particular government agencies or interest associations. From an institutional perspective, this mix is not a commodity to be possessed or engineered but a condition that reflects cultural consistency, normative backing, and conformity to agreed-upon rules. The inherent ambiguities of this multifaceted and dynamic condition make strategic intervention more a probabilistic than deterministic process. Even if it were possible to induce appropriate behaviors from the outside, by raising collective self-awareness and fostering trust, this would "not prove that there is even *one* [emphasis mine] sure ... way to actually extend trust when the actors believe it is in their interest to do so" (Sabel, 1992: 247).

The fact that trust makes collaboration possible, and vice versa, cannot necessarily be interpreted as evidence that it is institutionalized collaboration which explains district performance. Not all of the districts that have been studied so far are equally successful (Staber, 1996). Some of the districts are stagnating or declining, even though they seem to have some of the same structural features and institutional carriers as the more prosperous districts (Harrison, 1994; Zeitlin, 1992). That Baden-Württemberg, for example, has many technology transfer centers and joint research institutes is not proof that it is *these* organizations which are responsible for the success of this state's economy. Organizations of this sort also exist in other regions in Germany (Roth, 1994), without having led researchers to attribute their performance to district-type arrangements.

It is interesting to note that many of the regions in the "Third Italy" that have served as district models for replication elsewhere are now undergoing substantial transformations. But not in all cases are the changes endogenously controlled or do they follow a similar path. Business populations are changing in ways that introduce turbulence and uncertainty in districts, undermining their "negotiated order." In many regions, the pattern of business foundings in recent years has led to a process of resource deconcentration and economic polarization, quite in contrast to the predictions of the district model. Many of the new firms are marginal businesses operating in industries with limited scale economies and low barriers to entry, or they are small subcontractors dependent on the investment strategies of large corporations which act as if they are embedded more in global than local networks. To the extent that business foundings raise the heterogeneity of business populations with respect to organizational form, strategy, and employment quality, there is the possibility that development opportunities are becoming more, rather than less, segregated (Staber and Sharma, 1994). For some Italian districts it has been suggested that "the idea of a flexible system of production as a new form of labour organization and economic strategies (with all the implications of public policy) is strongly declining and, if the small firms are relatively profitable, this seems to reflect the prevalence of low wages and poor working conditions, rather than superior economic dynamism" (Fumagalli and Mussati, 1993: 32). In dynamic markets, district structures are not immutable and the distribution of costs and benefits is not fixed.

Recent developments in many industrial districts suggest intensified economic rivalry and greater reliance on conventional cost cutting measures, as small and large firms alike struggle to survive the onslaught of competition from low-wage countries. Observations of business networking in Baden-Württemberg indicate that vertically-integrated companies are just now beginning to experiment with district-type decentralization, while others attempt to reassert their power through traditional strategies of hierarchical control (Herrigel, 1993). Cooperation is not always desired and in some cases it would be actively resisted by firms if it were not for government intervention (Cooke et al., 1993). Business behavior has been so diverse and uneven in recent years of economic turbulence that it is difficult to predict whether the social organization of production in Baden-Württemberg is moving towards the district model or away from it. This is also true in many Italian districts where horizontal competition among firms is becoming fierce and vertical cooperation weak (Fumagalli and Mussati, 1993). The economic reality in many districts is that businesses are increasingly opportunistic, pursuing traditional cost-minimization strategies to survive in an intensely competitive market environment. Recent interview studies in Italian districts have detected a growing scepticism among business owners and service providers about the advantages of district-type small firm networking in an extremely volatile environment, under conditions that seem to call for greater centralization and vertical integration (Dunford et al., 1993).

Still, there is considerable and growing faith, at least in policy circles, in the contribution of industrial districts to regional economic development. Of course, some policy makers are aware of the possibility that there may not be a single organizational model of districts and that districts may not be the only way, or the best way, of organizing flexible production and exchange (Zeitlin, 1992). The diversity of institutional arrangements that has been uncovered in regional case studies, as well as their limited success, has led some commentators to argue that the most sensible public approach may be to create *broad* policy domains that provide *occasions* for private actors to jointly discover solutions to common problems, rather than to impose institutional structures (Sabel, 1992). Bull et al. (1991: 96-97), for example, conclude from their analysis of three textile districts that the provision of collective services by state agencies is only effective in those districts where local intervention is limited to *stimulating debates* among all economic actors. If local cultures and traditions are as important as many analysts suggest, policy interventions should be conceived in a way that reflects and builds upon local forces, for it is the local social milieu which defines whether policy initiatives are interpreted as benevolent or not (Kristensen, 1994).

Interventionist strategies to promote districts are likely to fail if they ignore local traditions when transplanting experiences from elsewhere without adjusting them to local circumstances. "Conditions for [district] growth are difficult to capture through even the most innovative policy measures, unless certain basic structures are already in place" (Amin and Thrift, 1992: 585). But these basic structures (i.e., institutional infrastructures supported by the appropriate cultural meaning systems) take time to consolidate. In the case of Baden-Württemberg, for example, the institutional agencies that today are prominent network players (such as cooperative banks, research institutes, and training centers) developed in the middle to late nineteenth century when the region first industrialized (Megerle, 1982). In Emilia-Romagna, one of the most celebrated industrial districts in Italy, it has taken small firm networks three to four decades to reach a stage where one can reasonably speak of economic success (Murray, 1987). In other Italian regions, the origins of district-relevant political traditions can be traced back to the beginning of this century (Trigilia, 1986). Districts in the Basque region of Spain are said to benefit from traditional skills dating back to the fifteenth century (Cooke and Imrie, 1989). The problem is that most policy makers do not want to wait for the appropriate district institutions to evolve "naturally," although these may be more effective in the long term than those which are engineered. In today's environment, public policy initiatives are expected to be expedient and bear fruit as quickly as possible, and so attempts to *create* institutional arrangements that support the right mix of cooperation and competition are understandable. But because the social fabric of an industrial district evolves over the long term, and the development of cooperative attitudes takes time, the ability of public intervention to unravel old relations that are no longer useful or to produce new relations "from scratch" is highly limited. Policy initiatives to create districts do not work, if they ignore historically sedimented structures and traditions.

One of the key points of the institutionalist perspective in sociology is that history matters, and often in unpredictable ways (W. Scott, 1995). The objective is to discover which historical processes matter more than others. Some outcomes are the result of a long series of events, as in the evolution of district structures. Other outcomes are path-dependent, in that developmental choices foreclose alternative possibilities. The problem with path-dependent processes is that they may cause human agents to ignore alternative options, including possibly superior ones. Outcomes generated by path-dependent processes may be relatively predictable but not necessarily historically efficient (Carroll and Harrison, 1994).

8.6 Conclusion

The picture that emerges from recent research suggests considerable (and possibly growing) variability in industrial district forms and network arrangements. This apparent variability challenges the assumption that the evolution and design of districts can be captured by a single and coherent model. The image of small firm owners strengthening regional economic competencies through a dynamic mix of cooperation and competition does not fit well the reality of many districts. This reality is far too heterogeneous and ambiguous to support a simple logic which runs from "proximity to experience to trust to collaboration to enhanced regional economic growth," as Harrison (1992: 478) noted in his critical review of the district model. There are multiple institutional carriers and elements which shape the development of district relations. Most industrial districts are not self-contained, but are more or less embedded in supra-regional, and even global, networks (Amin and Thrift, 1992). Global market forces put constant pressure on district players to reconfigure their connections and, if necessary, to substitute extra-regional linkages for local ones. Industrial districts are indeed dynamic, but not always in a manner that conforms to the model of local embeddedness and social integration. A sociological-institutional perspective on industrial districts suggests several areas for empirical research. I propose that research on district networks would benefit from (1) examining and comparing the effects of specific institutional mechanisms and carriers, (2) showing a concern for human agency and subjective experience, (3) studying institution building as a dynamic process, and (4) developing comparative models of district evolution.

First, the social embeddedness model of districts, while an improvement over standard economic approaches, suffers from theoretical vagueness. The observation that the outcomes of interfirm cooperation for firms and districts are uncertain because they depend on the particular way behavior is embedded in local social structures may be correct but is of limited use for predicting the effects of institutional changes. Ideally, policy makers would like to know what types of institutions have what kinds of outcomes, and whether some institutions are more likely to be self-sustaining than others. Research is needed to explicate the mechanisms by which institutions constrain or facilitate interfirm cooperation and innovation. Useful studies would flesh out the conditions under which particular institutional mechanisms and carriers exert their force.

Second, much of the previous research on small firm networks in industrial districts has followed a formal structuralist approach, without any consideration of the subjective aspects of network relations. While a structural analysis can lead to important insights, with high predictive power, it cannot provide a complete understanding of social structures, if it leaves culturally embedded categories unexplored (DiMaggio, 1992). The model must also capture actors' orientations toward one another and toward the society in which relations are embedded. The appropriate research strategy would be to complement relational analysis with ethnomethodological approaches, to study how actors make sense of opportunities for connecting with others. Such efforts may lead to insights into institutional possibilities for creating governance structures that can sustain the right balance of cooperation and competition. But care must be taken not to oversocialize the conception of economic action. Oversocialized models of networking posit that cultural beliefs predispose individuals to actions that are consistent with their beliefs, regardless of the situational context. The reality of industrial districts suggests otherwise. The mix of business cooperation and competition, as well as the composition of networks, can change substantially and quickly, as a result of unexpected disruptions in economic or political circumstances. The institutional order of districts is not immutable. The possibility of conflictual rules and inconsistent interpretations opens up room for discretion, and thus also for choice (March and Olsen, 1989).

Third, the social construction of district structures occurs through a dynamic process that cannot be captured in discrete snapshots. For example, we need better information about the processes by which institutional arrangements for business networks are created, transformed, and dissolved. Dynamic accounts of sense-making and trust-building require knowledge of changing interpersonal connections and changing motives. In research practice, such accounts are notoriously difficult to achieve, but even half-hearted attempts are better than the aggregate cross-sectional surveys of interfirm relations that we have now. Current cross-sectional research also suffers from a selection bias, as investigators study only those actors and relationships that have survived to the point of observation. A great deal can be learned by studying network attempts that have failed, or by comparing institutional strategies that were abandoned with those that were adopted.

Finally, there is a need for comparative models of district evolution. Comparative research on districts is very rare, and is limited to cross-sectional comparisons of global variables, such as forms of exchange or geographic distance between exchange partners. Researchers have tended to follow one of two extreme approaches. Either they have studied one case at a time and insisted on the (historical, cultural, economic, etc.) uniqueness of each case, or they have proposed a general (usually ideal-typical) model of industrial districts, without exploring systematic deviations from this model. Either approach is misleading and does little to advance a general theory of industrial districts. Without strictly comparative research designs it is impossible to explain the outcomes of variable institutional orders and interventions. Comparative studies are needed to formulate testable generalizations that are valid across time and space.

Comparative and dynamic research designs, especially if they are intended to capture the micro-foundations of district relations, present formidable challenges. But better research designs are necessary to remove the parochial and pedestrian character of some of the policy initiatives that are currently being tried. To be sure, comparative and longitudinal research suffers from important trade-offs. Broad comparative studies can only be done with rather simple and crude variables, thus missing the fine-grained variations in meaning systems and institutional processes. Institutionalist theorists interested in discovering the meaning of events will find it impossible to assemble the kinds of broad data sets that fascinate "positivist" researchers. But longitudinal research with crude variables, couched in a broad comparative framework, would still be a significant improvement over the current accumulation of isolated case studies of districts and networks.

In the final analysis, the future of district development and the contribution of business networks to their economic performance is very much an open question. To the extent that social reality is built from the bottom up, by actors whose preferences evolve in the process of constructing reality, there is room for chance, error, and creativity. There is always a certain degree of indeterminacy in the outcomes of policy initiatives to create collaborative structures or to adopt institutional solutions that have proven successful elsewhere. The problem is that the "particular historical details that lead to the success of a given institutional entrepreneur or group of entrepreneurs and the failure of another, defy theoretical prediction" (Zucker, 1988: 27-28). We may be able to explain ex post facto why some outcome has occurred, even though we could not have predicted, prior to the fact, that a particular sequence of events would be unfolding. It may be tempting to impose meaning on institution building processes from knowledge of outcomes, but to do so implies committing the retrospective fallacy. This tendency is illustrated in many accounts of district development. A sociological-institutional perspective, which is grounded empirically and accepts the indeterminacy of outcomes, would be a useful corrective.

9. Why Do Industries Cluster?

Peter B. Doeringer and David G. Terkla

9.1 Introduction

The history of state and local economic development policy has been marked by fads. In the 1960s, mature smokestack industries were the focus of industrial recruitment and retention efforts; attention shifted to high technology industries in the 1970s and early 1980s; and the attraction of foreign investment became popular in the latter half of the 1980s. The focus of development policy in the early 1990s is becoming "industrial clusters."

Industrial clusters are a revival of an old idea of industry agglomerations. In its new form, clusters represent a group of related industries that can tap advantages of co-location to lower costs and improve performance. In theory, targeting development policy on such clusters should permit firms to capture the externalities of co-location that would otherwise be unavailable to them. If the sources of clustering externalities can be identified, growth strategies based around the building of clusters can potentially avoid the pitfalls of inefficient subsidies and zero-sum competition for industries among states and regions.

State governments representing a diverse group, ranging from Arizona and Oregon in the west to the industrial states of Michigan and Pennsylvania to high-technology Massachusetts are now using some version of the industry cluster concept to organize their economic development policies. What appear to be lacking in these new policy efforts, however, are an understanding of the economics of industrial clustering and a methodology for translating the cluster concept into concrete growth policies tailored to specific businesses.

This chapter begins to fill this void by exploring what motivates industry clustering. Drawing primarily upon previous field research on the clustering of mature industries in local economies and on our current research on locational decisions of US and Japanese-owned manufacturing start-ups, we identify a set of "invisible" organizational advantages that contribute to the clustering of firms.

Three types of clustering forces are specified: (1) advantages based on production relationships among firms located within common "production channels," (2) advantages drawn from local factor markets, and (3) advantages derived from relationships with non-business institutions such as unions and governments. We will show how these forces can foster different types of clusters and how they affect the industrial boundaries of clusters.

The emphasis in this chapter is on the way that firms, rather than industries, interact with various regional environments. This emphasis underscores the importance of examining specific business strategies, rather than the behavior of broad industry aggregates, when defining clusters. It also highlights the importance of identifying unique regional strengths, instead of applying universal location criteria, when devising policies for nurturing clusters.

9.2 Competitive Advantage and Fuzzy Implementation

The concept of clusters is closely related to the economics of "competitive advantage." Michael Porter, for example, has argued that four key aspects of the business environment interact together to determine the competitive advantage of both regions and nations: factor market conditions, firm structure and rivalry, demand conditions, and the presence of related and supporting industries (Porter, 1990). Industry clusters are an extension of these principles.

Industry clusters are regional concentrations of industries that improve their combined economic advantage through co-location. According to Porter, clusters gain a competitive advantage from (1) operating in an innovative environment marked by vigorous competitive pressures from rival firms; (2) the presence of customers who pressure firms to innovate; (3) access to networks of local suppliers of specialized inputs who themselves are motivated to innovate constantly by fierce competition with local rivals; and (4) by the local availability of highly specialized labor and technology that meet the needs of cluster businesses (Porter, 1990). The cluster concept also embraces factors such as local research and development opportunities and the enhanced potential for developing important customer relationships.

Industry clusters are an appealing way to explore questions of state and local economic development policy because they seem to promise insights that go beyond traditional agglomeration considerations and other location influences such as relative factor prices, proximity to markets, and the quality of transportation and utility infrastructures. The cluster concept also highlights how regional growth can depend on non-export sectors, as well as on export base industries, in those instances where firms in both types of industries jointly contribute to the performance of the cluster (Tilly, 1993).

Unfortunately, there is a large gap between the general concept of industry clusters, spurred by competition and encouraged by public policies to tap various benefits of proximity, and the application of the concept to particular states and localities. Application requires pinpointing the specific types of benefits that are derived from co-location within different clusters, matching these benefits to the indigenous strengths of specific locations, and discovering the most effective policy levers for promoting cluster development.

Much of the literature on how states have constructed (or should construct) their industry clusters does not show evidence of such an understanding of the clustering process. Instead, clusters seem to emerge from *ad hoc* judgments based on broad industry growth forecasts, untested predictions regarding the business potential of particular technologies, and examples of particular cluster configurations that have been successful elsewhere. Little attention is paid to determining the critical factors in the clustering process or to formulating counterfactual questions about what would have occurred in the absence of any particular component in the development of the cluster.

A number of states are now adopting the cluster approach to economic development. In Arizona, for example, a public-private effort has identified nine key economic clusters which are now the focus of state economic development efforts, while Michigan, Pennsylvania, and Arkansas are focusing on the organization of networks of manufacturing firms within single industries (Waits, et al., 1992). These clusters tend to be defined in *ad hoc* ways and many are limited to a single industry, thus resembling previous industry-targeting practices.

The problem of translating cluster concepts into practice, however, is nowhere more evident than in Massachusetts (Commonwealth of Massachusetts, 1993). The blueprint for the current Massachusetts growth policy is provided by a recent study that specifies four major industry clusters – health care, information technology, financial services, and knowledge creation services – and several minor clusters in traditional two digit manufacturing industries such as plastics, machinery, and chemicals (Porter, 1991).

Rather than using criteria such as the frequency and character of business relationships or other elements of regional competitive advantage, these clusters are characterized as those "which compete nationally and internationally, and have the size, sophistication, productivity, and national and international positions to drive economic upgrading" (Porter, 1991: 14). There are no indicators of clustering benefits, no functional criteria for defining the industrial composition or boundaries of these clusters, and no indication of the degree to which the Massachusetts economy provides the rivalry and competitive pressure on these clusters that are supposed to stimulate high-performance. In fact, except for the information technology cluster, most of the industries within a cluster are from the same two or three digit Standard Industrial Classification (SIC), thereby excluding most vertical production relationships among firms.

Such *ad hoc* procedures are always a questionable basis for setting policy. It is hard to envision how either economic development analysts or business executives will be able to specify what pieces of a cluster are already present in a region and what types of new clusters could be attracted to it, let alone how they would determine how to recruit or nurture the elements of any particular cluster. At best, these efforts may help to document some of the location concerns of individual industries, but they do not deal effectively with cluster relationships *among* industries.

9.3 Towards a Business-Based Theory of Cluster Development

There is an emerging literature that provides some guidance on cluster formation (Sternberg, 1991). One branch of this literature has framed the analysis of clusters around specific industries and their input-output relationships (Markusen, 1986). Another branch has examined the evolution of industrial complexes ranging from those built around dominant central firms to more atomistic networks of small firms characterized by flexible specialization (Storper and Christopherson, 1987; Piore and Sabel, 1984; Sternberg, 1991; D'Cruz and Rugman, 1993).

Both of these approaches are moving the discussion of clusters in a productive direction, yet they each have limitations. The industry-based analyses continue to view relationships among industries through the distorting lens of relatively aggregate input-output relationships while neglecting intra-industry linkages and inter-industry linkages not based on product sales among firms. The studies of industrial complexes capture the details of business linkages and strategic networking, but often neglect other important dimensions of clustering such as common technologies and niche-seeking behavior.

9.3.1 Production Channels as an Economic Development Tool

An alternative way of thinking about clusters is in terms of *production channels*. Production channels are the chains of suppliers, manufacturers, and distributors that begin with basic inputs and end with the marketing of the final product. They involve relationships within industries as well as those that cut across industries. These include backward and forward production linkages, alliances among enterprises of different sizes, and informal networks of micro-enterprises and household production (Doeringer, et al., 1993). Production channels also incorporate an affiliated "infrastructure" of equipment vendors, information networks, transportation systems, and banking and financial institutions.

9.3.2 Beyond Industry-Level Relationships

Studying industrial location in terms of production channels has major advantages over using industries and industry-based input-output relationships as the unit of analysis. For example, location decisions made within the production channel framework do not depend simply on factor costs, proximity to markets, and arms-length exchanges among industries. They are also influenced by opportunities to redesign organizational relationships within these channels.

While there is an inter-industry dimension of such channels that can sometimes be detected in input-output tables, production channel relationships are fundamentally defined by strategic business decisions. Such strategic decisions are not likely to be uniform within industries, but will vary by size of firm, corporate structure, type of production process, and even nationality of ownership.

Take, for example, the factors affecting the location of the apparel industry. The apparel industry has shown a long-term trend toward relocating from industrialized countries to developing countries. The standard analysis identifies labor costs as the key determinant of these location shifts and suggests development policies that either offset high labor costs or otherwise protect uncompetitive domestic producers.

In contrast, the production channel approach treats the apparel industry as part of a larger textile-apparel production channel that begins with the spinning of natural or synthetic textile fibers and ends with retail clothing sales. In this broader perspective, labor costs in apparel manufacturing are becoming less important to its competitiveness while the rapid response of production to changing patterns of demand is becoming more important. This finding opens additional options for development policy that lie outside the narrow boundaries of the apparel industry.

The traditional apparel manufacturing process in the United States uses mass production techniques and highly-simplified jobs to assemble garments from "bundles" of components. This involves long production times and considerable buffer stocks between operations (Abernathy, n.d.; Dunlop and Weil, 1993). The labor intensity of the bundle system encourages mass production, the division of labor into very simple repetitive tasks, and the location of production in low-wage regions. However, the inventory costs of in-process work under the bundle system are quite large and it is difficult to reprogram production in response to shifting consumer tastes. As a result, clothing retailers have historically experienced frequent shortages or "stockouts" in particular sizes and colors coincident with high costs of carrying inventory stocks of less popular items and the consequent need to discount this unsold merchandise at the end of the selling season.

In recent years, there have been pressures from large clothing retailers to get apparel manufacturers to increase production response times so that retail inventories and stockouts can be reduced. Speeding time-to-market has entailed considerable restructuring of production within apparel plants (Dunlop and Weil, 1992, 1993; Bailey, 1988; Bailey, 1989). Experiments are now underway in the United States (and a number of other countries) to see if this system can be replaced with more flexible and responsive modular production, modeled after the Toyota Sewing Systems, in which large teams of multi-skilled workers assemble an entire garment. Pressures for more rapid production responses have also been transmitted to upstream US textile suppliers to encourage faster delivery times and sales of smaller lots of fabric. These changes have also been accompanied by new technologies and management practices, such as electronic data interchange, that are being adopted throughout the textile-apparel production channel.

These developments have moved the margin of competitiveness away from labor costs, where developing countries have an advantage, towards rapid response production and delivery where domestic producers have an edge. Paradoxically, many of these changes have actually required more production labor and higher labor costs, but these costs have been more than offset by inventory savings and the price premiums that retailers are willing to pay for shorter lead times on deliveries.

Such reforms have not occurred through arms-length rivalries, but have involved the formation of new business alliances all along the production channel. These alliances have blurred the traditional boundaries among firms at various stages in the production channel and have enhanced the responsiveness of the entire channel to shifting demand. In this reform process, it is the large retailers, rather than the manufacturers, that have initiated and guided change.

The bundle system technology is also used in the apparel industry in Great Britain. As in the United States, the British production channel is dominated by concentrated retailers who dictate standards for fashion, quality, and cost. However, rather than aggressively pushing British clothing manufacturers to innovate and restructure production, as is the case in the United States, these retailers have been content to see these manufacturers become "make-to-order" firms that compete on price with one another and foreign clothing producers. International differences in labor costs have, therefore, continued to adversely affect the location of apparel manufacturing in England.

9.3.3 Global Networks or Regional Industry Clusters?

The production channel relationships highlighted by the apparel examples do not necessarily imply a geographical clustering of firms. These relationships can also be formed through multinational enterprises which span the globe, piecing together production channel relationships from a number of different countries (Reich, 1991; D'Cruz and Rugman, 1993). In this view, national industries are subordinate to the strategies of multinational firms that assemble networks across national boundaries. Any geographic clustering of particular industries is coincident with historical factors that have little bearing on future business location. This view contrasts sharply with Porter's concept of the importance of clustering to a nation's competitiveness (Lazonick, 1993).

Yet, there are particular production channel relationships that appear to successfully develop only among firms in close geographic proximity to one another. One of the most cited of these is the example of industrial districts in Italy (Powell, 1990; Harrison, 1992; Piore and Sabel, 1984) consisting of small firms in a variety of industries – apparel, ceramics, machine tools, and metalworking – that group together to cooperate in producing for markets in which they are also competitors (Piore and Sabel, 1984; Best, 1990).

These collaborative arrangements within industries are complemented by a system that provides a flexible supply of components which is characterized by close cooperation among manufacturers, suppliers, and equipment vendors and by marketing and distribution networks often handled by a consortia of small firms that are independent of large retailers. This system is further supported by cooperation among government agencies, employer organizations, and banks.

None of our US studies has revealed such close collaboration among firms competing in the same product markets as is described in the case of the Italian industrial districts. In Italy, frequent contacts among competitors occur in local social and business settings, such as churches, social clubs, and advisory boards and seem to build bonds of trust that transcend competitive forces among firms in the market (Harrison, 1992). When local clustering is observed in the United States, it tends to occur almost exclusively around vertical business relationships within a production channel, rather than among firms in the same industry.

One explanation of the greater frequency of vertical over horizontal relationships within regions in the United States may be the regulatory climate created by relatively tough (compared to most European countries and Japan) antitrust policy in the United States (Best, 1990). A second reason, however, may lie in the nature of business rivalry in the United States.

9.4 Rivalry Versus Cooperation

Porter's widely-cited formulation of the cluster concept, although acknowledging some role for cooperative behavior among firms, places far greater stress on the importance of vigorous rivalry among firms as a goad to the formation of cluster networks (Porter, 1990; Lazonick, 1993). While this is a commonly-held view among many business executives in the United States, the well-known example of the US steel industry that chose a strategy of passive downsizing and disinvestment in response to international competitive pressures provides ample demonstration that competition is no guarantor of performance (Scherer, 1991). In fact, intense rivalry among firms within productions channels can be counterproductive to many of the performance improvements described above.

For example, the adoption of data-sharing and many of the other supportive relationships within the textile-apparel production channel in the United States was delayed, in part, by competitive rivalries among firms in the channel. Likewise, the promotion of vigorous cost competition among apparel manufacturers by large clothing retailers in Great Britain is inconsistent with the formation of high-performance collaborations within the production channel. There are two particularly notable exceptions to rivalry among successful industry clusters that illustrate the importance of cooperative interactions among firms in close geographic proximity to one another. One involves just-in-time supplier relationships and the other the creation of niche markets.

9.4.1 Just-In-Time Production

Our recent study of Japanese manufacturing investment in the United State (Doeringer and Terkla, 1992; Doeringer, Evans, and Terkla, 1992) along with others (Chang, 1989; Mair, Florida and Kenney, 1988; Kenney and Florida, 1993) confirm the importance of geographical proximity to location decisions in some industries. New automotive parts suppliers and suppliers of plastics for consumer electronics considered only locations sufficiently close to their customers to permit just-in-time delivery schedules and to facilitate the development of rapid response capabilities for adjusting to changing product specifications.

9.4.2 Building Niche Markets

The close physical proximity between manufacturers and supplier firms can often expose previously undiscovered niche markets based on quality and speed of delivery, especially where just-in-time inventory practices and frequent design changes make for frequent interactions between suppliers and buyers. These niche markets may not be available to suppliers at more distant locations.

For example, our study of a mature manufacturing region in central Massachusetts revealed wide variations in performance among manufacturing firms in a diverse group of industries ranging from furniture and apparel to machine tools and plastics (Doeringer and Terkla, 1990). One common characteristic shared by the successful firms in each of these industries was the ability to produce customized products for niche markets provided by other firms within their production channel.

These firms were constantly searching for niche markets and developing specialized products and services through close interactions with their primary customers and suppliers. The typical niche-seeking firm was small to medium-sized (fewer than 100 employees) and was found in such diverse product lines as moldmaking of custom-designed artificial limbs and joints, machinery and metal fabrication of prototype products for the defense industry, customized plastic fabrication, and some specialized furniture manufacturing.

Some of these production channel relationships were based on close geographical proximity to suppliers and customers. Proximity generated "collaboration economies" – the ability to participate in, and respond rapidly to, changing design and manufacturing practices among firms that buy and sell from one another – and to resolve problems over product specifications and schedules quickly. For example, custom molding firms frequently worked with their resin firm suppliers to develop specialized materials for particular product runs and also worked closely on the designing of molds with the precision fabricators of the final product. This importance of innovative home-based suppliers has also been documented in Italy, Germany, and Sweden (Porter, 1990.

9.5 Factor Market Relationships

A second set of factors that promotes geographical clustering originates in local and regional markets for technology and labor. In the case of technology, proximity among firms can influence the direction in which technologies evolve, create an environment that yields externalities of technology diffusion, and even provide a basis for encouraging stronger production channel relationships that enhance the competitive advantage of local firms. Local labor markets can foster generic workforce qualities that favor certain kinds of economic agglomerations that cut across industries.

9.5.1 Technology Transfer

One set of examples of business clusters formed around a technology comes from our study of Japanese plant locations. In the plastics industry, we found several instances of new production channel linkages being formed through technology transfer that were mediated through relationships with local universities and through joint ventures with US companies. For example, a Japanese firm with limited strengths in diskette technology formed a joint venture with a counterpart German firm with a complementary technology that had chosen to locate close to a university with a strong science and electronic engineering faculty. Both firms continued to draw upon the university-based research and to develop a shared technology.

A second example involves the clustering of optics and imaging firms in the Rochester, New York area (Sternberg, 1991). The technology transfer occurred among a group of small firms (distributed across a wide range of SIC categories including telecommunications, computer peripherals, and medical equipment) that had only minimal input-output relationships with one another or with Eastman Kodak or Xerox, the two large related manufacturers in the area. Rather, the cluster evolved around a core technology that developed from the interaction among local universities and large corporations in the area. This technology was spread to smaller companies, not through supplier relationships and niche markets, but through the swapping of employees within the common pool of skilled and technical labor that developed around the core technology in the region.

9.5.2 Workforce Quality

Local labor markets provide a second source of bonding for certain types of business clusters. One of the apparent anomalies in the industrial location literature is that wage differences are often found to be unimportant in influencing firms' location decisions (Terkla and Doeringer, 1991; Bartik, 1991). One reason is that wages are only one piece of the labor cost equation; true labor costs must be adjusted for labor productivity. Labor productivity is influenced by basic education and job skills, but also by employee attitudes and the flexibility with which the labor force can adapt to shifting job assignments and job content on the shop floor.

9.5.3 Skills

While schools and training programs can contribute to the skill base of a regional economy, and have often been used as a part of state development strategies for recruiting new firms (Gittell and Flynn, 1993), their effect is strongest on younger workers who hold entry level jobs. Our studies of mature industries and of plant locations have consistently shown that skill is often more important than educational level as a source of shop-floor labor productivity. Moreover, it is also widely-documented that most productivity-building skills are learned on-the-job (Doeringer and Piore, 1971; Veum, 1993). This means that the skills of the labor force are intimately related to the existing industrial mix of a region.

For example, one manager of a large machine tool company in the greater Cincinnati area said the most important agglomeration economy in his decision to locate in the area was a trained and experienced labor force. The machine tool industry had historically developed in the area around a large inflow of skilled German immigrants. The demand for these skills has been perpetuated by the many machine tool plants in the area and these employers have ensured that vocational schools maintain an appropriate curriculum so that a trained workforce would be readily available.

9.5.4 Work Attitudes

Other productive qualities (such as motivation, work attitudes, and flexibility) are also learned locally, partly through socialization processes at home and in school, but also at the workplace. In our mature industry study, the work commitment of the local labor force was widely cited by employers as a crucial ingredient of their success in customized production. This was especially the case with those managers who where able to make comparisons with worker attitudes in similar facilities located elsewhere. A strong work ethic was particularly important in maintaining a rapid response production capability and in sustaining product quality.

Worker attitudes are also frequently cited as being crucial by managers of Japanese start-ups in a variety of industries interviewed in Georgia and Kentucky (Doeringer and Terkla, 1992). These firms defined labor quality in terms of flexibility, adaptability, loyalty, motivation, and problem-solving capacity. Managers devoted substantial time and resources to testing and screening large numbers of job applicants in order to discover these hard-to-observe worker traits.

Interestingly these criteria of labor quality seem to be associated with Japanese management styles, rather than with particular industries. Managers of US start-ups in the same industries and locales were more concerned with factors such as education and skill, personal references, and prior work experience. They interviewed far fewer applicants for a particular job vacancy than their Japanese counterparts. Thus, in this case, the key factor clustering firms around attitudinal characteristics of the local workforce is nationality of ownership.

Since generic skills and attitudes are built on-the-job, regions that have concentrated in mass production are likely to have a different mix of workforce qualities from those that have been dominated by firms that produce batch or customized products. These differences in workforce qualities are then likely to translate into differences in the types of business clusters that regions will be able to attract.

Such workforce-based clustering will be more strongly correlated with hard-to-observe, firm-specific factors – position in the product cycle, human resource management strategies, and length of production runs (mass vs. customized production) – than with particular industries. For example, skills that focus around the ability to form and shape material may be generated through on-the-job training in any number of different product lines – furniture, plastics fabrication, and metalworking, to name a few. These skills often involve the ability to achieve high accuracy and precision in production and to modify production techniques to fit changing product specifications. The extent to which workers have these qualities does not depend on which material forming industry has employed them, but on the organization of work and the degree of precision demanded by specific firms. Where these skills are present, they will be an attraction to firms in any number of industries that do precision forming.

Standard industry definitions are less likely to be a good guide to identifying the types of firms that will value such skills than are considerations such as whether a firm is in the innovative or mature phase of the product cycle or whether it serves customized or mass markets. In the case of the successful mature manufacturing firms that we studied, the presence of a skilled labor pool (developed through on-the-job training and reinforced through strong local cultural traditions such as father-son transfers of machining and woodworking skills) was key to business prosperity and promoted the clustering of such firms in the local economy (Doeringer and Terkla, 1990).

Similarly, the contribution of a highly skilled labor force to clustering is apparent in the development of the optics and imaging firms in the Rochester example described above (Sternberg, 1991). Although Rochester accounts for only 0.4 per cent of the nation's population, 21 per cent of the national membership of the Society of Imaging Science and Technology lives in the area and is a major attraction to firms in a wide range of industries.

9.6 Institutional Relationships

A third set of hard-to-measure clustering considerations is embedded in the local environment of economic and governmental institutions. The role of schools and skill training institutions has been widely studied and has been briefly noted above. This section will examine the importance of two other types of institutions – trade unions and state and local governments.

9.6.1 Labor-Management Relations

Quantitative location studies have often identified union militancy as a deterrent to business location and the importance of the quality of labor-management relations has been confirmed by qualitative studies (Doeringer, Terkla and Topakian, 1987; Doeringer and Terkla, 1992; Doeringer, Evans and Terkla, 1992). When unionized firms speak of a healthy labor-management environment, they are less-concerned with union pressures on wage rates than with the willingness of unions to accommodate day-to-day issues of work rules, safety, and flexibility in the utilization of labor. Nonunionized firms often cite these same characteristics as advantages to not being unionized.

Flexible labor relations appear to be most easily achieved by small and medium-sized firms. These firms are not bound by rigid organizational rules and often have more personalized labor relations which enable them to realize more fully the potential flexibility of their work force. This flexibility enhances their ability to compete in markets that require frequent production line changes in order to respond rapidly to changing customer demands and to be able to exploit new niches in the product market as they are discovered. In this sense, flexibility may reinforce other elements in the clustering process, such as the formation of production channel relationships and the diffusion of technology.

9.6.2 Civic Capacity

Taxes, expenditure patterns, and the "business climate" have traditionally been mentioned as key governmental qualities that may influence the location of particular firms (Bartik, 1991), but these factors are not usually associated with the potential clustering of industries. Even the recent state economic development strategies that are intended to promote industrial clusters are not sharply focused on the attraction of clusters, *per se*, but instead are centered around generic issues such as regulatory policy, workforce training, and investment in education likely to be attractive to all firms.

For example, in Arizona, the key policy recommendations for developing the state's nine identified clusters include: improving educational and job opportunities, creating world-class educational and research resources in the state, and the expansion of trade between in-state firms and foreign countries (Waits, *et al.*, 1992). Likewise, in Massachusetts, the focus is on improving the basic and higher education systems, improving workforce training, development of industrial extension services, encouraging networking and technology transfer among firms, and expanding export sales and access to capital (Commonwealth of Massachusetts, 1993).

Our field research, however, reveals certain governmental qualities that can influence clustering in much the same way as workforce quality. In the case of Japanese business location decisions, for example, we found that the clustering of start-ups in the United States is sensitive to the degree of civic organization and business "security" provided by government officials and leaders of civic organizations.

Many Japanese firms seem to look for evidence of a willingness among governments and communities to make economic and political accommodations if unanticipated problems should arise in the future. Japanese executives typically emphasized the quality and effectiveness of the state government mechanisms for coordinating industrial recruiting, the degree of civic organization provided by business and government leaders at the local level, and the hospitality of government officials (Doeringer and Terkla, 1992). Managers repeatedly commented on the capacity of state and local government and of civic organizations to provide for civic stability and resolve community problems that might affect their plants.

In contrast, domestic companies placed less emphasis on such potential accommodations than on the quality of community amenities. In the words of one manager of a domestic company that had recently relocated, "what makes a difference in the location decision is what feels best for our people, particularly for people that you relocate." There are, however, examples of domestic business locations that have responded to the ability of local governments to reform difficult labor-management environments and to upgrade the quality of schools (Gittell, 1992).

9.7 Conclusion: Building Cluster Potential at the State and Local Level

The concept of industry clusters promises a new way for states and local communities to initiate policies to attract new firms without relying on traditional zero-sum methods such as direct subsidies. Developing industry clusters requires understanding the unique advantages inherent in specific regional economies that provide a basis for externality benefits from the clustering of firms. These advantages are often intangible and can be incorporated in development strategies at a much lower cost than traditional tax rebates and direct subsidies.

However, the trend in current state policies toward *ad hoc* definitions of industry clusters runs the risk of wasting development resources by focusing on the wrong group of industries for future economic development and by missing important linkages among firms that cut across industries. Our research indicates that industry clusters are not likely to be correctly identified by examining employment and export performance data classified by industry. Instead, our findings point to the need for state and local economic development policies that are based on the "cluster potential" of their economies.

Cluster potential should be determined from an understanding of where existing firms in a region fit into their larger production channels. Analyzing production channel relationships is a way of identifying opportunities for collaborative relationships among firms, both vertically and across product lines. It must be remembered, however, that collaborative relationships do not occur automatically, but must be developed in a climate that is not aggressively competitive.

Moreover, not all beneficial production channel relationships depend on geographic proximity. Multinational firms operating through production channels can prosper by spreading their facilities around the world, while still linking key operations together within the corporation. However, the development of niche-seeking strategies through production channel relationships is greatly enhanced by geographic proximity.

Regional clusters can also be formed among firms that are not part of the same production channel. Opportunities for technology sharing and generic skills and attitudes of the regional labor force can also contribute to the clustering of firms, often in ways that cut across traditional industry categories.

Using industrial clusters as an approach to regional economic development requires a deep understanding of business strategy and management practice of the kind acquired by business "insiders" and world-class management consultants. This understanding must begin with the analysis of high performing firms in established industries, both to gain a sense of what relationships lead to competitive advantage at the firm level and what clustering strengths are available in the regional economy.

Once this knowledge-base is created, development officials should embark on a dual strategy of (1) filling in the gaps in existing clusters and (2) laying the foundation for attracting new clusters. This strategy can be guided by looking at other states and localities, as well as at their own regions, to determine what types of production channels include firms with similar production processes (but not necessarily similar products) to those already in the industrial base; how these channels generate efficiency benefits for member firms; what types of business linkages, factor market qualities, and non-business institutional relationships they value; and by asking what adaptations might have to be made to accommodate the clustering process.

Finally, clustering can be encouraged by savvy and enlightened leadership in institutions such as trade unions and government agencies whose actions can affect the economic flexibility and political security of the business community. In this process, one of the biggest challenges facing states and local communities will be the fostering of an environment that encourages collaboration among competing firms. In the long run, this may be the critical element in the civic capacity of government to promote growth.

10. Regional Clusters and Economic Development: A Research Agenda

Michael J. Enright

10.1 Introduction

Interest in regional clusters and their role in economic development has grown substantially over the last several years among academics, economic development professionals, and firm managers. The main reasons have been the increased intensity of interregional and international competition in the world economy, the apparent shortcomings of traditional regional development models and policies, and the emergence of successful clusters of firms and industries in many nations around the world. Intensified competition has placed firms and regions under increasing pressure, especially in the context of the economic stagnation experienced in both developed and developing nations in the 1980s and early 1990s. Traditional regional development models involving attempts to attract or create large firms have been called into question as the cost of attracting companies has increased, as large firms in North America, Europe, and Japan have experienced difficulties, and as traditional regional development models have shown mixed results. Within firms, location decisions based on financial incentives have also been called into question as many firms have found that such incentives have not proven to be as much of an advantage as was once believed. Meanwhile, examples of successful clusters of high technology firms and small and medium-sized craft firms have highlighted alternatives to development through large managerial firms. Firms themselves have found other aspects of the location decision as important or more important to their competitive success than traditional financial incentives.

In this chapter, I will highlight some recent work on regional clusters, identify some of the gaps in our present knowledge of the clustering phenomenon, and suggest an agenda for further research. The particular set of issues covered is idiosyncratic rather than exhaustive, reflecting my own research interests and drawing on results, preliminary results, and stylized facts that have emerged in my own research as well as the literature. The purpose is to begin to map a research agenda that will help academics, development professionals, and managers develop a better understanding of this important phenomenon.

10.2 Some Definitions

Many terms have been used to describe geographic agglomerations of firms in an industry or related industries. Terms with somewhat different meanings are sometimes used interchangeably, creating confusion and a need for more precise definitions. In particular, it is important to distinguish between industrial clusters, regional clusters, industrial districts, and business networks. An industrial cluster (see Porter 1990) is a set of industries related through buyer-supplier and supplier-buyer relationships, or by common technologies, common buyers or distribution channels, or common labor pools. A regional cluster is an industrial cluster in which member firms are in close geographic proximity to each other. Industrial districts (such as the Italian industrial districts described in Becattini 1987, 1989b; Goodman and Bamford 1990; and Pyke, Becattini, and Sengenberger 1992) are concentrations of firms involved in interdependent production processes, often in the same industry or industry segment, that are embedded in the local community (Becattini 1989a) and delimited by daily travel to work distances (Sforzi 1992). A business network consists of several firms that have ongoing communication and interaction, and might have a certain level of interdependence, but that need not operate in related industries or be geographically concentrated in space. Business networks will not be addressed directly in this paper (see Sydow, in this volume, for discussions of business networks).

Regional clusters, as defined here, include industrial districts of small and medium sized craft firms, concentrations of high technology firms related through the development and use of common technologies, and production systems that contain large hub firms and their local suppliers and spinoffs. Regional clusters also subsume the spatial manifestations of the "production channels" of Doeringer and Terkla (in this volume), the "flexible production complexes" of Scott and Storper (1989), and the "innovative milieu" of Maillat (1991). Given the extensive literature on industrial districts, the distinction between regional clusters and industrial districts (a subset of regional clusters) is worth highlighting. Whereas the focal point of an industrial district is often a single industry or even a single industry segment, regional clusters generally involve a range of related industries.

The rationale for using the relatively broad term, regional cluster, is that all of the terms alluded to describe geographic agglomerations of firms in the same or related industries and as such are used to describe aspects of the same broad phenomenon. In addition, there are distinct similarities in the explanations for the development and persistence of the differently named agglomerations in the literature, particularly in the reliance on externalities and localized information flows. This is not to say that we should ignore the differences between different types of regional clusters, but rather that we should explore in detail both their similarities and differences.

10.3 The Economics of Clustering

The whole notion of regional clusters relies on the fact that production patterns are not uniform over space, that production in at least some industries is geographically concentrated. The economic rationales for the geographic concentration of industries have been explored by a number of authors dating back to Weber (1929) and Marshall (1920a, 1920b). Recent reviews include Krugman (1991), Harrison (1992), Enright (1990), and Doeringer and Terkla (in this volume). The economic rationales for such geographic concentration involve externalities and agglomeration economies including technological spillovers, information sharing, labor pooling, and access to natural resources or specialized inputs, among others. I will not repeat the conclusions of this literature here.

One question that arises with respect to the economics of clustering is which industries tend toward geographic concentration, and therefore regional clustering, and which do not. Enright (1993a) reports the results of a cross-sectional econometric study of the determinants of geographic concentration of employment and establishments in United States manufacturing industries. This study uses a series of geographic concentration indices as dependent variables and variables reflecting industry and firm structure, skill intensities, use of raw materials and specialized inputs, and product differentiation as explanatory variables.

Strong results were found for variables reflecting fewness of firms, employment of medium skilled workers, the intense use of advertising and non-advertising selling efforts (all of which were associated with higher levels of geographic concentration), and large purchases that were made to order (which was associated with lower levels of geographic concentration). Weaker results were obtained for utilization of raw materials and specialized inputs, use of sales and technical service in marketing, use of outside experts in marketing, research intensity (positive contribution to geographic concentration), and the importance of large establishments of large firms (negative contribution to geographic concentration). This last result indicates that, on average, the large establishments of large US manufacturing firms repel, rather than attract, the establishments of other firms in the same industry. Intensive use of highly skilled and unskilled production labor had no significant effect on geographic concentration.

The study showed a close relationship between industrial organization and geographic concentration in industry. In addition, it showed that variables that addressed information flows within an industry have an important influence on the geographic profile of US manufacturing industries. The implications for cluster development are clear. Some industries do not cluster; any attempts to make them do so through policy are bound to fail. Some industries cluster near particular sources of raw materials or particular downstream markets; attempts to foster clusters of such industries in the absence of these features are bound to fail. Improved information flow between a geographic cluster and the outside world can increase or decrease the tendency of an industry to cluster. Easier transmis-

Figure 10.1 Italian regions

provinces of Milan (31 per cent of total employment), Varese (13 per cent), and Bergamo (10 per cent) as the leading centers. Four regions, Lombardy, Emilia-Romagna, Veneto, and Tuscany, accounted for 73 per cent of the nation's employment in the knitwear and hosiery industries. Modena (including the industrial district of Carpi) was the leading province with 9 per cent of national employment. The province of Como, in Lombardy, dominated the Italian silk industry with more than 90 per cent of industry employment. Lombardy accounted for 52 per cent of employment in the textile machinery industry; Milan and Brescia were the main centers. Although there were no good statistics for the design industry, Milan is the recognized center of Italian fashion, with Florence and Rome a distant second and third, respectively.

The location of the local apparel and textile/apparel retailing industries gives one a picture of the location of local demand for textile products. Although the Italian apparel and textile/apparel retailing industries were less geographically concentrated than the textile and textile machinery industries, they were still very

Table 10.1 Employment in the Italian textile cluster, selected regions, 1981 (in %)

Region	Population	Wool textile	Cotton textile	Knitware	Total textile	Textile machinery	Apparel	Textile-apparel retailing
Piedmont	8	30	10	7	14	14	9	8
Lombardy	16	7	66	28	37	52	23	30
Veneto	8	15	7	15	11	4	17	8
Friuli-Venezia	2	0	2	1	1	16	1	2
Emilia-Romagna	7	1	0	19	8	3	9	10
Tuscany	6	43	2	11	16	9	13	9
Total	47	96	87	81	87	98	72	67

Note: Percentages refer to percent of national population or employment.

Source: Calculated from ISTAT, Census of Industry, 1981.

Figure 10.2 Italian provinces

much centered in the textile producing regions (see Table 10.1). Milan, the Italian center of fashion and design, had disproportionate representation in both apparel manufacturing (7 per cent of national employment) and textile/apparel retailing (17 per cent of the national total) employment.

In this view of the Italian textile sector, one can appreciate the geographic concentration of particular industries and segments, like the wool textile industry and its segments, but one rapidly reaches the conclusion that these localized industries all draw upon a much larger textile subculture, infrastructure, and skill base that spans much of north-central Italy. The skills, machinery, design, and customer

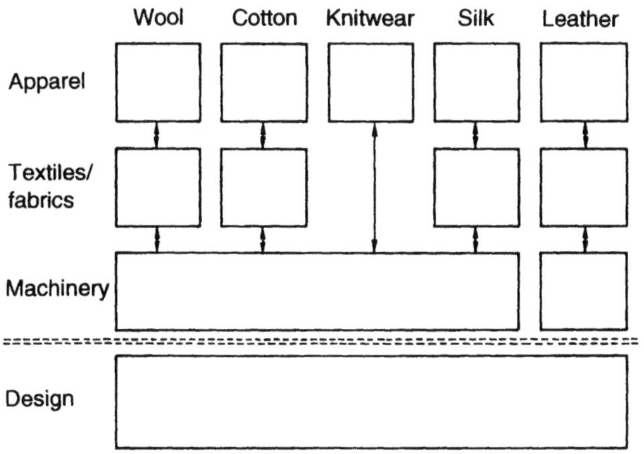

Figure 10.3 The Italian textile cluster

base that contribute to each textile industry and segment are spread across areas larger than the localized industrial districts themselves. The individual industrial districts are well worth understanding in their own right, but when placed in context, they appear as specialized components of a larger structure, the regional cluster, as peaks in a mountain range, rather than islands in an ocean.

Judgments about the geographic scope of a regional cluster cannot be divorced from judgments about the sectoral extent of the cluster. In order to determine the geographic and sectoral scope of a regional cluster, one must trace the flows of inputs, knowledge, and information that contribute to the cluster's ability to compete in interregional or international competition. Porter's framework provides one way of organizing such a search, though use of his framework requires judgment. Particularly important are judgments concerning the sources of the key skills and capabilities that are necessary for the industries within the clusters to succeed (see also Doeringer and Terkla, in this volume). The nature of the information and judgments necessary to determine the sectoral and geographic scope of a regional cluster limit the usefulness of input-output relations and cross-sectional analysis to describe the geographic or sectoral scope of regional clusters. Such relations and analyses, however, can be used as starting points for a more detailed assessments of the relative importance of different linkages or potential linkages among industries in the cluster.

This section suggests that research that focuses exclusively on developments within the narrow geographic areas of industrial districts might provide important insights concerning the internal operation of the districts themselves, but perhaps miss some of the important competitive advantages provided by the larger regional clusters of which they are part. This, in turn, suggests that policies that aim to stimulate the development of regional clusters or regional economies must look beyond narrowly defined industry segments to the larger set of skills, capabilities, and influences that contribute to competitive advantage. Efforts that focus on a single segment of an industry without regard for the varied general and specific skills necessary to compete in that segment and related segments might well fail to bring about the desired results. In addition, we must also take into account the fact that local environments or milieu (Maillat 1991) are embedded in national macroeconomic, legal, and innovation systems (Ettlinger 1994), as well as regimes governing labor relations (Gertler and Rutherford, in this volume).

Research into the geographic and sectoral scope of regional clusters would seek to address several related questions. One such question involves the nature of the links between industrial districts, defined as groups of firms in the same industry in a tightly circumscribed geographical location, and regional clusters, which can encompass larger geographical areas and a range of closely related industries. A second question is the extent to which the two different, but related, phenomena contribute to economic development. Although several studies of individual industries and individual regions address the importance of districts or clusters, there has been relatively little work that provides a quantitative assessment of their contribution to overall national economic growth and development (Sforzi 1992 is an exception). A third question concerns the link between the national environment and regional clusters and industrial districts. The prominence of regional clusters and industrial districts in some nations, for example, might lead one to look for particular national characteristics that could foster clustering. Research into these and related questions should tell us much about the optimal level (both in geographic and sectoral terms) for regional development policy and firm strategies to develop or take advantage of regional clusters.

10.5 Competition and Cooperation in Regional Clusters

Paradoxically, regional clusters appear to entail both greater cooperation and greater competition among direct competitors than geographically dispersed industries. Greater cooperation can come about through the fact that there are simply more activities that firms in close proximity can share, such as bulk purchasing, joint infrastructure investments, environmental control, and basic training, than can be shared by dispersed firms. In addition, firms in close proximity are more likely to be interdependent and recognize this interdependence than dispersed firms. At the same time, there is greater scope for competition among firms in close proximity than among dispersed firms. This is due to the greater visibility of local competitors as well as the potential for interpersonal competition among the economic actors within regional clusters (Enright 1990).

There has been much debate over the relative value of competition and cooperation in contributing to the competitiveness, and presumably the development potential, of regional clusters. The arguments for cooperation among direct competitors tend to focus on the inefficiencies that can result if decentralized competitors do not coordinate their actions (Scott 1992). Porter (1990), on the other hand, emphasizes the role that competition among local firms has in stimulating innovation and improvement in international competitiveness. He claims that local competitors provide stimulation above and beyond that provided by foreign competitors. Some researchers, such as Granovetter (1985), have reminded us that economic activity is embedded in a larger set of social relationships. We should remember that competition is just as much a social process as cooperation. In many geographic clusters, competition for position in the local social hierarchy results in tougher economic competition among firms inside the cluster. This is especially true in industries in which the owners of the leading firms are the leading citizens of the same city or town.

In assessing the relative importance of competition and cooperation in the development of regional clusters, it is important to define what is meant by competition and what is meant by cooperation. Some researchers, Best (1990) and Piore and Sabel (1984), for example, seem to extend the notion of cooperation to include a rough local consensus on the appropriate competitive variables (differentiating features as opposed to price). A rough agreement on the "rules of the game," however, does not preclude tough competition within those rules. In attempting to identify the role of cooperation in the development of regional clusters, it is important to understand whether it is the rules or the competition that fosters innovation and improvement.

In assessing the importance of competition and cooperation in the development of regional clusters, it is also important to distinguish between vertical relationships (those with buyers and suppliers) and horizontal relationships (those with direct competitors). Though some authors take great care to emphasize this distinction (Brusco 1992a, for example), others (Lazonick 1993, for example) virtually ignore it. The distinction is important because the arguments for vertical cooperation and horizontal cooperation are different, as are the potential benefits and costs. The arguments for cooperation with buyers or suppliers, in terms of sharing information that can contribute to new product and process developments or to gains through better coordination of activities, are relatively well understood (Russo 1985, for example). As indicated above, there is less consensus on the value of cooperation versus competition among direct competitors.

My own research indicates that the appropriate question for firms in regional clusters (and policy makers that influence them) is not whether to compete or cooperate, but rather on what dimensions to compete and on what dimensions to cooperate. In many successful clusters, there is cooperation among direct competitors in some activities, such as lobbying, foreign market research, joint export promotion, participation in trade fairs, and investments in industry-specific infrastructure, while other activities, such as company-specific marketing, production, sales, new product development, and process improvements, tend to be done in a competitive fashion. The Zurich Gold Pool, for example, was set up by the Swiss banks in order to create a larger, more efficient market for gold trading in the city. The banks then competed actively for business in the market that subsequently developed. The local industry associations in Prato and Biella sponsor trade fairs that bring in buyers from around the world. The companies cooperate to put on the show, but compete aggressively within the show. The Italian packaging machinery industry association commissions market research and carries out generic promotion in foreign markets. The Italian ceramic tile industry association also provides payroll, bulk purchasing, research on materials, and basic training services. At the same time, member companies compete aggressively in the marketplace. There are numerous other examples of similar behavior.

The interesting research question is to try to identify the optimal mix of competition and cooperation for a given regional cluster, or for regional clusters in general. In particular, which activities are best carried out competitively and which are best carried out cooperatively? For firms, cooperation with direct competitors involves the tradeoff between access to greater resources versus the potential for loss of proprietary information or the creation of stronger competitors. For policy makers, the tradeoff is between the advantages of cooperation versus the stimulus provided by tough local competition. The optimal levels and forms of competition and cooperation will be those that optimize across these tradeoffs.

Optimal levels and forms of competition and cooperation will vary by industry and by region. Simply put, there are some types of cooperation that will be beneficial in some industries and some locations, but would not be beneficial in other industries with different economic and business imperatives, or in other locations with different institutions and histories. Different regions have different potentials for truly cooperative or competitive undertakings (Gertler and Rutherford; Gittell et al.; and Staber, in this volume) due to differences in cultural norms, legal regimes, political considerations, and historical circumstances. It is not enough to suggest that since certain competitive or cooperative structures have arisen in one nation or region that they can or should be copied elsewhere. Instead, we need to develop an understanding of what types of competitive or cooperative behavior are feasible and desirable under differing circumstances.

10.6 Governing Relations in Regional Clusters

The nature of relations and governance of transactions within regional clusters and industrial districts has also received a great deal of attention. Different types of regional clusters have different structures and different mechanisms for governing transactions and broader relations. Storper and Harrison (1991), for example, propose a typology of structures of production systems by the extent of division of labor, the size of individual production units, the degree of connection among units, the territorial extent of the production system, and governance structures (power relationships among firms). Enright (1995) describes an alternative typology based on the length and nature of the relationships among transacting parties. In this typology, transactions take place on spot markets, through short term coalitions, through long term relationships, or within hierarchical structures. Each type of transaction is organized by a different type of coordinating agent and employs different coordinating mechanisms. Kamann (1991) and Johansson (1991) conclude that power considerations are extremely important characteristics of the interaction firms within networks. Power considerations include the power to exclude potential members and power to decide who suffers in downturns, among others.

Different types of regional clusters entail different types and degrees of centralization of decision making, which, in turn, influence the ability of the cluster to coordinate its activities. Some of the most interesting coordination issues arise in the context of fragmented local industry structures with decentralized decision making processes. Of particular interest are mechanisms to govern transactions in regional clusters that limit opportunistic behavior on the part of different economic actors. There are two basic approaches that researchers have taken to describe the governance of transactions within relatively fragmented clusters. One, based on recent work on institutional economics (Williamson 1985, for example), is the transaction cost framework. In the transaction cost framework, reputational effects and the potential for sanctions are invoked to explain the limits to opportunistic behavior by transacting partners often found in regional clusters. Scott (1986), Enright (1990, 1995), and Lundvall (1993), among others, discuss the role of transaction cost considerations in regional clusters.

The second approach to describing the governance of transactions within regional clusters, based on work on the sociology of regional clusters, focuses on trust between local economic actors. In this view, cultural similarities, community cohesiveness, interdependence among local firms, repeated interaction, and familiarity allow transaction partners to trust that their counterparts will not act opportunistically. It is this trust that allows for the smooth function of fragmented regional clusters made up of many participants. Harrison (1992), Piore and Sabel (1984), Sabel (1992), Becattini (1989b), and Best (1990), among others, discuss the role of trust in regional clusters. Staber (in this volume) provides a useful overview.

Some of the work on trust in regional clusters appears to give short shrift to any economic explanation for transaction governance in regional clusters. My own experience (based on formal and informal discussions and interviews with managers, consultants, industry association representatives, and government officials involved in regional clusters in a dozen nations), however, tells me that such trust is often both overstated and overrated. I have come across instances of managers spying on competitors with telescopes, of price fixing agreements that have been violated before the completion of the meetings that set them, and of industry associations that are not allowed to compile statistics from the annual reports of member companies even though the reports are public information. All of these were in regional clusters that one or more researchers have concluded have relationships primarily based on interfirm trust. In my own work, I have yet to see a case in which trust has caused behavior that was inconsistent with the parties' economic self-interest. This implies that what is often called trust in regional clusters is part of economic self-interest, not a replacement for it.

Authors who might claim that the trust they see in regional clusters is something significantly different from (and seemingly unrelated to) economic self-interest usually do not take into account the repeated nature of economic interaction, the importance of reputation in economic transactions, and the ability to punish short-run opportunistic behavior inherent in most geographic clusters. In other words, an economic view of regional clusters is sometimes equated with a straw man of a one-shot, anonymous transaction, a model no serious economist would use in such circumstances. The corresponding straw man on the other end of the spectrum is rarely identified. It is useful to do so, since, after all, a utopian form of local capitalism in which everyone within a regional cluster cooperates and operates on the basis of trust divorced from medium-term economic self interest is at least as far from reality as a Hobbesian form of local capitalism in which everyone within a regional cluster acts opportunistically in each transaction. A complete description of transaction governance in regional clusters must clearly incorporate both economic and sociological forces.

The research questions that come out of this literature involve investigations of the patterns of relationships among economic actors in different regional clusters and the role of economic self-interest as opposed to trust that cannot be framed in terms of economic self-interest. In this regard, if the challenge for the economist is to show that his or her model of behavior is *sufficient* to explain the economic behavior of actors in regional clusters, then the challenge for the sociologist is to show that his or her model of behavior is *necessary* to explain the economic behavior of such actors. Trying to differentiate economic self-interest that takes into account reputational effects and the ability of local agents to sanction opportunistic behavior from relationships built on trust would be an extremely useful exercise, even though, should the economic behavior predicted by both views be the same, it might turn out to be a distinction without a meaningful difference.

10.7 Globalization-Localization Tensions

The recent literature on regional clusters and localization in industry appears to conflict with recent literature on the multinational firm. The latter increasingly focuses on global or transnational firms which reportedly transcend and diminish the economic role of nations and regions (see Bartlett and Ghoshal 1989, for example). According to Cooke and Imrie (1989), globalization has broken down formerly strong local and regional economic identities. Amin and Robbins (1990) conclude that globalization is a powerful tendency that runs counter to localization of production into industrial districts. On the other hand, much of the literature on industrial districts and the "renaissance of regional economies" (Sabel 1989: 22-31) focuses on the development of localized industrial districts or regional clusters of firms and industries. Storper (1992, p.62), for example, concludes that in many industries, "the key collections of physical capital, labor, and information resources are almost always highly geographically concentrated in one, or a few, subnational regions of their respective leader countries." Thus, in his view, the advantages of local production systems and technology districts limit the globalization of industry.

This seeming contradiction leads to questions over how long regions will have a distinct economic role. Enright (1993b) claims that regions will matter as long as the sources of competitive advantage in industries vary from place to place. Regions will matter as long as there are significant regional differences in tastes, patterns of local demand, institutions, firm strategies and structures, related and supporting industries, rivalry among firms, and government policies. In this view, globalization does not mean economic homogenization, particularly when the path-dependence of local economic development is taken into account. Enright (1993b, p.100) claims, "For regions to lose their distinctive economies, trade and investment barriers must fall more slowly than changes in capabilities, tastes, institutions, and economic organizations that provide the underlying sources of competitive advantage." Otherwise, local differences actually should become more, rather than less, important in determining the location of production.

The apparent tension between globalizing and localizing tendencies also leads to questions concerning the interaction of global firms and local economies. Some authors view the emergence of global firms with the power to extract rents from local authorities as a threat to regions, which must compete for a place in an economic hierarchy dictated by the strategies of transnational companies (TNCs). Dicken (1994, p.123), for example, states, "Ultimately, therefore, it may be that, because of the immense asymmetry of power between TNCs and *local* institutions, there is little that such institutions can do on their own other than to provide an attractive business environment or to attempt to stimulate the kinds of local businesses that might eventually be embedded in a TNC network." Such conclusions have resulted in calls for more active regional economic development policies (Cooke and Imrie 1989, for example) so that a given region might be included, as opposed to excluded, from TNC networks.

Some nations that have relied on foreign direct investment for economic growth have apparently been able to develop clusters with the aid of such investment. In other nations, foreign owned firms are found in enclaves with relatively little spillover into the local economy. In 1989, for example, Ireland's foreign owned firms accounted for 44 per cent of the nation's manufacturing employment, 55 per cent of manufacturing output, and 75 per cent of manufacturing exports (O'Malley et al. 1992). Despite these figures, many believe that foreign owned firms have made only limited contributions to the development of indigenous industry. Non-food foreign owned companies imported 80 per cent of the inputs and 30 per cent of all the services they used. A recent review of Ireland's industrial policy concluded that foreign owned firms had generated only limited contacts with local companies and had not contributed to the development of self-sustaining clusters of local firms (Industrial Policy Review Group 1992). While there are clearly examples in which "outsider" firms have contributed to the development of regional clusters, there has been little systematic work that would allow us to conclude that vibrant regional clusters can be developed solely, or mostly, through the attraction of "outsider" firms. A major question for firms is how they might take advantage of the existence of regional clusters (Enright 1994). There has been relatively little work that explores the nature of the benefits that firms from outside the cluster can obtain from locating a facility within a cluster. The issue is not whether a multinational firm can use its existing network of subsidiaries to generate and transfer knowledge within the corporation, but whether the outsider firm can truly take advantage of the skills and knowledge bases found in the cluster. Several European pharmaceutical companies, including Hoffmann-La Roche, Novo Industri, Rhone Poulenc, Sandoz, and Ciba-Geigy, for example, have recently acquired interests in United States biotechnology clusters. Though these firms are usually kept as stand alone operations, the clear intent is for the pharmaceutical firms to use their acquisitions as a window into the new technology. These investments have helped some companies fill their product pipeline. My own informal discussions with company managers, however, indicate that knowledge has generally not been transferred back to the rest of the company to the extent desired.

Kenney and Florida (1994) conclude that most Japanese research and development investment in the United States is in support of customizing or adapting new products for the US market or to support other US activities such as manufacturing. It is not clear whether investments made in clusters with significant expertise in the United States (by auto, electronics, and biotechnology firms) have truly resulted in the transfer of specialized knowledge back to the rest of the company. The purchases of United States motion picture studios by Sony and Matsushita, on the other hand, represent a very different type of investment. These investments have not been designed to (nor are they likely to) transfer motion picture production and distribution knowledge back into the Japanese operations of the two companies.

The global-local nexus described in this section provides a rich set of research questions. The first involves the relative importance of globalizing and localizing tendencies and the extent to which globalization of markets might contribute to the localization of production. A second involves the evaluation of regional policies to build clusters around investments from outside the region. Although there has been a great deal of effort expended by local authorities on attracting investment from firms from other nations and regions, there has been relatively little work that explicitly links these efforts with the role that "outsiders" play in cluster development. To what extent do outside firms contribute to or hinder the development of clusters and to what extent can outsiders tap into regional clusters for their own advantage?

A third question involves the extent to which a firm can "buy into" a regional cluster, and how the likelihood of success might differ from industry to industry or country to country. One might expect, for example, that the artisan and "high tech cottage industries" of northern Italy, with their relatively closed social structures, would be more difficult for outsiders to penetrate than the high technology clusters of the United States, with their relatively open social structures. The extent to which "outsider" firms can take advantage of the expertise present in a regional cluster clearly depends on the type of information that is available in the cluster and the freedom of information flow within the cluster. The extent to which "outsider" firms can take advantage of regional clusters far from their home region or nation might also depend on the nationality of the company and region in question. According to Dicken (1994), transnational companies (TNCs) are not placeless. He concludes that all TNCs have an identifiable home base that embeds it in a particular national environment, that ultimate decision making authority is usually concentrated at home, that very few TNCs have moved ultimate decision making authority outside their home nation, and that similarities among TNCs from a given nation are usually more important than their differences. This implies that firms from a particular nation might be better or worse at assimilating knowledge from foreign clusters than those from other nations.

10.8 The Failure Modes of Geographic Clusters

Almost lost in the recent literature on successful regional clusters and localized industries has been the fact that many regional clusters of firms and industries do not succeed and that many that do succeed for a time eventually fail. In particular, there has been relatively little recent work on the failure modes or potential failure modes of once successful regional clusters of firms and industries. Notable exceptions include Amin and Robbins (1990), Grabher (1993a), Dunford et al. (1993), Harrison (1994), and Enright (1995). There appear to be five basic failure mechanisms developed in the literature: falling demand for a cluster's products, organizational obsolescence, competition from similar clusters, loss of the ability to coordinate activities, and loss of internal dynamism through ossification.

Falling demand through product obsolescence can cause hardship for geographic clusters. The detachable collar industry of Troy, New York, for example, is a distant memory (Krugman 1991). A less distant memory is the minicomputer, which was a major pillar of the development of the Route 128 area outside of Boston. Digital Equipment Company, Data General, Prime Computer, and Wang Laboratories have all suffered as personal computers and workstations replace the minicomputer. DEC was forced to end a thirty-three year no layoff policy and will reduce its worldwide employment from 130,000 in 1989 to a projected 80,000 by 1995. Data General has already reduced its workforce from 18,000 to 7,000. Wang Laboratories has gone through a painful bankruptcy and restructuring. Employment at Wang was projected to fall to 6,000 in 1994, down from approximately 17,000 in 1991. Wang and Prime have chosen to focus on providing software and service and are no longer manufacturing minicomputers. DEC and Data General have scrambled to reposition their products (Information taken from corporate reports and announcements). The decline of the minicomputer and lower defense spending have helped put an end to the "miracle" days the Massachusetts economy experienced in the 1980s. Similar declines in demand have hurt the military aerospace cluster of Southern California (Scott and Bergman, in this volume) and the coal, iron, and steel cluster of the Ruhr (Grabher 1993b), among others.

A second failure mode for regional clusters is what one might term organizational obsolescence. The best known examples of this mechanism are those in which mass production by integrated firms has replaced artisan production within regional clusters. The gun quarter of Birmingham, for example, was made obsolete by mass produced firearms made with interchangeable parts (Wise 1949). In more recent times, Dunford et al. (1993) have questioned the continued vitality of the Vigevano shoe cluster in Italy on grounds of the obsolescence of the small firm cluster. The product life cycle (Vernon 1966, Markusen 1985) can also make geographic clusters obsolete. As the knowledge necessary to produce a given product or set of products diffuses over time, either through a natural diffusion process or through the actions of firms, the importance of location near pools of expertise and leading edge customers decreases, as does the advantage of the variety of strategies and technological choices often present in geographic clusters.

Regional clusters often represent an early stage of development of larger, integrated firms. Comau, Fiat's factory automation equipment subsidiary, for example, was once an association of twenty machine tool and machinery suppliers to Fiat. The "Big Three" United States auto companies absorbed several other local companies in their early years, as did the "Big Three" German chemical companies. Harrison (1994) recounts attempts to internalize the externalities of regional clusters by expansion through acquisition by Sasib, the Italian engineering and metal-mechanical firm. Though not necessarily the sign of economic failure, in fact the conventional wisdom is that such evolution is associated with economic progress (Chandler 1990), such developments might call into question the stability and development potential of regional clusters of small and medium-sized firms.

Regional clusters of firms are sometimes displaced by similarly structured clusters in other locations. In the eighteenth century, Sheffield (United Kingdom) was the world's leading supplier of cutlery. Sheffield was known as the "factory without walls" due to its concentration of many small cutlery firms and suppliers. In the late nineteenth century, Sheffield was overtaken by its rival, Solingen, a similarly structured cluster in Germany. In the latter portion of the twentieth century, as Sheffield faded, a new challenger emerged for Solingen. Seki (Japan), which has been called the "Japanese Solingen," is home to yet another cluster of small and medium sized firms. In the early 1990s, there were approximately 300 cutlery firms in Solingen and 600 cutlery firms in Seki. Japan and Germany have been neck and neck as the world's leading exporters of cutlery since the 1970s (van der Linde 1991).

A fourth failure mode, or at least potential failure mode, for regional clusters cited in the literature is the loss of cooperative relationships and information flows within clusters. Florida and Kenney (1990a) claim that the increase in litigation among Silicon Valley firms attempting to protect intellectual property and guard against competition from spinoff firms is a sign of potential decay. Harrison (1994) traces the difficulty that the Prato industrial district has experienced in the 1990s in part to a failure to institutionalize new forms of cooperative undertakings, including the failure of attempts to create area-wide information systems to speed order processing and coordination of production. In these two case, however, the ultimate impact of the lack of cooperation is not clear.

The fifth, and in many ways most interesting failure mode for regional clusters of firms is loss of dynamism through ossification. In comparing the evolution of Silicon Valley and Route 128 in the 1980s, Saxenian (1994, p.162) has concluded that "industrial systems built on regional networks are more flexible and technologically dynamic than those in which experimentation and learning are confined to individual firms." While this might be an apt conclusion for Silicon Valley and Route 128, even industrial systems built on regional networks can lack the flexibility they need to adjust to discontinuous change. In some regional clusters, close relationships eliminate the need for firms to develop certain functional specialties, such as marketing, that are carried out through personal relationships within clusters. The lack of such functional skills can be a detriment to adaptability when circumstances change. The same geographically impacted information that allows for the formation of regional clusters in the first place sometimes prevents firms from reacting quickly and effectively to stimulus from outside the cluster. In addition, in some clusters, labor, management, and local politicians develop methods of operation and perquisites that make it difficult for the cluster to change with the times. Entrenched interests often divert resources that could be utilized in new industries to prop up older, failing industries.

Grabher (1993b) has termed these three types of failure "functional lock-in," "cognitive lock-in," and "political lock-in." In his study of the coal, iron, and steel complex of the Ruhr, Grabher concludes that close relationships among industry participants had disastrous long term consequences for the region's adaptability, since they prevented local firms from developing certain types of expertise. In addition, a common worldview allowed industry participants to confuse secular trends with cyclical downturns. Finally, political lock-in occurred as planning authorities, unions, and professional associations pushed for support of an industry trajectory that had become a dead end. Grabher concludes that the Ruhr suffered from a "consensus culture, from lack of constructive conflict, and [from a lack of] creative chaos." (Grabher, 1993b: 275) The very types of relationships that many researchers extol had become liabilities.

There are a number of similar examples. The Swiss watch industry, for example, was unable to respond to the development of the tuning fork watch in the 1960s and quartz movement in the 1970s, even though both were invented by Swiss engineers. The structure of the Swiss industry had been largely frozen in the 1930s by the cooperation among local industry participants that resulted in several cartel arrangements that were cemented by laws governing the sector. By the mid-1960s, the cartels had been abolished, but the structure that remained, fragmented firms with a limited amount of coordination within two loose holding companies, made it difficult for the Swiss firms to respond to the emergence of US and Japanese companies. It was not until the dismantling of many of the industry's traditional structures and the advent of SMH, a vertically integrated, managerial company, in the early 1980s that the Swiss watch industry was able to regain its position in low and medium-priced watches (Enright 1995).

The point of this section is that regional clusters of industries do not always grow and that existing clusters do not always persist. Geographic clusters fail when their strengths (decentralized structures, geographically impacted information, localized routines, self-awareness, interdependence, and ties between local firms and institutions) become their weaknesses. Although the industry studies reported here and elsewhere suggest that geographic clusters of firms can be very flexible in the face of incremental change, they also suggest that such clusters can be rather inflexible in the face of radical change. The failure mechanisms of regional clusters are generally well-known, but often seem to be overlooked in the current discussions of clusters among academics and policy makers.

There are several research questions posed by the failure modes of regional clusters. The first involves determining the relative importance of the different failure mechanisms across a sample of regional clusters. Such studies might allow firms and policy makers to be on guard for particular types of decline. A second line of research would assess at what point coordination of activities among the actors in an industry cluster turns from an advantage to a disadvantage. This is particularly important given the calls for increased cooperation and business-government interaction typically found in many if not most articles and papers on regional clusters. Further work could focus on mechanisms for the actors within regional clusters to break out of functional, cognitive, and political forms of lock-in when they occur. The difficulty that some traditional industrial areas have faced in the last few decades heightens the importance of a thorough understanding of such mechanisms. Relation of experiences with different strategies and policies that help clusters adapt and persist in the face of discontinuous change would also be welcome.

10.9 Government, Regional Clusters, and the Nature of Regional Policy

In order to understand the interest in regional clusters among policy makers, it is useful to recall the changes in government policy toward regional development over the last several decades (Scott 1992). The traditional aim of regional development policy in most nations has been to eliminate differences in income levels, unemployment, and standard of living. In the 1950s and 1960s, "growth pole" policies tried to stimulate development through large infrastructure projects and by encouraging the migration of large companies and multinationals to peripheral locations. The goal was to take advantage of the multiplier effects of large facilities through their backward and forward linkages with local economies. Infrastructure provision, interest rate subsidies for private investment, capital subsidies, investment credit guarantees, and support in developing industrial land were all used as development tools.

Attempts to create new growth poles, however, met with limited success. Donckels and Courtmans (1990), for example, conclude that the growth pole strategies followed in the Kempen area in Belgium did not result in the improvement of the local economy. The firms that were attracted were not integrated into the local economy and that the relocation of facilities based on financial incentives was often not permanent. According to Bull, Pitt, and Szarka (1991, p.85), the failure of the growth pole approach in France, as evidenced by the failure of the iron and steel agglomeration at Fos, near Marseilles, to meet expectations and in Italy, where the approach failed to industrialize the South in the 1960s and early 1970s, helped cause the "abandonment of local development induced by exogenous means." Eventually, local governments began to look for alternatives to economic development strategies that relied on attracting manufacturing investments from outside the area.

By the 1980s, the success of the high technology clusters in Silicon Valley and on Route 128 outside of Boston led to a wide variety of efforts to stimulate local development by promoting the growth of local high technology industries. Governments promoted science parks, high technology incubators, venture capital funds, and attempts to form linkages between high technology university research and local firms. A number of local governments made investments in amenities that were designed to make life attractive for a mobile, skilled, high technology, work force. Some authors provided detailed prescriptions for "growing the next Silicon Valley" (Miller and Côté 1987, for example). Although some centers developed fairly rapidly, such as Research Triangle, North Carolina; Austin, Texas; and Sophia Antipolis, France, the overall results of such policies have been at best mixed (Preer 1992, Castells and Hall 1994). Relatively few regions have been able to generate new, innovative technology-based industries. This has been due in part to the difficulties of choosing which sectors would grow, in part to the difficulties in duplicating research infrastructures that had taken decades to develop, in part to the prior existence of competing centers that had arisen organically, and in part to competition among a large number of regions attempting to promote the same set of high technology industries.

The 1990s have seen the emergence of development strategies based on regional clusters. Québec (Ferland et al., in this volume), Arizona (Waits et al. 1992), and Massachusetts, among other states, provinces, and regions, have explicitly begun to base their development efforts on cluster formation and extension. Such policies have also been suggested at the national level in Ireland (Industrial Policy Review Group 1992) and elsewhere. It should be noted that the earlier policies described above have similarities with cluster based development strategies. All try to take advantage of the stimulus that an industry can have on its supplier industries, buyer industries, and industries related through common technologies. The biggest difference in the more recent approaches is a greater emphasis on building on the skills, capabilities, and industrial base found in particular regions. The goal has been development that builds incrementally on a region's economic base through the creation and enhancement of institutions that allow for greater interfirm communication, greater information sharing, the pooling of resources to create localized public goods, the creation of supporting research and service centers, and the tailoring of local educational efforts to the needs of the local economy. Many of these activities have placed governmental agencies in supporting roles, rather than lead roles, in local development, though there is a substantial variety in the nature of government involvement in regional cluster development strategies.

Enright (1992) provides four basic steps for fostering the development of regional clusters. These steps are: 1) Identify existing or potential clusters of successful industries within the nation. Potential clusters may be those that incorporate a specific technology in which the region is a leader, or which are particularly well suited to the skills of the local workforce, or which satisfy a demand that is particularly sophisticated within the nation. 2) Invest in developing the major technologies and capabilities that cut across the industries in the cluster. Such investments will have the greatest leverage in deepening and broadening the cluster. They should include development of indigenous technology as well as acquiring best practice technology from abroad. 3) Identify the "holes" in the cluster, the supplier and related industries that are not well developed in the region. Such "holes" will tend to weaken the entire cluster and might provide opportunities for the region's firms. Filling these holes through the organic development of local firms or the targeted attraction of outside investment, will strengthen the cluster as a whole. 4) Ensure that rivalry permeates the cluster. Cooperation within a cluster should not reduce rivalry to the point where the cluster becomes vulnerable to firms in more dynamic environments. Several authors (Ferland et al., in this volume, and Waits et al. 1992, for example) have provided more detailed descriptions of actual cluster development policies or policy suggestions.

As mentioned above, many governments at the national, regional, and local levels have become interested in supporting economic growth through the development of regional clusters. The interest in development policies based on regional clusters is due to the perceived failures of earlier policies and the perceived success of certain regional clusters. There is a danger, however, that governments will view regional clusters as the next panacea for problems of economic development and simply repeat the mistakes of the past by all trying to foster clusters in the same set of industries (a limited set of high technology industries, for example) and by forming policy without regard to the local context. Competitive advantage comes from uniqueness, not from the same policies aimed at the same industries. Unless the policy or program builds on some unique feature of the local environment, it is unlikely to be the source of sustained success. The main difference between the more creative current approaches for development based on regional clusters and earlier efforts is a greater emphasis on real as well as potential linkages with local economic, industrial, skill, and institutional bases. If this difference is lost, then development strategies based on regional clusters will be no more or less effective than the strategies they were meant to replace.

There is also a danger that governments will forget that their role in cluster development is at best partial. It will be difficult for governments to create competitive clusters out of thin air, just as it proved difficult for governments to create dynamic growth poles or dynamic technopolises. If an advantage could be created on one region or nation exclusively through the use of policy, then what is to stop another nation or region from using the same policy mix to foster development of a competing industry? Government can help or hurt the process, but it seems less able to create vibrant clusters on its own.

There are, of course, several research questions that should be addressed regarding government's role in cluster formation. The first is the extent to which government can influence the formation of regional clusters. Most of the regional clusters of which I am aware developed organically, often with relatively limited direct input from government, which sometimes became involved after the fact. The second question is the nature of the policies that ultimately promote development and those that do not. There has been relatively little in the way of systematic post-audits of governmental policies toward regional clusters. This will have to be remedied if we are to develop solid overall guidelines for such policies.

Another fruitful avenue for research is the potential conflict between national policies that attempt to decentralize productive activities and local policies that attempt to build on local advantages. Increasingly, nations cannot, or will not, hurt strong industries and areas in order to help weaker industries and areas. Attempts to decentralize particular industries on the part of national governments often fly in the face of development based on regional clusters. In Canada, for example, the Québec Government has made efforts to stimulate further development of its aerospace industry, while the National Government has made efforts to disperse the industry through its purchasing practices. Similarly, political negotiations caused a Canadian plan to support a limited number of centers of excellence in microelectronics to result in the establishment of a center of excellence in microelectronics in each province. Thus, an effort to bring together a critical mass of expertise did just the opposite until most of the centers were closed. The lesson appears to be that nations should not attempt to make all regions look alike. Instead, they should allow and encourage different regions to develop different specialties.

Finally, despite the interest in regional development policies and the large number of case studies of individual regional policies, in Ettlinger's (1994: 144) words, "We lack comparative analysis of localized development planning to extrapolate general principles of effective business-government relations and local development." Such comparative analysis that attempts to isolate the impact of regional policies from other influences on regional development would go a long way toward allowing us to draw better conclusions and recommendations regarding regional policies.

10.10 Conclusion

The virtual explosion of research on regional clusters in recent years has dramatically improved our understanding of the phenomenon. There are, however, a number of issues which have yet to be fully explored. Several of these have been highlighted in this chapter. Promising areas for future research include the types of industries that tend to be parts of regional clusters, the geographic and sectoral scope of regional clusters, the optimal mix of competition and cooperation in regional cluster, the governance of transactions and broader relations within regional clusters, the seeming tension between globalizing and localizing tendencies, the failure modes of regional clusters, and the appropriate role for government policy in fostering regional clusters.

In terms of methodology, there is ample room for more competitive and comparative studies of regional clusters. Most studies of regional clusters seem to focus on the internal operations of the clusters with little regard for the external influences that will help determine its success or failure. The nature of competition between a particular cluster and clustered or dispersed firms in other locations is frequently ignored. Since the success or failure of a cluster is determined by its ability to succeed against outside competitors, the conclusions and suggestions of such studies must be questioned. *Competitive* studies, studies that provide a detailed assessment of regional clusters and outside competitors, would provide additional, valued perspectives. Although *comparative* studies of regional clusters in the same industry or types of industry are more common (see Preer 1992, Castells and Hall 1994, and Storper 1992 on high technology agglomerations and Bull, Pitt, and Szarka 1991 on the textile industry, for example), significant additional insights can be gained through further studies in which clusters in the same industry, or similar industries, are examined across several nations.

There is also room for a greater focus on what we might call *ex ante* academic studies and *ex post* policy studies. Nearly all academic studies of regional clusters are *ex post* studies that attempt to explain the success, failure, or structure of a given regional cluster or small set of clusters. Relatively few academic studies use present knowledge of regional clusters to provide *ex ante* predictions of the success or failure of a given cluster in a particular region, or the clusters that are likely to emerge in a particular region. Scott and Bergman (in this volume), in their work on the potential for the development of a ground transportation cluster in the Los Angeles area, is a notable exception. Whereas academics tend to focus on *ex post* explanations, rather than *ex ante* predictions, policy makers have the opposite tendency. Policy makers tend to engage in *ex ante* prophesies with little in the way of *ex post* accounting. The result is that policies are often not subjected to rigorous performance evaluations that would allow for a full understanding of their consequences.

This chapter has attempted to summarize at least part of the recent literature on regional clusters and related phenomena and to map out an agenda for future research. Improvements in our knowledge in each of the areas identified will add, not only to an academic understanding of regional clustering, but also to the ability of policy makers and managers to formulate strategies to help develop and take advantage of regional clusters.

References

Abernathy, F. W. "The U.S. Apparel Industry: Response to Global Markets," unpublished manuscript.

Ahmad, M. 1993. "Economic Cooperation in Southern Growth Triangle: An Indonesian Perspective," in T. M. Heng and L. Low (eds.) *Regional Cooperation and Growth Triangles in ASEAN*. Singapore: Times Academic Press, 92-118.

Aldrich, H. 1979. *Organizations and Environments*. Englewood Cliffs: Prentice-Hall.

Aldrich, H. 1989. "Networking among Women Entrepreneurs," in O. Hagan, C. Rivchun, and D. Sexton (eds.) *Women-Owned Businesses*. New York: Praeger, 103-132.

Aldrich, H. and M. Fiol. 1994. "Fools Rush In? The Institutional Context of Industry Creation," *Academy of Management Journal*, 19, 645-670.

Aldrich, H. and T. Sasaki. 1995a. "Governance Structure and Technology Transfer Management in R&D Consortia in the United States and Japan," in J. Liker, J. Ettlie, and J. Campbell (eds.) *Managing Technology Development and Deployment in Manufacturing: U. S. and Japan Comparisons*, (forthcoming).

Aldrich, H. and T. Sasaki. 1995b. "R&D Consortia in the United States and Japan," *Research Policy*, (forthcoming).

Alter, C. and J. Hage. 1993. *Building Cooperation Between Organizations*. Lexington: D. C. Heath.

Amin, A. 1993. "The Globalization of the Economy: An Erosion of Regional Networks?" in G. Grabher (ed.) *The Embedded Firm*. London: Routledge, 278-295.

Amin, A. and K. Robbins. 1990. "The Re-Emergence of Regional Economies? The Mythical Geography of Flexible Accumulation," *Environment and Planning D: Society and Space*, 8, 7-34.

Amin, A. and N. Thrift. 1992. "Neo-Marshallian Nodes in Global Networks," *International Journal of Urban and Regional Research*, 16, 571-587.

Ash, R. F. and Y. Y. Kueh. 1993. "Economic Integration within Greater China: Trade and Investment Flows between China, Hong Kong, and Taiwan," *The China Quarterly*, 136, 711-745.

Astley, G. and C. Fombrun. 1983. "Collective Strategy: Social Ecology of Organizational Environments," *Academy of Management Review*, 8, 576-587.

Axelrod, R. 1984. *The Evolution of Cooperation*. New York: Basic Books.

Aydalot, P. and D. Keeble (eds.). 1988. *High Technology Industry and Innovative Environments*. Andover, Hants.: Routledge & Kegan Paul.

Badaracco, J. L. 1991. *The Knowledge Link*. Boston: Harvard Business School.

Bade, F. 1983. "Large Corporations and Regional Development," *Regional Studies*, 17, 315-326.

Bailey, T. 1988. "Education and the Transformation of Markets and Technology in the Textile Industry," *Conservation of Human Resources,* Technical Paper No. 2, New York: Columbia University.

Bailey, T. 1989. "Technology, Skills, and Education in the Apparel Industry," *Conservation of Human Resources*, Technical Paper No. 7, New York: Columbia University.

Bartik, T. J. 1991. *Who Benefits from State and Local Economic Development Policies*? Kalamazoo, Michigan: W. E. Upjohn Institute for Employment Research.

Bartlett, C. A. and S. Ghoshal. 1989. *Managing across Borders*. Boston: Harvard Business School Press.

Becattini, G. (ed.). 1987. *Mercato e Forze Locali: il Distretto Industriale*. Bologna: il Mulino.

Becattini, G. (ed.). 1989a. *Modelli Locali di Sviluppo*. Bologna: il Mulino.

Becattini, G. 1989b. "Sectors and/or Districts: Some Remarks on the Conceptual Foundations of Industrial Economics," in E. Goodman, J. Bamford, and P. Saynor (eds.) *Small Firms and Industrial Districts in Italy*. London: Routledge, 123-136.

Behrens, B. and R. Böhmer. 1993. "Team ist Trumpf," *Wirtschaftswoche*, 47, 14-22.

Bellandi, M. and M. Romagnoli. 1994. "Case Study II: Prato and the Textile Industry," in R. Leonardi and R. Nanetti (eds.) *Regional Development in a Modern European Economy: The Case of Tuscany*. London: Pinter, 145-169.

Belzer, V. 1993. *Kooperationspraxis im Verarbeitenden Gewerbe – Erfahrungen aus Nordrhein-Westfalen*, Arbeitspapier IAT-DS 01 des Instituts für Arbeit und Technik, Gelsenkirchen.

Benson, K. 1975. "The Interorganizational Network as a Political Economy," *Administrative Science Quarterly*, 20, 229-249.

Bergman, E. M., G. Maier, and F. Tödtling (eds.). 1991. *Regions Reconsidered: Economic Networks, Innovation, and Local Development in Industrialized Countries*. London: Mansell.

Best, M. H. 1990. *The New Competition*. Cambridge, MA: Harvard University Press.

Bianchi, P. and N. Bellini. 1991. "Public Policies for Local Networks of Innovators," *Research Policy*, 20, 487-497.

Bluestone, B. and I. Bluestone. 1992. "Workers (and Managers) of the World Unite," *Technology Review*, 95, 30-40.

Boelcke, W. 1986. "Die Industrialisierung: Bedingtheiten im Südwesten," in R. Rinker and W. Setzler (eds.) *Die Geschichte Baden-Württembergs*. Stuttgart: Konrad Theiss, 254-263.

Boelcke, W. 1987. "Organisation und Politik von Industrie, Handwerk und Handel," in H. Schneider (ed.) *Verbände in Baden-Württemberg. Schriften zur Politischen Landeskunde Baden-Württembergs*. Stuttgart: Kohlhammer, 14, 136-165.

Booz-Allen and Hamilton Inc. 1992. *Regional Economic Analysis of the Thirty-Year Plan*. A Report Submitted to the Los Angeles County Transportation Commission. Los Angeles: Transportation Consulting Division, Booz-Allen and Hamilton.

Boyer, R. 1989. *Global Competition, Firm Organization and Total Factor Productivity: A Micro-Perspective*. Paris: OECD.

Brown, L. D. 1983. *Managing Conflict at Organizational Interfaces*. Reading, Mass: Addison-Wesley.

Brusco, S. 1982. "The Emilian Model: Productive Decentralisation and Social Integration," *Cambridge Journal of Economics*, 6, 167-184.

Brusco, S. 1992a. "The Idea of the Industrial District: Its Genesis," in F. Pyke, G. Becattini, and W. Sengenberger (eds.) *Industrial Districts and Inter-Firm Co-Operation in Italy.* Geneva: ILO, 10-19.

Brusco, S. 1992b. "Small Firms and the Provision of Real Services," in F. Pyke and W. Sengenberger (eds.) *Industrial Districts and Local Economic Regeneration.* Geneva: ILO, 177-196.

Bryson, J., P. Wood, and D. Keeble. 1993. "Business Networks, Small Firm Flexibility and Regional Development in the U.K. Business Services," *Entrepreneurship and Regional Development*, 5, 265-277.

Bull, A., M. Pitt, and J. Szarka. 1991. "Small Firms and Industrial Districts: Structural Explanations of Small Firm Viability in Three Countries," *Entrepreneurship and Regional Development*, 3, 83-99.

Buono, A. F. and G. A. Hachey. 1993. "Ethical Gaps in Financial Services Networks: Lessons from the Mortgage Banking Industry," *Business and the Contemporary World*, 5, 140-152.

Burt, R. 1992. *Structural Holes: The Social Structure of Competition.* Cambridge: Harvard University Press.

California Council on Competitiveness. 1992. *California's Future and Jobs.* Sacramento: Office of the Governor.

Carroll, G. and J. R. Harrison. 1994. "On the Historical Efficiency of Competition between Organizational Populations," *American Journal of Sociology*, 100, 720-749.

Casson, M. 1991. *The Economics of Business Culture.* Oxford: Oxford University Press.

Castells, M. and Y. Aoyama. 1994. "Paths towards the Informational Society: Employment Structure in G-7 Countries, 1920-90," *International Labour Review*, 133, 5-31.

Castells, M. and P. Hall. 1994. *Technopoles of the World: The Making of 21st Century Industrial Complexes.* London: Routledge.

Chandler, A. 1990. *Scale and Scope: The Dynamics of Industrial Capitalism.* Cambridge, MA: Harvard University Press.

Chang, K. 1989. "Japan's Direct Manufacturing Investment in the United States," *The Professional Geographer*, 41, 315-328.

Chia, S. Y. 1993. "Foreign Direct Investment in ASEAN Economies," *Asian Development Review*, 11, 60-102.

Chinitz, B. 1961. "Contrasts in Agglomeration: New York and Pittsburgh," *American Economics Association Paper Proceedings*, (73rd Meeting), 51, 279-289.

Christopherson, S. 1993. "Market Rules and Territorial Outcomes: The Case of the United States," *International Journal of Urban and Regional Research*, 17, 274-288.

Christopherson, S. and B. Redfield. 1993. "The False Promise of Industrial Districts for Rural Economic Development," in A. Bernat and M. Frederick (eds.) *Rural America and the Changing Structure of Manufacturing: Spatial Implications of New Technology and Organization.* Washington: U.S. Department of Agriculture, 107-118.

Chubb, J. 1988. "Institutions, the Economy, and the Dynamics of State Elections," *American Political Science Review*, 79-96.

Clarke, M. and E. Dobson. 1992. *Increasing the Competitiveness of America's Manufacturers: A Review of State Industrial Extension Programs.* National Governors' Association.

Commonwealth of Massachusetts. 1993. *Choosing to Compete: A Statewide Strategy for Job Creation and Economic Growth.* Executive Office of Economic Affairs.

Cooke, P. and R. Imrie. 1989. "Little Victories: Local Economic Development in European Regions," *Entrepreneurship and Regional Development*, 1, 313-327.

Cooke, P. and K. Morgan. 1991. "The Network Paradigm: New Departures in Corporate and Regional Development," *Regional Industrial Research,* Cardiff: University of Wales College.

Cooke, P. and K. Morgan. 1993. "The Network Paradigm: New Departures in Corporate and Regional Development," *Environment and Planning D: Society and Space*, 11, 543-564.

Cooke, P., K. Morgan, and A. Price. 1993. "The Future of the Mittelstand: Collaboration Versus Competition," *Regional Industrial Research Report*, 13, Cardiff: University of Wales College.

Côté, S., N. Bordeleau, and N. Pellerin. 1993. "La Stratégie du Développement des Grappes Industrielles et le Développement Economique des Régions," paper presented to the working group on industrial clusters and regional development, at the conference La Prospérité à travers la Technologie, Montréal, 3rd February.

Cummings, T. G. 1984. "Transorganizational Development," in B. Staw and L. L. Cummings (eds.) *Research in Organizational Behavior*, 6, Greenwich, Conn.: JAI-Press, 323-338.

D'Cruz, J. and A. Rugman. 1992a. *New Compacts for Competitiveness.* Report commissioned by Kodak Canada Inc., Toronto.

D'Cruz, J. and A. Rugman. 1992b. "Business Networks for International Competitiveness," *Business Quarterly*, 101-107.

D'Cruz, J. and A. Rugman. 1993. "Business Networks, Telecommunications, and International Competitiveness," unpublished manuscript, Toronto: Faculty of Management, University of Toronto.

De Jong, M. W., K. Machielse, and P. A. de Ruijter. 1992. "Producer Services and Flexible Networks in the Netherlands," in H. Ernste and V. Meier (eds.) *Regional Development and Contemporary Industrial Response.* London: Belhaven, 147-162.

DeBresson, C. and F. Amesse. 1991. "Networks of Innovators: A Review and Introduction to the Issue," *Research Policy*, 20, 363-379.

Dei Ottati, G. 1994. "Case Study I: Prato and Its Evolution in a European Context," in R. Leonardi and R. Nanetti (eds.) *Regional Development in a Modern European Economy: The Case of Tuscany.* London: Pinter, 116-144.

Dertouzos, M., R. Lester, and R. Solow. 1989. *Made in America: Regaining the Productive Edge.* Cambridge, MA: MIT Press.

Dicken, P. 1994. "Global-Local Tensions: Firms and States in the Global Space-Economy," *Economic Geography*, 70, 101-128.

DiMaggio, P. 1992. "Nadel's Paradox Revisited: Relational and Cultural Aspects of Organizational Structure," in N. Nohria and R. Eccles (eds.) *Networks and Organizations.* Boston: Harvard Business School Press, 118-142.

DiMaggio, P. and W. Powell. 1983. "The Iron Cage Revisited: Institutional Isomorphism and Collective Rationality in Organizational Fields," *American Sociological Review*, 48, 147-160.

Doeringer, P. B. and M. J. Piore. 1971. *Internal Labor Markets and Manpower Analysis.* Lexington, MA: D.C. Heath.

Doeringer, P. B. and D. G. Terkla. 1990. "Turning Around Local Economies: Managerial Strategies and Community Assets," *Journal of Policy Analysis and Management*, 9, 487-506.

Doeringer, P. B. and D. G. Terkla. 1992. "Japanese Direct Investment and Economic Development Policy," *Economic Development Quarterly*, 6, 255-272.

Doeringer, P. B., C. Evans, and D. G. Terkla. 1992. "Is Japanese Investment the Answer for State and Local Economic Development?," paper presented at the Meetings of the International Regional Science Association, Chicago.

Doeringer, P. B., P. Moss, and D. G. Terkla. 1986. "Capitalism and Kinship: Do Institutions Matter in the Labor Market?," *Industrial and Labor Relations Review*, 40, 48-60.

Doeringer, P. B., D. G. Terkla, and G. C. Topakian. 1987. *Invisible Factors in Local Economic Development*. New York: Oxford University Press.

Doeringer, P. B., M. J. Piore, G. Rogers, and W. Sengenberger. 1993. "Industry in Crisis: Production Channels, Labor Institutions, and Industrial Performance 'MDNM'," unpublished manuscript.

Donckels, R. and A. Courtmans. 1990. "Big Brother Is Watching Over You: The Counselling of Growing SMEs in Belgium," *Entrepreneurship and Regional Development*, 2, 211-223.

Dunford, M., A. Fernandes, B. Musyck, B. Sadowski, M. Cho, and S. Tsenkova. 1993. "The Organization of Production and Territory: Small Firm Systems," *International Journal of Urban and Regional Research*, 17, 132-136.

Dunlop, J. T. and D. Weil. 1992. "Human Resource Innovations in the Apparel Industry: An Industrial Relations System Perspective," unpublished manuscript, Harvard University/ Boston University.

Dunlop, J. T. and D. Weil. 1993. "Labor Productivity and Competitiveness: The Lessons of Apparel," paper presented at the meetings of the Eastern Economic Association.

Eccles, R. G. 1981. "The Quasi Firm in the Construction Industry," *Journal of Economic Behaviour and Organizations*, 2, 335-357.

Eccles, R. G. and D. B. Crane. 1987. "Managing through Networks in Investment Banking," *California Management Review*, 30, 176-194.

Economic Roundtable. 1992. *Fuel Cell Commercialization: Developing Fuel Cell Power Plants in Southern California*. Los Angeles: Economic Roundtable and the Loker Hydrocarbon Institute, University of Southern California.

Edgar, Dunn, and Co. 1992. *Status of Fuel Cell Technology for Transit Applications: Report to the Southern California Rapid Transit District and Los Angeles County Transportation Commission*. Los Angeles: ICF Kaiser Engineers.

Eisinger, P. 1988. *The Rise of the Entrepreneurial State: State and Local Economic Development Policy in the United States*. Madison: University of Wisconsin Press.

Enright, M. J. 1990. "Geographic Concentration and Industrial Organization," Ph.D. Dissertation, Cambridge, MA: Harvard University.

Enright, M. J. 1992. "Why Local Clusters Are the Way to Win the Game," *World Link*, 5, 24-25.

Enright, M. J. 1993a. "The Determinants of Geographic Concentration in Industry," Working Paper 93-052, Cambridge, MA: Division of Research, Harvard Business School.

Enright, M. J. 1993b. "The Geographic Scope of Competitive Advantage," in E. Dirven, J. Groenewegen, and S. van Hoof (eds.) *Stuck in the Region?: Changing Scales of Regional Identity*. Utrecht: Netherlands Geographical Studies 155, 87-102.

Enright, M. J. 1994. "Regional Clusters and Firm Strategy," Working Paper 94-074, Cambridge, MA: Division of Research, Harvard Business School.

Enright, M. J. 1995. "Organization and Coordination in Geographically Concentrated Industries," in N. Lamoreux and D. Raff (eds.) *Coordination and Information: Historical Perspectives on the Organization of Enterprise*. Chicago: Chicago University Press, 103-142.

Enright, M. J., A. Francés, and E. Scott Saavedra. 1994. *Venezuela: el Reto de la Competitividad*. Fondo Fintec/Ediciones IESA.

Ernste, H. and V. Meier (eds.). 1992. *Regional Development and Contemporary Industrial Response*. London: Belhaven Press.

Ettlinger, N. 1994. "The Localization of Development in Comparative Perspective," *Economic Geography*, 70, 144-166.

European Network for SME Research. 1994. *The European Observatory for Small and Medium-Sized Enterprises* (Second Annual Report). Zoetermeer: ENSR.

Faini, R., G. Galli, and C. Giannini. 1993. "Finance and Development: The Case of Southern Italy," in A. Giovannini (ed.) *Finance and Development: Issues and Experience*. Cambridge: Cambridge University Press, 120-139.

Fallows, J. 1995. *Looking at the Sun: The Rise of the New East Asian Economic and Political System*. New York: Vintage Press.

Feld, S. 1981. "The Focused Organization of Social Ties," *American Journal of Sociology*, 86, 1015-1035.

Feller, I. 1992. "American State Governments As Models for National Science Policy," *Journal of Policy Analysis and Management*, 11-26.

Ferguson, R. and H. S. Ladd. 1988. "Massachusetts," in R. S. Fosler (ed.) *The New Economic Role of American States*. New York: Oxford University Press.

Florida, R. and M. Kenney. 1990a. *The Breakthrough Illusion*. New York: Basic Books.

Florida, R. and M. Kenney. 1990b. "High-Technology Restructuring in the USA and Japan," *Environment and Planning A*, 22, 233-252.

Fombrun, C. and W. G. Astley. 1983. "Strategies of Collective Action: The Case of the Financial Services Industry," *Advances in Strategic Management*, 2, 125-139.

Forrest, J. 1992. "Management Aspects of Strategic Partnering," *Journal of General Management*, 17, 25-40.

Fournier, B., H. Munro, and H. Noori. 1992. *The Role of Business Networks in SME Competitiveness*, Report to Industry, Science and Technology Canada.

Freeman, R. B. and J. Medoff. 1984. *What Do Unions Do?* New York: Basic Books.

Frenkel, S. 1993. "Theoretical Frameworks and Empirical Contexts of Trade Unionism," in S. Frenkel (ed.) *Organized Labour in the Asia-Pacific Region*. Ithaca, NY: ILR Press, 3-55.

Friedland, R. and A. F. Robertson (eds.). 1990. *Beyond the Marketplace: Rethinking Economy and Society*. New York: Aldine de Gruyter.

Friedmann, D. 1993. "Getting Industry to Stick: Enhancing High Value-Added Production in California," in A. J. Scott (ed.) *Policy Options for Southern California*, Working Paper No. 4. Los Angeles: Lewis Center for Regional Policy Studies, University of California, 135-177.

Frobel, F., J. Heinrichs, and O. Kreye. 1980. *The New International Division of Labour*. New York: Cambridge University Press.

Fujita, K. and R. Hill. 1995. "Global Toyotaism and Local Development," *International Journal of Urban and Regional Research*, 19, 7-22.

Fumagalli, A. and G. Mussati. 1993. "Italian Industrial Dynamics from the 1970s to the 1980s: Some Reflections on Entrepreneurial Activity," *Entrepreneurship and Regional Development*, 5, 25-37.

Gagné P. and M. Lefèvre M. 1993. "L'Entreprise à Valeur Ajoutée: le Modèle Québécois," Montréal, Public-Relais.

Gagnon, J. E. 1993. "Condensé de la Politique Gouvernementale en Matière de Développement Régional et la Stratégie Industrielle du Québec," Secrétariat aux Affaires régionales, (November).

Galaskiewicz, J. and S. Wasserman. 1989. "Mimetic Processes within an Interorganizational Field: An Empirical Test," *Administrative Science Quarterly*, 34, 454-479.

Garnsey, E. W. and A. Cannon-Brookes. 1993. "The 'Cambridge Phenomenon' Revisited: Aggregate Change among Cambridge High-Technology Companies since 1985," *Entrepreneurship and Regional Development*, 5, 179-207.

Garnsey, E. W., S. C. Galloway, and S. A. Mathisen. 1994. "Flexibility and Specialization in Question: Birth, Growth and Death Rates of Cambridge New Technology-Based Firms 1988-92," *Entrepreneurship and Regional Development*, 6, 81-107.

Geertz, C. 1973. *The Interpretation of Cultures*. New York: Basic Books.

Gentle, C. J. S. 1993. *The Financial Service Industry: The Impact of Corporate Reorganisation on Regional Economic Development*. Aldershot: Avebury.

Gertler, M. S. "Implementing Advanced Manufacturing Technologies in Mature Industrial Regions," *Regional Studies*, 27, (forthcoming).

Giddens, A. 1984. *The Constitution of Society*. Cambridge: Polity Press.

Giddens, A. 1987. *Social Theory and Modern Society*. Stanford: Stanford University Press.

Gilpin, Robert. 1987. *The Political Economy of International Relations*. Princeton, NJ: Princeton University Press.

Gittell, R. 1992. *Renewing Cities*. Princeton, NJ: Princeton University Press.

Gittell, R. and P. Flynn. 1993. "Looking Forward: Massachusetts Business Climate from a Comparative and Historical Perspective," Report to the Massachusetts Industrial Finance Agency.

Glasmeier, A. 1993. "Flexible Districts, Flexible Regions? The Institutional and Cultural Limits to Districts in an Era of Globalization and Technological Paradigm Shifts," Working paper, University Park: Pennsylvania State University.

Goldstein, H. A. 1987. *The State and Local Industrial Policy Question*. Chicago: Planners Press.

Goodman, E. and J. Bamford (eds.). 1990. Small Firms and Industrial Districts in Italy. London: Routledge.

Grabher, G. 1989. "Regionalpolitik gegen De-Industrialisierung? Der Umbau des Montankomplexes im Ruhrgebiet," *Jahrbuch für Regionalwissenschaft*, 9/10, 94-110.

Grabher, G. (ed.). 1993a. *The Embedded Firm: On the Socioeconomics of Industrial Networks*. London: Routledge.

Grabher, G. 1993b. "The Weakness of Strong Ties: The Lock-In of Regional Development in the Ruhr Area," in G. Grabher (ed.) *The Embedded Firm: On the Socioeconomics of Industrial Networks*. London: Routledge, 255-277.

Granovetter, M. 1982. "The Strength of Weak Ties: A Network Theory Revisited," in P. Marsden and N. Lin (eds.) *Social Structure and Network Analysis*. Beverly Hills: Sage, 105-130.

Granovetter, M. 1985. "Economic Action and Social Structure: The Problem of Embeddedness," *American Journal of Sociology*, 91, 481-510.
Granovetter, M. 1992. "Problems of Explanation in Economic Sociology," in N. Nohria and R. Eccles (eds.) *Networks and Organizations*. Boston: Harvard Business School Press, 25-56.
Granovetter, M. 1993. "The Nature of Economic Relationships," in R. Swedberg (ed.) *Explorations in Economic Sociology*. New York: Russell Sage Foundation, 3-41.
Gray, B. 1990. "Building Interorganizational Alliances: Planned Change in a Global Environment," in W. A. Pasmore and R. W. Woodman (eds.) *Research in Organizational Change and Development*, 4. Greenwich, Conn.: JAI-Press, 101-140.
Grote, J. 1995. "Relevance of Size and Territory for the Organization of Business Interests in Europe," in J. Greenwood (ed.) *European Casebook on Business Alliances*. London: Prentice-Hall, 237-258.
Groupe de Recherche en Économie et Gestion des PME (GREPME). 1994. *Les PME: Bilan et Perspectives*. Cap-Rouge: Les Presses Inter-Universitaires, Economica.
Guilhon, B. and P. Gianfoldini. 1990. "Chaînes de Compétences et Réseaux," *Revue d'Économie Industrielle*, 97-112.
Guillouet, A. 1990. *Booming Economies of South East Asia*. Singapore: Longman Singapore Publishers.
Hall, R. and R. Quinn (eds.). 1983. *Organizational Theory and Public Policy*. Beverly Hills: Sage.
Hardill, I., D. Fletcher, and S. Montagne-Villette. 1995. "Small Firms' 'Distinctive Capabilities' and the Socio-Economic Milieu: Findings from Case Studies in Le Choletais (France) and the East Midlands (UK)," *Entrepreneurship and Regional Development*, 7, 167-186.
Hardin, R. 1982. *Collective Action*. Baltimore: Johns Hopkins University Press.
Harrigan, K. 1988. "Strategic Alliances and Partner Asymmetries," in F. Contractor and P. Lorange (eds.) *Cooperative Strategies in International Business*. Lexington: Lexington Books, 205-225.
Harrison, B. 1992. "Industrial Districts: Old Wine in New Bottles?" *Regional Studies*, 26, 469-483.
Harrison, B. 1994. *Lean and Mean: The Changing Landscape of Corporate Power in the Age of Flexibility*. New York: Basic Books.
Hatch, R. 1991. "The Ties That Bind: Networks and the Making of Denmark's Competitive Edge," *Entrepreneurial Economy Review*, (Spring), 13-18.
Herrigel, G. 1993. "Power and the Redefinition of Industrial Districts: The Case of Baden-Württemberg," in G. Grabher (ed.) *The Embedded Firm*. London: Routledge, 227-251.
Hill, R. C. 1989. "Divisions of Labour in Global Manufacturing: The Case of the Automobile Industry," in A. MacEwan and W. K. Tabb (eds.) *Instability and Change in the World Economy*. New York: Monthly Review Press, 166-186.
Hirst, P. and J. Zeitlin (eds.). 1989. *Reversing Industrial Decline? Industrial Structure and Policy in Britain and Her Competitors*. Oxford: Berg.
Hyman, R. 1994. "Industrial Relations in Western Europe: An Era of Ambiguity?," *Industrial Relations*, 33, 1-24.
Illeris, S. 1992. "The Herning-Ikast Textile Industry: An Industrial District in West Jutland," *Entrepreneurship and Regional Development*, 4, 73-84.

Industrial Policy Review Group (Ireland). 1992. *A Time for Change: Industrial Policy for the 1990s.* Dublin: The Stationery Office.

Inzerelli, G. 1990. "The Italian Alternative: Flexible Organization and Social Management," *International Studies of Management and Organization*, 20, 6-21.

Isard, W. 1956. *Location and Space-Economy.* Cambridge: MIT Press.

Jarillo, J. 1988. "On Strategic Networks," *Strategic Management Journal*, 9, 31-41.

Jepperson, R. 1991. "Institutions, Institutional Effects, and Institutionalism," in W. Powell and P. DiMaggio (eds.) *The New Institutionalism in Organizational Analysis.* Chicago: Chicago University Press, 143-163.

Johansson, B. 1991. "Economic Networks and Self-Organization," in E. M. Bergman, G. Maier, and F. Tödtling (eds.) *Regions Reconsidered: Economic Networks, Innovation, and Local Development in Industrialized Countries.* London: Mansell, 17-34.

Jones, R. S., R. E. King, and M. Klein. 1992. "The Chinese Economic Area: Economic Integration without a Free Trade Agreement," Working Papers No. 124, Paris: OECD, Economics Department, 1-42.

Jones, R. S., R. E. King and M. Klein. 1993. "Economic Integration between Hong Kong, Taiwan and the Coastal Provinces of China," *OECD Economic Studies*, 20, 115-144.

Kamann, D. J. 1991. "The Distribution of Dominance in Networks and Its Spatial Implications," in E. M. Bergman, G. Maier, and F. Tödtling (eds.) *Regions Reconsidered: Economic Networks, Innovation, and Local Development in Industrialized Countries.* London: Mansell, 35-57.

Kanter, R. and R. G. Eccles. 1992. "Conclusion: Making Network Research Relevant to Practice," in N. Nohria and R. G. Eccles (eds.) *Networks and Organizations: Structure, Form, and Action.* Boston: Harvard Business School Press, 521-527.

Katz, M. L. and C. Shapiro. 1985. "Network Externalities, Competition and Compatibility," *American Economic Review*, 75, 424-440.

Katzenstein, P. 1985. *Small States in World Markets.* Ithaca: Cornell University Press.

Kaufman, A., R. Gittell, M. Merenda, W. N. Naumes, and C. W. Wood. 1994. "Porter's Model for Geographic Competitive Advantage: The Case of New Hampshire," *Economic Development Quarterly*, 8, 43-66.

Kelley, M. and B. Harrison. 1991. "Unions, Technology, and Labor-Management Cooperation," in L. Mishel and P. Voos (eds.) *Unions and Economic Consequences.* White Plains, NY: ME Sharpe.

Kelley, M. R. and A. Arora. 1995. "Service Provider or Institution Builder? An Assessment of the Role of Industrial Modernization Programs in U. S. Technology Policy," *Research Policy*, (forthcoming).

Kenney, M. and R. Florida. 1993. *Beyond Mass Production: The Japanese System and Its Transfer to the U. S.* New York: Oxford University Press.

Kenney, M. and R. Florida. 1994. "The Globalization of Japanese R&D: The Economic Geography of Japanese R&D Investment in the United States," *Economic Geography*, 70, 344-369.

Kiely, R. 1994. "Development Theory and Industrialisation: Beyond the Impasse," *Journal of Contemporary Asia*, 24, 133-160.

Kilper, H. and D. Rehfeld. 1991. *Vom Konzept der Agglomerationsvorteile zum Industrial District.* Arbeitspapier IAT-PS 03 des Instituts für Arbeit und Technik, Gelsenkirchen.

Kingdon, J. 1984. *Agendas, Alternatives, and Public Policies.* Boston: Little, Brown and Company.

Kochan, T. A., H. C. Katz, and R. McKersie. 1986. *The Transformation of American Industrial Relations*. New York: Basic Books.

Kogut, B. 1988. "A Study of the Life Cycle of Joint Ventures," in F. Contractor and P. Lorange (eds.) *Cooperative Strategies in International Business*. Lexington: Lexington Books, 169-332.

KPMG Peat Marwick Policy Economic Group. 1992. "A Study of the New Hampshire State and Local Revenue Structure," submitted to the New Hampshire State Legislature.

Kraar, L. 1992. "Asia's Hot New Growth Triangle," *Fortune*, 126(7), 136-142.

Kreiner, K. and M. Schultz. 1993. "Informal Collaboration in R&D. The Formation of Networks across Organizations," *Organization Studies*, 14, 189-209.

Kristensen, P. 1992. "Industrial District in West Jutland, Denmark," in F. Pyke and W. Sengenberger (eds.) *Industrial Districts and Local Economic Regeneration*. Geneva: International Institute for Labour Studies, 219-232.

Kristensen, P. 1994. "Spectator Communities and Entrepreneurial Districts," *Entrepreneurship and Regional Development*, 6, 177-198.

Krugman, P. 1991. *Geography and Trade*. Cambridge: MIT Press.

Larson, A. 1992. "Network Dyads in Entrepreneurial Settings: A Study of the Governance of Exchange Relationships," *Administrative Science Quarterly*, 37, 76-104.

Laumann, E. and D. Knoke. 1987. *The Organizational State: Social Choice in National Policy Domains*. Madison: University of Wisconsin Press.

Lazerson, M. 1995. "A New Phoenix?: Modern Putting-Out in the Modena Knitwear Industry," *Administrative Science Quarterly*, 40, 34-59.

Lazonick, W. 1993. "Industry Clusters versus Global Webs: Organizational Capabilities in the American Economy," *Industrial and Corporate Change*, 2, 1-24.

Lipparini, A. and M. Sobrero. 1994. "The Glue and the Pieces: Entrepreneurship and Innovation in Small-Firm Networks," *Journal of Business Venturing*, 9, 125-140.

Locke, R. M. 1989. "Local Politics and Industrial Adjustment: The Political Economy of Italy in the 1980s," Ph.D. Dissertation, Massachusetts Institute of Technology.

Lomi, A. 1995. "The Population Ecology of Organizational Founding: Location Dependence and Unobserved Heterogeneity," *Administrative Science Quarterly*, 40, 111-144.

Lorenz, E. H. 1989. "The Search for Flexibility: Subcontracting Networks in British and French Engineering," in P. Hirst and J. Zeitlin (eds.) *Reversing Industrial Decline?* Oxford: Berg, 122-132.

Los Angeles County Transportation Commission (LACTC). 1992. *LACTC Proposed 30-Year Integrated Transportation Plan*. Los Angeles: LACTC.

Lundvall, B. A. 1993. "Explaining Interfirm Cooperation and Innovation: The Limits of the Transaction Cost Approach," in G. Grabher (ed.) *The Embedded Firm*. London: Routledge, 52-64.

Lyons, M. 1991. "Joint-Ventures as Strategic Choice – A Literature Review," *Long Range Planning*, 24, 130-144.

Mahon, R. 1987. "From Fordism To... ?: New Technology, Labour Markets and Unions," *Economic and Industrial Democracy*, 8, 5-60.

Maier, H. E. 1987. "*Das Modell Baden-Württemberg: Über institutionelle Voraussetzungen differenzierter Qualitätsproduktion*," Discussion paper IIM/LMP 87-10a, Wissenschaftszentrum Berlin.

Maillat, D. 1991. "The Innovation Process and the Role of the Milieu," in E. M. Bergman, G. Maier, and F. Tödtling, (eds.) *Regions Reconsidered: Economic Networks, Innovation, and Local Development in Industrialized Countries*. London: Mansell, 103-118.

Maillat, D. 1995. "Territorial Dynamic, Innovative Milieus and Regional Policy," *Entrepreneurship and Regional Development*, 7, 157-165.

Maillat, D. and B. Lecoq. 1992. "New Technologies and Transformation of Regional Structures in Europe: The Role of the Milieu," *Entrepreneurship and Regional Development*, 4, 1-20.

Maillat, D. and J.-Y. Vasserot. 1988. "Economic and Territorial Conditions for Indigenous Revival in Europe's Industrial Regions," in P. Aydalot and D. Keeble (eds.) *High Technology Industry and Innovative Environments*. Andover, Hants.: Routledge & Kegan Paul, 163-183.

Mair, A., R. Florida, and M. Kenney. 1988. "The New Geography of Automobile Production: Japanese Transplants in North America," *Economic Geography*, October, 352-373.

March, J. and J. Olsen. 1989. *Rediscovering Institutions: The Organizational Basis of Politics*. New York: Free Press.

Markusen, A. 1985. *Profit Cycles, Oligopoly, and Regional Development*. Cambridge: MIT Press.

Markusen, A. 1986. "Neither Ore, Nor Coal, Nor Markets: A Policy-Oriented View of Steel Sites in the USA," *Regional Studies*, 20, 449-61.

Marsden, P. 1990. "Network Data and Measurement," *Annual Review of Sociology*, 16, 435-463.

Marshall, A. 1890. *Principles of Economics*. Basingstoke: Macmillan.

Marshall, A. 1920a. *Industry and Trade* (3rd ed.). London: Macmillan.

Marshall, A. 1920b. *Principles of Economics* (8th ed.). London: Macmillan.

Marshall, R. 1992. "Unions and Competitiveness," in *Empowering Workers in the Global Economy: A Labour Agenda for the 1990s*. Toronto: United Steelworkers of America, 75-98.

Marton, A., T. McGee, and D. G. Paterson. 1995. "Northeast Asian Economic Cooperation and the Tumen River Area Development Project," *Pacific Affairs*, 68, 9-33.

Masten, S. 1986. "The Economic Institutions of Capitalism: A Review Article," *Journal of Institutional and Theoretical Economics*, 142, 445-451.

Megerle, K. 1982. *Württemberg im Industrialisierungsprozess Deutschlands*. Stuttgart: Klett-Cotta.

Meurer, S., D. Sobel, and D. Wolfe. 1987. *Challenging Technology's Myths*. Toronto: Labour Council of Metropolitan Toronto.

Miller, R. and M. Côté. 1987. *Growing the Next Silicon Valley: A Guide for Successful Regional Planning*. Lexington, MA: Lexington Books.

Ministry of Industry, Commerce, Science, and Technology, Canada (MICST). 1994. "Les PME au Québec, Etat de la Situation 1992-1993," Groupe d'analyse sur les PME et les régions.

Ministry of Industry, Commerce, and Technology, Canada (MICT). 1992. "La Stratégie Industrielle du Gouvernement du Québec: Rétrospective et Perspectives," (September).

Ministry of Industry, Commerce, and Technology, Canada (MICT). 1993a. "Focus: Québec," (3rd quarter).

Ministry of Industry, Commerce, and Technology, Canada (MICT). 1993b. "Mesures pour le Soutien et la Création d'Emplois," Internal document (November).

Morales, R., M. Storper, M. Cisternas, C. Quandt, A. J. Scott, J. Slifko, W. Thomas, M. Wachs, and S. Zakhor. 1991. "*Prospects for Alternative Fuel Vehicle Use and Production in Southern California: Environmental Quality and Economic Development*," Working Paper No. 2. Los Angeles: University of California, Lewis Center for Regional Policy Studies.

Morrison, D. C. 1995. "Technology Tussle," *National Journal*, April 1, p.30.

Moss-Kanter R. 1994. "Collaborative Advantage," *Harvard Business Review*, (July-August), 96-108.

Murray, F. 1987. "Flexible Specialization in the Third Italy," *Capital and Class*, 33, 84-95.

Muster, M. 1992. "Achieving Co-Determination," in Empowering Workers in the Global Economy: A Labour Agenda for the 1990s. Background Paper and Conference Proceedings, October 22-23, 1991. Toronto: United Steelworkers of America, 139-141.

Myers, K. 1990. "Analysis of New Hampshire's Legislative Parties," Masters Thesis, University of New Hampshire.

National Governors' Association, United States. 1992. *Going Global: A Governor's Guide to International Trade.*

New Hampshire Department of Resources and Economic Development. 1991. *Biennial Report: 1990-1991.*

New Hampshire Post-Secondary Technical Education. 1993. "Draft: Technology Development Centers, a Vision of the Future at New Hampshire's Technical Colleges/Institutes."

New Hampshire Post-Secondary Technical Education System. 1992. *Annual Report, 1991.*

Niskanen, W. A. 1971. *Bureaucracy and Representative Government*. Chicago: Aldine-Altherton.

Nohria, N. 1992. "Information and Search in the Creation of New Business Ventures: The Case of the 128 Venture Group," in N. Nohria and R. G. Eccles (eds.) *Networks and Organizations*. Boston: Harvard Business School Press, 240-261.

Nonara, I. 1991. "The Knowledge-Creating Company," *Harvard Business Review*, (November/December), 96-104.

O'Malley, E., K. A. Kennedy, and R. O'Donnell. 1992. *Report to the Industrial Policy Review Group on the Impact of the Industrial Development Agencies*. Dublin: The Stationery Office.

Ohmae, K. 1993. "The Rise of the Region State," *Foreign Affairs*, 72, 78-87.

Olson, M. 1982. *The Rise and Decline of Nations*. New Haven: Yale University.

Orru, M. 1991. "The Institutional Logic of Small-Firm Economies in Italy and Taiwan," *Studies in Comparative International Development*, 26, 3-28.

Osborne, D. 1988. *Laboratories of Democracy*. Boston: Harvard Business School Press.

Osborne, D. 1990. "Refining State Technology Programs," *Issues in Science and Technology*, 6, 55-61.

Pellerin, N. 1992. "La Stratégie des Grappes Industrielles et le Développement Régional," Excerpts from Minister Tremblay's (Minister of Industry, Commerce, and Technology) speech (February).

Peltzman, S. 1987. "Economic Conditions and Gubernatorial Elections," *American Economic Review*, 293-297.

Pennsylvania Economy League, Inc. 1993. "Executive Summary: Impacts of Ben Franklin Center."

Perrow, C. 1981. "Markets, Hierarchies and Hegemony," in A. Van de Ven and W. Joyce (eds.) *Perspectives on Organization Design and Behavior*. New York: Wiley, 371-386.

Perrow, C. 1986. *Complex Organizations* (3rd ed.). New York: Random House.

Perrow, C. 1992. "Small-Firm Networks," in N. Nohria and R. G. Eccles (eds.) *Network and Organizations*. Boston: Harvard Business School Press, 445-470.

Pfeffer, J. and G. Salancik. 1978. *The External Control of Organizations*. New York: Harper and Row.

Pillai, M. G. G. 1992. "Emerging Trade Alliances in Asia," *Economic and Political Weekly*, 27, 199.

Piore, M. and C. Sabel. 1984. *The Second Industrial Divide: Possibilities for Prosperity*. New York: Basic Books.

Popovic, A. 1994. "Kooperation – Spiel ohne Verlierer?" in D. Ahlert and G. Dieckheuer (eds.) *Kooperation in der Textilwirtschaft: Perspektiven und Konzepte zur Zusammenarbeit zwischen Industrie und Handel*. Münster: FATM, 215-231.

Porac, J., H. Thomas, F. Wilson, D. Paton, and A. Kanfer. 1995. "Rivalry and the Industry Model of Scottish Knitwear Producers," *Administrative Science Quarterly*, 40, 203-227.

Porter, M. E. (ed.) 1986. *Competition in Global Industries*. Cambridge: Harvard Business School Press.

Porter, M. E. 1990. *The Competitive Advantage of Nations*. New York: Free Press.

Porter, M. E. 1991. *Canada at the Crossroads*. Ottawa: BCNI and Industry, Science and Technology Canada.

Porter, M. E., in collaboration with Monitor Company, Inc. 1991. *The Competitive Advantage of Massachusetts*. Harvard Business School.

Portes, A. and J. Sensenbrenner. 1993. "Embeddedness and Immigration: Notes on the Social Determinants of Economic Action," *American Journal of Sociology*, 98, 1320-1350.

Poulin, D., B. Montreuil, and S. Gauvin. 1994. "L'Entreprise-Réseau: Bâtir Aujourd'hui l'Organisation de Demain," Montréal Public-Relais.

Powell, W. 1990. "Neither Market nor Hierarchy: Network Forms of Organization," *Research in Organizational Behavior*, 12, 295-336.

Powell, W. and P. DiMaggio (eds.). 1991. *The New Institutionalism in Organizational Analysis*. Chicago: University of Chicago Press.

Prahalad, C. K. and G. Hamel. 1990. "The Core Competence of the Corporation," *Harvard Business Review*, 68, 79-91.

Preer, R. 1992. *The Emergence of Technopolis: Knowledge-Intensive Technologies and Regional Development*. New York: Praeger.

Project California. 1992. *Advanced Transportation Business Analysis: Summary Presentation*. Los Angeles: Monitor Company.

Province of Ontario. 1986. *Final Report and Recommendations of the Advisory Committee on Resource Dependent Communities in Northern Ontario, Toronto.*

Province of Ontario. 1990. *People and Skills in the New Global Economy*. Report of the Premier's Council on Technology, Toronto.

Putnam, R. 1993. *Making Democracy Work*. Princeton: Princeton University Press.

Pyke, F., G. Becattini, and W. Sengenberger (eds.). 1990. *Industrial Districts and Inter-Firm Co-Operation in Italy*. Geneva: ILO.

Pyke, F. and W. Sengenberger. 1990. "Introduction," in F. Pyke, G. Becattini, and W. Sengenberger (eds.) *Industrial Districts and Inter-Firm Co-Operation in Italy*. Geneva: ILO, 1-9.

Pyke, F. and W. Sengenberger (eds.). 1992. *Industrial Districts and Local Economic Regeneration*. Geneva: ILO.

Quinn, J. B. 1992. *Intelligent Enterprise: A Knowledge and Service Based Paradigm for Industry*. New York: Free Press.
Reed, M. 1992. *The Disorganized Society and the Future of Organisations*. London: Sage.
Rees, G. and M. Thomas. 1989. "From Coalminers to Entrepreneurs? A Case-Study in the Sociology of Re-Industrialisation," paper presented at the British Sociological Association, Brighton, England.
Rehfeld, D. 1994. "Produktionscluster und räumliche Entwicklung – Beispiele und Konsequenzen," in W. Krumbein (ed.) *Ökonomische und politische Netzwerke in Regionen*. Münster: Lit-Verlag, 187-205.
Reich, R. B. 1991. *The Work of Nations: Preparing Ourselves for 21st-Century Capitalism*. New York: Knopf.
Ring, P. S. and A. H. Van de Ven. 1994. "Developmental Processes of Co operative Interorganizational Relationships," *Academy of Management Review*, 19, 90-118.
Rodan, G. 1993. "Reconstructing Divisions of Labour: Singapore's New Regional Emphasis," in R. Higgott, R. Leaver, and J. Ravenhill (eds.) *Pacific Economic Relations in the 1990s: Cooperation or Conflict?* St. Leonards, NSW: Allen and Unwin, 223-249.
Romer, P. M. 1986. "Increasing Returns and Long-Run Growth," *Journal of Political Economy*, 94, 1002-1037.
Rosenberg, N. 1963. "Technological Change in the Machine Tool Industry, 1840-1910," *Journal of Economic History*, 23, 413-443.
Rosenfeld, S. 1991. "Rural Perspectives: Linking Networks and Economic Development," *The Entrepreneurial Economy Review*, 9, 28-31.
Rosenfeld, S. and B. Bosworth. 1992. *Significant Others: Exploring the Potential of Manufacturing Networks*. Aspen, Colorado: The Aspen Institute.
Rosenfeld, S., P. Shapira, and J. T. Williams. 1992. *Smart Firms in Small Towns*. Washington, DC: The Aspen Institute.
Roth, S. 1994. "Kooperationsnetzwerke: Gewerkschaftliche Aktivitäten in der Automobil- und Zulieferindustrie," *Industrielle Beziehungen*, 1, 374-384.
Russo, M. 1985. "Technical Change and the Industrial District: The Role of Interfirm Relations in the Growth and Transformation of Ceramic Tile Production in Italy," *Research Policy*, 14, 329-343.
Sabel, C. 1989. "Flexible Specialisation and the Re-Emergence of Regional Economies," in P. Hirst and J. Zeitlin (eds.) *Reversing Economic Decline?: Industrial Structure and Policy in Britain and Her Competitors*, Oxford: Berg, 17-70.
Sabel, C. 1992. "Studied Trust: Building New Forms of Co-Operation in a Volatile Economy," in F. Pyke and W. Sengenberger (eds.) *Industrial Districts and Local Economic Regeneration*. Geneva: ILO, 215-250.
Sabel, C., G. B. Herrigel, R. Deeg, and R. Kazis. 1989. "Regional Prosperities Compared: Massachusetts and Baden-Württemberg in the 1980s," *Economy and Society*, 18, 374-404.
Salancik, G. 1995."Wanted: A Good Network Theory of Organization," *Administrative Science Quarterly*, 40, 345-349.
Saunders, J. 1995. "Bob Rae: Mr. Bailout," *The Globe and Mail*, 27 May, B1-B4.
Saxenian, A. 1989. "In Search of Power: The Organization of Business Interests in Silicon Valley and Route 128," *Economy and Society*, 18, 25-70.
Saxenian, A. 1990. "Regional Networks and the Resurgence of the Silicon Valley," *California Management Review*, 33, 89-112.

Saxenian, A. 1994. *Regional Advantage: Culture and Competition in Silicon Valley and Route 128.* Cambridge, MA: Harvard University Press.

Sayer, A. 1989. "Postfordism in Question," *International Journal of Urban and Regional Research*, 13, 666-695.

Schaefer, N. and J. Roy (eds.). 1993. *The Power of Clusters and Business Networks Can Make Your Business Competitive in World Markets.* Fredericton: Centre for International Marketing and Entrepreneurship, University of New Brunswick.

Scherer, F. M. 1991. "Research, Development, and Technological Innovation," in I. Yamazawa and A. Hirata (eds.) *Industrial Adjustment in Developed Countries and Its Implications for Developing Countries.* Tokyo: Institute of Developing Economies.

Schmitz, H. 1992. "Industrial Districts: Model and Reality in Baden-Württemberg," in F. Pyke and W. Sengenberger (eds.) *Industrial Districts and Local Economic Regeneration.* Geneva: ILO, 87-121.

Schumpeter, J. 1934. *The Theory of Economic Development.* Cambridge, MA: Harvard University Press.

Scitovsky, T. 1954. "Two Concepts of External Economies," *Journal of Political Economy*, 143-151.

Scott, A. J. 1986. "Industrial Organization and Location: Division of Labor, the Firm, and Spatial Process," *Economic Geography*, 63, 214-231.

Scott, A. J. 1988a. "Flexible Production Systems and Regional Development: The Rise of New Industrial Spaces in North America and Western Europe," *International Journal of Urban and Regional Research*, 12, 171-186.

Scott, A. J. 1988b. *New Industrial Spaces: Flexible Production Organization and Regional Development in North America and Western Europe.* London: Pion.

Scott, A. J. 1992. "The Collective Order of Flexible Production Agglomerations: Lessons for Local Economic Development Policy and Strategic Choice," *Economic Geography*, 68, 219-233.

Scott, A. J. (ed.). 1993a. "Electric Vehicle Manufacturing in Southern California: Current Developments, Future Prospects," Working Paper No. 5. Los Angeles: University of California, Lewis Center for Regional Policy Studies.

Scott, A. J. 1993b. "The New Southern California Economy: Pathways to Industrial Resurgence," *Economic Development Quarterly*, 7, 296-309.

Scott, A. J. 1993c. *Technopolis: High-Technology Industry and Regional Development in Southern California.* Berkeley: University of California Press.

Scott, A. J. and D. Bergman. 1993. "Advanced Ground Transportation Equipment Manufacturing and Local Economic Development: Lessons for Southern California," Working Paper No. 8. Los Angeles: University of California, Lewis Center for Regional Policy Studies.

Scott, A. J. and D. Bergman. 1995. "The Industrial Resurgence of Southern California?: Advanced Ground Transportation Equipment Manufacturing and Local Economic Development," *Environment and Planning C: Government and Policy*, 13, 97-124.

Scott, A. J. and A. Paul. 1990. "Collective Order and Economic Coordination in Industrial Agglomerations: The Technopoles of Southern California," *Environment and Planning C: Government and Policy*, 8, 179-193.

Scott, A. J. and M. Storper. 1989. "The Geographical Foundations and Social Regulation of Flexible Production Systems," in J. Wolch and M. Dear (eds.) *The Power of Geography: How Territory Shapes Social Life.* Boston: Unwin Hyman, 21-40.

Scott, A. J. and M. Storper. 1992. "Regional Development Reconsidered," in H. Ernste and V. Meier (eds.) *Regional Development and Contemporary Industrial Response*. London: Belhaven Press, 3-24.

Scott, B. and G. Lodge. 1985. *U. S. Competitiveness in the World Economy*. Boston: Harvard Business School Press.

Scott, W. R. 1994. "Institutions and Organizations," in W. R. Scott and J. Meyer (eds.) *Institutional Environments and Organizations*. Thousand Oaks: Sage, 55-80.

Scott, W. R. 1995. *Institutions and Organizations*. Thousand Oaks: Sage.

Sedatis, H. 1979. *Liberalismus und Handwerk in Südwestdeutschland*. Stuttgart: Klett-Cotta.

Semlinger, K. 1993. "Economic Development and Industrial Policy in Baden-Württemberg: Small Firms in a Benevolent Environment," *European Planning Studies*, 1, 435-463.

Semlinger, K. 1994. "Industrial-District-Politik in Baden-Württemberg: Zwischen Neubesinnung und Neuanfang," Arbeitsbericht Nr. 39 der Akademie für Technologieabschätzung in Baden-Württemberg, Stuttgart.

Sengenberger, W. 1993. "Local Development and International Economic Competition," *International Labour Review*, 132, 313-329.

Sforzi, F. 1992. "The Quantitative Importance of Marshallian Industrial Districts in the Italian Economy," in F. Pyke, G. Becattini, and W. Sengenberger (eds.) *Industrial Districts and Inter-Firm Co-Operation in Italy*. Geneva: ILO, 75-107.

Shapira, P. 1990. *Modernising Manufacturing: New Policies to Build Industrial Extension Services*. Washington, DC: Economic Policy Institute.

Sharma, B. 1991. "Industrialization and Strategy Shifts in Industrial Relations," in S. Tyson and C. Brewster (eds.) *International Comparisons in Human Resource Management*. London: Pitman Books, 92-109.

Simmel, G. 1955. *Conflict and the Web of Group Affiliations*. Glencoe: Free Press.

Sink, D. W. 1991. "Transorganizational Development in Urban Policy Coalitions," *Human Relations*, 44, 1179-1195.

Slifko, J. P. 1993. "Technology Policy Issues in Building an Electric Vehicle Manufacturing Base in Southern California," in A. J. Scott (ed.) *Electric Vehicle Manufacturing in Southern California: Current Developments, Future Prospects, Working Paper No. 5*. Los Angeles: University of California, Lewis Center for Regional Policy Studies, 173-215.

Smilor, R. W., G. Kozmetsky, and D. V. Gibson. 1988. "The Austin-San Antonio Corridor: The Dynamics of a Developing Technopolis," in R. W. Smilor, G. Kozmetsky, and D. V. Gibson (eds.) *Creating the Technopolis: Linking Technology, Commercialization, and Economic Development*. Cambridge, MA.: Ballinger, 145-183.

Smith, H., K. Dickson, and S. Smith. 1991. "'There are Two Sides to Every Story': Innovation and Collaboration Within Networks of Large and Small Firms," *Research Policy*, 20, 457-468.

Solinas, G. 1982. "Labour Market Segmentation and Workers' Careers: The Case of the Italian Knitwear Industry," *Cambridge Journal of Economics*, 6, 331-352.

Sorge, A. and W. Streeck. 1988. "Industrial Relations and Technological Change: The Case for an Extended Perspective," in R. Hyman and W. Streeck (eds.) *New Technology and Industrial Relations*. Oxford: Basil Blackwell, 19-47.

Southall, R. 1988. "Introduction: At Issue: Third World Trade Unions in the Changing International Division of Labour," in R. Southall (ed.) *Trade Unions and the New Industrialization of the Third World*. London: Zed Books, 1-34.

Southern California Association of Governments (SCAG). 1993. "Economic Component, SCAG Regional Comprehensive Plan," Preliminary draft. Los Angeles: SCAG.

Spence, A. M. and H. Hazard (eds.). 1988. *International Competitiveness*. Cambridge, MA: Ballinger.

Staber, U. 1987. "Corporatism and the Governance Structure of American Trade Associations," *Political Studies*, 35, 278-288.

Staber, U. 1992. "Organizational Interdependence and Organizational Mortality in the Cooperative Sector: A Community Ecology Perspective," *Human Relations*, 45, 1191-1212.

Staber, U. 1996. "Accounting for Variations in the Performance of Industrial Districts: The Case of Baden-Württemberg," *International Journal of Urban and Regional Research*, 20, 299-316.

Staber, U. and H. Aldrich. 1983. "Trade Association Stability and Public Policy," in R. Hall and R. Quinn (eds.) *Organizational Theory and Public Policy*. Beverly Hills: Sage, 163-178.

Staber, U. and H. Aldrich. 1995. "Cross-National Similarities in the Personal Networks of Small Business Owners: A Comparison of Two Regions in North America," *Canadian Journal of Sociology*, 20, 441-467.

Staber, U. and B. Sharma. 1994. "The Employment Regimes of Industrial Districts: Promises, Myths, and Realities," *Industrielle Beziehungen*, 1, 321-346.

Starbuck, W. H. 1992. "Learning by Knowledge-Intensive Firms," *Journal of Management Studies*, 29, 713-740.

Stata, R. 1989. "Organizational Learning: The Key to Management Innovation," *Sloan Management Review*, (Spring), 43-49.

State of New Hampshire. 1991. *Strategic Plan for Economic Development: A Blueprint for the 1990s*. Department of Resources and Economic Development, Office of Business and Industrial Development.

Sternberg, E. 1991. "The Sectoral Cluster in Economic Development Policy: Lessons from Rochester and Buffalo, New York," *Economic Development Quarterly*, 5, 342-356.

Stewart, T. P. and M. L. H. Png. 1993. "The Growth Triangle of Singapore, Malaysia and Indonesia," *Georgia Journal of International and Comparative Law*, 23, 1-61.

Stigler, G. J. 1951. "The Division of Labor is Limited by the Extent of the Market," *Journal of Political Economy*, 69, 213-225.

Stohr, W. (ed.). 1990. *Global Challenge and Local Response: Initiatives for Economic Regeneration in Contemporary Europe*. New York: The United Nations University.

Storper, M. 1991. *Industrialization, Economic Development, and the Regional Question in the Third World*. London: Pion.

Storper, M. 1992. "The Limits to Globalization: Technology Districts and International Trade," *Economic Geography*, 68, 60-96.

Storper, M. and S. Christopherson. 1987. "Flexible Specialization and Regional Industrial Agglomeration: The Case of the U. S. Motion Picture Industry," *Annals of the Association of American Geographers*, 77, 104-117.

Storper, M. and B. Harrison. 1991. "Flexibility, Hierarchy and Regional Development: The Changing Structure of Industrial Production Systems and Their Forms of Governance in the 1990s," *Research Policy*, 20, 407-422.

Storper, M. and A. J. Scott. 1992. *Pathways to Industrialization and Regional Development.* London: Routledge.

Streeck, W. 1986. "Industrial Relations and Industrial Change in the Motor Industry: An International View," Working paper, University of Warwick, School of Industrial Relations.

Streeck, W. 1990. "On the Institutional Conditions of Diversified Quality Production," Working paper, Madison: University of Wisconsin.

Streeck, W. 1992. "Klasse, Beruf, Unternehmen, Distrikt: Organisationsgrundlagen industrieller Beziehungen im europäischen Binnenmarkt," Discussion paper, Wissenschaftszentrum Berlin.

Swedberg, R. 1990. *Economics and Sociology.* Princeton: Princeton University Press.

Sydow, J. 1992a. "Enterprise Networks and Co-Determination: The Case of the Federal Republic of Germany," in D. Campbell and W. Sengenberger (eds.) *Is the Single Firm Vanishing?* Geneva: ILO, 34-65.

Sydow, J. 1992b. "On the Management of Strategic Networks," in H. Ernste and V. Meier (eds.) *Regional Development and Contemporary Industrial Response.* London: Belhaven, 113-130.

Sydow, J. and A. Windeler. 1996. "Managing Interfirm Networks: A Structurationist Perspective," in C. G. A. Bryant and D. Jary (eds.) *Anthony Giddens.* London: Routledge, (forthcoming).

Sydow, J., A. Windeler, M. Krebs, A. Loose, and B. van Well. 1995. *Organisation von Netzwerken.* Opladen: Westdeutscher Verlag.

Taplin, I. 1989. "Segmentation and the Organisation of Work in the Italian Apparel Industry," *Social Science Quarterly*, 70, 408-424.

Teal, G. 1995. "The IMS (Indonesia-Malaysia-Singapore) Growth Triangle," unpublished Manuscript, Singapore: National University of Singapore.

Terkla, D. G. and P.B. Doeringer. 1991. "Explaining Variations in Employment Growth: Structural and Cyclical Change among States and Local Areas," *Journal of Urban Economics*, 29, 329-348.

Thorelli, H. 1986. "Networks: Between Markets and Hierarchies," *Strategic Management Journal*, 7, 37-51.

Tiebout, C. 1956. "A Pure Theory of Public Expenditures," *Journal of Political Economy*, 64, 416-424.

Tilly, C. 1993. "State Strategy for Developing Base Industries: A Massachusetts Case Study," *New England Journal of Public Policy*, 9, 33-50.

Topolsky J. and A. Bernstein. 1992. "Flexible Business Networks: Cooperating to Compete in the Global Marketplace," German Marshall Fund of the United States, New York.

Traxler, J., M. M. Fischer, A. Nöst, and U. Schubert. 1991. "Producer Service Networks in the Metropolitan Region of Vienna," in E. Bergman, G. Maier, and F. Tödtling (eds.) *Regions Reconsidered.* London: Mansell, 197-212.

Trigilia, C. 1986. "Small-Firm Development and Political Subcultures in Italy," *European Sociological Review*, 2, 161-175.

Trigilia, C. 1990. "Work and Politics in the Third Italy's Industrial Districts," in F. Pyke, G. Becattini, and W. Sengenberger (eds.) *Industrial Districts and Interfirm Cooperation in Italy.* Geneva: International Institute for Labour Studies, 173-197.

United States Department of Commerce. 1991. *Technology Administration: Strategic View.* Washington, D.C.: Department of Commerce.

United States Department of Commerce. Bureau of Economic Analysis, Economics and Statistics Administration. 1991. *The 1982 Benchmark Input-Output Accounts of the United States*. Washington D.C.: Bureau of Economic Analysis.

United States Department of Commerce. Bureau of the Census. 1990. *County Business Patterns*. Washington D.C.: Bureau of the Census.

United States General Accounting Office. 1991. *Technology Transfer, Federal Efforts to Enhance the Competitiveness of Small and Medium-Sized Manufacturers*.

United Steelworkers of America. 1992. *Empowering Workers in the Global Economy: A Labour Agenda for the 1990s*. Background paper and Conference Proceedings, October 22-23, 1991.

van der Linde, C. 1991. "The Competitive Advantage of Germany," Ph.D. Dissertation, University of St. Gallen.

Vatikiotis, M. 1993. "Three's Company: Malaysia, Thailand, Indonesia Forge Development Zone," *Far Eastern Economic Review*, 158 (31), 58-59.

Verma, A. and B. Sharma. 1993. "Beyond Corporatism and Repression: Economic Development and the Evolution of Employment Relations," paper presented at the Conference on Asian Business, University of Michigan.

Vernon, R. 1966. "International Investment and International Trade in the Product Cycle," *Quarterly Journal of Economics*, 80, 190-207.

Veum, J. R. 1993. "Training among Young Adults: Who, What Kind, and for How Long?" *Monthly Labor Review*, August, 27-32.

Waits, M. J., K. Kahalley, and R. Heffernon. 1992. "Organizing for Economic Development: New Realities Call for New Rules," *Public Administration Review*, 52, 612-616.

Weber, A. 1929. *Theory of the Location of Industries*. Chicago: University of Chicago Press.

Williamson, O. 1975. *Markets and Hierarchies*. New York: Free Press.

Williamson, O. 1985. *The Economic Institutions of Capitalism*. New York: Free Press.

Williamson, O. and W. Ouchi. 1981. "The Markets and Hierarchies Program of Research: Origins, Implications, Prospects," in A. Van de Ven and W. Joyce (eds.) *Perspectives on Organization Design and Behavior*. New York: Wiley & Sons, 347-370.

Windolf, P. 1985. "Industrial Robots in West Germany," *Politics and Society*, 459-495.

Wise, M. J. 1949. "On the Evolution of the Jewellery and Gun Quarters in Birmingham," *Transactions of the Institute of British Geographers*, 15, 57-72.

Wolfe, D. 1993. "The Wealth of Regions: Rethinking Industrial Policy," paper read at the Annual Meeting of the Canadian Political Science Association, Ottawa.

Zeitlin, J. 1992. "Industrial Districts and Local Economic Regeneration: Overview and Comment," in F. Pyke and W. Sengenberger (eds.) *Industrial Districts and Local Economic Regeneration*. Geneva: ILO, 279-294.

Zucker, L. 1986. "Production of Trust: Institutional Sources of Economic Structure," in L. L. Cummings and B. Staw (eds.) *Research in Organizational Behavior*, 8, Greenwich, Conn: JAI Press, 53-111.

Zucker, L. 1987. "Institutional Theories of Organization," *Annual Review of Sociology*, 13, 443-464.

Zucker, L. 1988. "Where Do Institutional Patterns Come From?" in L. Zucker (ed.) *Institutional Patterns and Organizations*. Cambridge: Ballinger, 23-49.

List of Contributors

David Bergman is Graduate Student in the Department of Geography, University of California, Los Angeles, USA.

Peter B. Doeringer is Professor in the Department of Economics, Boston University, and in the John F. Kennedy School of Government, Harvard University, Boston, USA.

Michael J. Enright is Assistant Professor in the Graduate School of Business Administration, Harvard University, Boston, USA.

Marc Ferland is Coordinator for the implementation of industrial strategy in the Ministry of Industry, Science, Commerce, and Technology, Government of Québec, Canada.

Meric S. Gertler is Professor in the Department of Geography, University of Toronto, Toronto, Canada.

Ross Gittell is Professor in the Whittemore School of Business and Economics, University of New Hampshire, Durham, USA.

Allen Kaufman is Professor in the Whittemore School of Business and Economics, University of New Hampshire, Durham, USA.

Sarosh Kuruvilla is Associate Professor in the New York State School of Industrial and Labor Relations, Cornell University, Ithaca, USA.

Michael Merenda is Professor in the Whittemore School of Business and Economics, University of New Hampshire, Durham, USA.

Benoit Montreuil is Associate Professor in the Department of Operations and Decision Systems, and Research Professor in the SORCIIER Research Center, Laval University, Québec City, Canada.

Diane Poulin is Associate Professor in the Department of Management, and Research Professor in the SORCIIER Research Center, Laval University, Québec City, Canada.

Tod D. Rutherford is Professor in the Department of Geography, University of Waterloo, Waterloo, Canada.

N. V. Schaefer is Professor in the Faculty of Administration, University of New Brunswick, Fredericton, Canada.

Allen J. Scott is Professor in the Department of Geography and Director of the Lewis Center for Regional Policy Studies, University of California, Los Angeles, USA.

Basu Sharma is Professor in the Faculty of Administration, University of New Brunswick, Fredericton, Canada.

Udo Staber is Professor in the Faculty of Administration, University of New Brunswick, Fredericton, Canada.

Jörg Sydow is Professor in the Institute of Management, Free University of Berlin, Germany.

David G. Terkla is Professor in the Department of Economics, University of Massachusetts, Boston, USA.

Anil Verma is Associate Professor in the Faculty of Management and the Center for Industrial Relations, University of Toronto, Canada.

Index

Bei Fragen zur Produktsicherheit wenden Sie sich bitte an:
If you have any questions regarding product safety,
please contact:

Walter de Gruyter GmbH
Genthiner Straße 13
10785 Berlin
productsafety@degruyterbrill.com